DARK AGE BRITAIN

WHAT TO SEE AND WHERE

DARK AGE BRITAIN

WHAT TO SEE AND WHERE

Robert Jackson

 Patrick Stephens, Cambridge

First published in 1984

British Library Cataloguing in Publication Data

Jackson, Robert
Dark Age Britain.
1. Great Britain—History—To 1066
I. Title
941.01

ISBN 0-85059-622-X

Photoset in 9 on 10 pt and 10 on 11 pt Garamond by
Manuset Limited, Baldock, Herts. Printed in
Great Britain on 115 gsm Fineblade coated cartridge,
and bound, by William Clowes Limited, Beccles,
Suffolk, for the publishers, Patrick Stephens Limited,
Bar Hill, Cambridge, CB3 8EL, England.

Contents

List of sites which may be visited   6
Introduction   9

Part One: The British resistance 410-642 AD   19

Chapter 1 Britain alone   20
Chapter 2 Ambrosius Imperator   31
Chapter 3 Arthur: the fact and the legend   40
Chapter 4 The British collapse   56

Part Two: The Anglo-Saxon kingdoms 642-800 AD   71

Chapter 5 Northumbria and Mercia: the power struggle   72
Chapter 6 The conversion of the English   81
Chapter 7 'A dyke from sea to sea'   97
Chapter 8 The rise of Wessex   109

Part Three: 'From the fury of the Northmen, O Lord, deliver us'   123

Chapter 9 The coming of the Northmen   124
Chapter 10 The high tide—and the turn   135
Chapter 11 The English on the offensive   150
Chapter 12 The years of darkness   169
Chapter 13 The end of the beginning   182

Part Four: Scotland in the Dark Ages   189

Chapter 14 The painted warriors   190
Chapter 15 The Dalriada Scots   202

Index   207

List of sites which may be visited

Page numbers in Roman type **refer to text**, those in *italics* **refer to illustrations**

Abernethy 196
Abercorn 195
Alkborough *172*, 178
Alton Barnes 115
Ardwall Isle 199
Aspatria 165
Athelney 141
Badbury 45, *45*, 46
Bakewell 74
Barnack *25*, 150
Barton-on-Humber *141*, 150
Beachamwell 185
Bedford 153
Bewcastle 75
Bichamditch 35
Binchester 43, 44, *44*
Boarhunt 151
Bokerley Dyke 37
Bolam 148, *148*
Bosham 151
Bracebridge 176
Bradford-on-Avon 99
Bradwell-on-Sea 94
Branston *68*, 176
Breamore 151
Brechin 200
Brecon 58
Breedon-on-the-Hill 95
Brent Ditch 37
Brigstock *27*, 130
Brisco *62*, 62
Britford 155
Brixworth 95, *128*
Broch of Gurness 190
Brompton 126, *126*
Brough of Birsay 190
Broughton *140*, 180
Bryncir 55
Burgh Castle 86
Burghhead 197
Bygrave 166
Bywell 114
Cabourne 138, *138*
Cadbury 28

Caistor *14*, 180
Camboglanna 53, *54*
Cambridge 184
Canterbury 83, *103-5*
Caratacus Stone 55
Cardiff 143
Cardinham 171
Carew 183
Carlisle *61*, 62
Castle Dore 29
'Castle Guinnion' 43
Castle Haven 199
Catterick 84, *85*
Chapel Finian *192*, 199
Chester 44
Chun Castle 29
Cissbury 28
Clapham *23*, 153
Cockley Cley *18*
Codford St Peter 125
Colchester 184
Corbridge 92, *116-7*
Corhampton 171
Corringham 177, 186
Craig Phadrig 198
Cricklade 142
Croft 121
Cubert 56
Dacre 82
Daglingworth 173
Dalmahoy 197
Dearham 162
Deerhurst 99
Degsastan 65
Devil's Dyke 38, *38*
Diddlebury 174
Dinas Emrys 33
Dover 153
'Dubglas', River 43
Dumfries 193
Dumyat 197
Dunadd 199
Dundurn 196
Earl's Barton *126-7*, 157

East Lexham 185, *185*
Edenham *136*, 180
Edinburgh 201, *205*
Eglwys-Cymmyn 58
Eilach na Naoimh 200
Eliseg's Pillar 153
Escomb 106, *151*
Eyam 84
Farr 198
Fleam Dyke 39, *39*
Geddington *18*, 118
Glastonbury 52
Glen, River 42, *42*
Glentworth *175*, 180
Gosforth 126
Govan 196
Great Dunham *11*, 185
Great Paxton 163, *182*
Great Tey 184
Greenstead 159
Guestwick 184
Hackness 80, *88*
Haddiscoe Thorpe 187
Halton 130
Halwell 142
Heapham *68-9*, 180
Hexham *68*, 79, 92
Heysham 121
Holton-le-Clay 147, *147*
Hough on the Hill 154
Hovingham 87, *87*
Ilkley 162
Iona 199
Islay 199
Jarlshof 193
Jarrow 96
Jedburgh 190
Keillmore 190
Kildonan 190
Kingarth 190
Kirby Hill *155*, 163
Kirkdale *87*, 164
Kirk Hammerton 112, *122*
Kirkleavington 76, 130

Kirkmadrine 198
Langford 76
Ledsham 112
Leicester 178
Lewannick 58
Liddington Castle 47-8, *47-9*
Lincoln 33, *185*
Lindisfarne 129
'Linnuis' battle 42, *42*
Liskeard 107
Little Bardfield 75
Liverpool 121
Llanaelhaearn 55
Llanerfyl 58
Llangadwaladr 59
Llangian 53
Llangollen 24
Llangybi 55
Llantwit Major 149
London 112
Lydford 145
Lyminge 84
Maen Madoc 59
Maes Howe 193
Margram 114
Marton 177, *183*
Masham 80
Mayburgh 155
Melbury Osmond 125
Melsonby 121
Men Scryfa Down 58
Middleton *88*, 167
Military Zone (Roman North)
  12, 21
Moncrieffe Hill 196
Monkwearmouth 95
Mote of Mark 199
Nettleton 145, *145*
Nevern 59
Newent 100
Newton by Castleacre *66*, 185
North Elmham *110-11*, 167

Norwich 183
Nunburnholme 165
Offa's Dyke 97, *100-101*
Oldbury Camp 28
Old Sarum 147
Orphir 190
Ovingham 161
Oxford 174
Penally 107
Penmachno 60
Penrith 164
Penzance 171
Pictish Stones 195
Piercebridge 21, *21*
Pilton 145
Portchester 133
Ramsbury 115
Reculver 74
Repton 95
Restenneth 198
Ring of Brodgar 190
Ripon 95, *159*
Rothwell 146, *146*
Roughton 184
Ruthwell 195
St Albans 22
St Andrews 200
St David's 59
St Just 54
Sancreed 169
Sandbach 84
Scartho 180
Seaham 109
Shelford 176
Singleton 136
Skipwith 80
Sockburn 114
Solsbury Hill 45, *51*
Somerford Keynes 76
Somerton 137
Sompting 169
Sourton 60

South Cadbury 50
Springthorpe *57*, 177
Stanton Lacy 176
Stanwick 63-4, *63-4*, 70, *160*
Stapleford 176
Stonegrave *85*, *163*
Stoughton 183
Stow 77, *93*
Strethall 184
Swansea 77
Taplow 72
Tavistock 60
Thanet 24
Thornhill 200
Tintagel 41, *41*
Towyn 106
Traprain Law 197, *204*
Trusty's Hill 195
Tynron Doon 205, *205*
Votadini (territory of) 26
Waithe 144, *144*
Wallingford 147
Wansdyke 69
Warden 163
Wareham 142
Wat's Dyke 98, *98*
Weaverthorpe 88, *88*
West Stow 23, *23*
Wharram le Street *90*, 163
Whitby *70*, *73*, 95
Whithorn *188*, *192*, 198, *203*
Wickham 170
Winchester 117
Wing 107
Winterbourne Steepleton 171
Wootton Wawen 175
Worth 170
Wroxeter 31-2, *31-2*, 34-7,
  34-7
Yeavering Bell 65
York 8, *58*, *102*, *118*, *119*, 120,
  163, *164-5*

York Minster, seen from the mediaeval walls. One of Britain's first centres of Christianity, York's religious fortunes were to change during successive centuries, as the city was occupied by later Scandinavian pagan invaders.

Introduction

The Roman fort of Birdoswald is one of the most striking fortifications of Hadrian's Wall, Designed to guard the bridge over the River Irthing and to command the road which once ran to the outpost fort of Bewcastle, it was sited with the utmost care in one of the finest strategic positions along the whole of the Wall's 70-mile course. Lying a little under 2 miles to the west of Gilsland village, its northern approaches are guarded by a valley into which spills Midgeholm Moss, a quagmire which, in Roman times, must have been virtually impassable. There was once an extensive bog on the western flank, too, while to the south the land falls away in a steep escarpment to the valley of the Irthing. To stand on the edge of that escarpment, and look down into that crooked, tree-shrouded gorge is an experience in itself, for it was this view that gave the fort its Roman name of Camboglanna, the Crooked Glen. It is a name which, as we shall see, may be of tremendous historical and romantic significance.

Camboglanna—and it is preferable to use that name, rather than the one bestowed on it later by the English—was occupied until late in the fourth century by the First Cohort of Dacians, hardy soldiers from what is now Romania. It is intriguing to imagine, standing within the perimeter of the fort, what those men from far off must have thought and felt as the dwindling Wall garrison, and indeed the whole population of Roman Britain, lived through the twilight years of a great civilization; years that marked the frontier of the period we know today as the Dark Ages. In theory, the Dark Age period encompasses the time between the departure of the Romans from Britain and the establishment of the English kingdoms some three centuries later. Yet this in itself is a misleading definition, for there was never a real end to Roman administration and influence in Britain; the assets brought to the province by the Romans were to a considerable degree assimilated by the so-called barbarians who presided over Rome's decline, and they stamped their own imprint upon them.

The decline of the Roman Empire had been inevitable for centuries; in fact, it was a miracle that it had lasted so long. For a start, the more the empire expanded, the greater became the problems of defence; there were never enough legions to defend the vast land frontiers, let alone to mount big punitive expeditions against the hostile barbarian tribes which pressed against those frontiers with growing vigour. In the early days of empire this thin defensive screen was adequate, for there was no concert between the barbarian tribes and the military qualities of the Roman Army were superior in every respect; only when the barbarians began to use the Romans' own tactics against them, and to achieve parity in weapons technology, did the threat assume serious proportions. Even so, this in itself need not have spelled disaster, for the Roman administration skilfully employed some barbarian peoples in a defensive role, settling them within the boundaries of the empire as allies and integrating them into the defensive structure in return for grants of land.

Defence apart, the most massive problem to beset the Roman Empire throughout its lengthy existence was one of economy. Only an industrial economy could have adequately supported an empire of such magnitude, and Rome's economy was primarily agricultural. The financial structure was unsound, too, for real wealth lay in the hands of a comparative few in the upper layers of the social pyramid, and more often than not this wealth was used for the acquisition of land rather than for the expansion of trade or in a quest for innovations which might have brought prosperity and vigour to the empire as a whole. Rome's flair for administration and government is beyond question; but her statesmen were debaters and speculators, not scientists or inventors, and in any case the plentiful supply of slave labour did not encourage invention. The Romans would have argued that it was pointless to construct some labour-saving device when ten slaves were readily available to perform the task for which it was intended.

The inadequacies of the imperial structure were sharply revealed in the middle of the third century, when a succession of barbarian invasions smashed the old frontiers. The worst and most traumatic of these invasions was a massive assault across the Rhine by Germanic tribes, who overran and devastated much of Gaul. It was as though the barbarians, learning of the internal power struggles that were going on within the empire at the time, had sensed that the time was ripe for them to strike. The empire might have collapsed in ruin then, but a succession of strong military governments saved the situation, expelled the invaders and restored the frontiers.

In 284 AD, the Emperor Diocletian began a thorough reorganisation of the empire, driving a wedge between the civil and military administrations and abolishing the old Roman provinces, replacing them by smaller territorial units which were grouped into four large prefectures. He remodelled the army too, replacing the old static frontier defences by a more workable and effective defence in depth. The emphasis now was on a large and mobile field army, equipped with cavalry and able to move rapidly to any trouble spot. Diocletian's work was carried on by Constantine I (306–337), who moved the seat of government from Rome to Constantinople and who made Christianity the official religion of the Roman world.

By a strange twist of fortune, the devastation of Gaul's rich agricultural lands by the barbarians helped to bring a new-found prosperity to Britain. Hitherto, Gaul had supplied much of the provisions required by the soldiers on the long Rhine frontier; but with Gaul wasted the legions were forced to look elsewhere, and they turned to Britain. The result was the rise in Britain of the villa economy, with huge agricultural estates—and the huge fortunes that went with them—being created in a remarkably short time.

So far, Britain had escaped the attentions of the barbarians on the scale Gaul had suffered. By the middle of the third century, however, her Channel coastline was coming under increasing threat from Saxon and Frankish sea-raiders, and in 285 a man named Marcus Aurelius Carausius was given a naval command and ordered to deal with them. This new command, in fact, was part of a much wider scheme of things, for the man who created it was the Caesar Maximian, who was shortly to become co-emperor with Diocletian and who at that time was waging a successful campaign against revolutionaries in northern Gaul. Carausius, who was no mean seafarer, set up his headquarters at Boulogne, and within a remarkably short time his fleet had secured the Channel area, destroying large numbers of raiders and capturing their booty. It was then that he made a fatal mistake; instead of returning the plunder his men had taken to its rightful owners, or handing it over to the imperial treasury, he kept it. On learning of this, Maximian accused the naval commander of treason and ordered his arrest.

Carausius' immediate reaction was to strengthen his hold on the vital port of Boulogne, declare himself emperor and call upon the Roman forces in Britain—to which his fleet controlled all access—to rally to him. He appears to have had considerable British support, strengthened presumably by those merchants who applauded his actions in ridding the Channel of the Saxon and Frankish pirates. Maximian prepared a fleet of his own, and in 289 this set sail down the Rhine, the intention being to enter the North Sea and

The church of St Andrew at Great Dunham, Norfolk, is one of Norfolk's finest Anglo-Saxon structures. Inside, the very fine arches are of Roman brick.

then sail down the Channel to bring Carausius to battle. The attempt failed for reasons which are not recorded, and it was five years before Carausius' separatist rule in Britain was once again challenged. In 293, Maximian—who now presided as emperor over the western part of the empire, Diocletian controlling the eastern part—appointed a deputy named Constantius, whose army marched on the naval base at Boulogne, laid siege to it and eventually captured it, isolating Carausius in Britain. This must have been disastrous for British commerce, and the sudden cessation of trade with the continent probably contributed greatly to the next turn of events. Soon after the fall of Boulogne, there was a political coup in Britain; Carausius was assassinated and replaced by an economist named Allectus, who had been his finance minister.

Allectus, however, was no military genius, and was certainly no match for the tactics of the very experienced Constantius. In 296, the latter launched a two-pronged naval assault on Britain, one fleet sailing from Boulogne to land on the Isle of Wight, the other heading out from the estuary of the Seine. The Isle of Wight force marched on London and Allectus hurried to confront them with an army which seems to have been composed mainly of German mercenaries; they were no match for regular legionaries and were quickly defeated, their leader being killed. The remains of his army, streaming back towards London, were wiped out by Constantius' second expeditionary force, which had sailed up the Thames. Constantius restored Britain to Roman rule after ten years of severance. He also rebuilt the economy and strengthened the defences of the *Litus Saxonicum*, the Saxon Shore, where the construction of forts at strategic points had been started before the time of Carausius. What part Carausius himself played in the building of these strongpoints—which stretched in a great arc round the coast from Portus Adurni (Portsmouth) to Branodunum (Brancaster, at the mouth of the Wash)—is not certain, although some historians think it

unlikely that a man whose success had been achieved by naval tactics would spend time and effort on the construction of static defences which were vulnerable to siege.

The decade of Carausius' rule in Britain is important, for it showed that the island could exist independently of the empire for a lengthy period. It also proved that both civil and military leaders in Britain were not slow in giving their support to a man they believed to be right for Britain, even if it meant going in the face of the empire as a whole. More important still, it marked the beginning of a rift between Britain and the empire; a rift that was never to be fully healed. Constantius, newly created emperor following the retirement of Diocletian and Maximian, returned to Britain in 305 to strengthen the northern defences against Caledonian incursions from beyond the

The last frontier. In the early Dark Age period, Hadrian's Wall, northern boundary of the Military Zone, may still have had a significant defensive role, Several Dark Age battles were fought in its vicinity, right up to the time of Scandinavian settlement.

throughout the empire. What new threat presented itself to Britain is not known; what is known is that Constans, Constantine's successor in the west, visited the island in 342-3, arriving in the middle of winter—a far from ideal time to come to Britain, and certainly not one an emperor would have chosen had it not been for some dire emergency. Constans is thought to have set up an extensive intelligence network in northern Britain, with agents known as *areani* reporting on the movements and intentions of the Caledonian tribes, the most warlike of whom appear to have been the Picts. Contrary to popular belief, the Picts did not inhabit the area immediately north of the Wall; their homeland was beyond the Firth of Forth and they were only one of several northern tribes, although they were presumably the most influential. Either Constans or the man who followed him to Britain to rule over the island with the title of Comes (Count) Gratian—whose son was to become the emperor Valentinian—concluded some kind of treaty with the Picts and probably with other warlike tribes too, because in 360 they broke it, attacking the northern frontier once again. The British administration appealed to Julian, who was then Caesar in the west and who was fighting the Alemanni in Gaul; he had his hands full, but he despatched a senior commander, Lupicinus, with a field force to restore the situation.

Wall. Several key forts on the Wall—including Camboglanna—had been allowed to fall into disrepair, and Constantius not only refurbished them but also reinstated some forts south of the Wall, deepening the northern defences. He died in York in 306, and it was there that the Army of Britain proclaimed his son Constantine emperor.

What followed then, as Constantine climbed the ladder to an awesome pinnacle of imperial power, was a period of relative quiet for Britain, although there is no reason to suppose that pirate attacks on her frontiers suddenly ceased. What does appear to have happened is that, under Constantine's rule, the defence-in-depth system continued to be strengthened, possibly at the expense of weakening the garrisons on the Wall and other frontiers. There is no real record of the external threats which confronted Britain at this time, although the Saxon sea-raiders and the Caledonian tribes must have been prominent; there is no mention, yet, of raiders from across the Irish Sea, although a list of Roman provinces (the so-called Verona List, prepared in 312-14) does mention the Scotti of Ireland as a hostile tribe.

Constantine's death in 337 seemed to be the signal for a resurgence of barbarian attacks

It was only the beginning. In 367—Julian having in the meantime died in a Persian campaign and the empire having been divided between Valentinian in the west and Valens in the east—three separate groups of barbarians reportedly attacked Britain simultaneously. For several years the Saxons had been advancing steadily along the German coast from their original home in Schleswig-Holstein; now they came sweeping across the North Sea to strike at the East Coast. At the same time, the Picts stormed into the north and the Scotti from Ireland into the west; the concerted attacks smashed the defences and for months savage warrior bands, their numbers swollen presumably by runaway slaves and renegade mercenary soldiers, roamed the countryside, burning and pillaging.

This fierce barbarian raid may, in fact, have been linked in some way to a revolt that broke out in Britain about the same time. It was led by a man named Valentinus, who had been an official in Pannonia (what is now Hungary) before being banished to Britain for some misdemeanour. The possibility that troops had to be withdrawn from vital frontier areas to crush the revolt, so leaving the defences dangerously weak and giving the barbarians a chance to break through, is far more likely than the alternative: that the barbarians formed some sort of alliance in order to launch their great raid. Our source of information on the raid, the historian Ammianus, tells us that an army was hastily assembled under the command of Theodosius and thrown across the Channel. It landed at Richborough and marched on London, where Theodosius divided his forces and sent them off to deal with the bands of raiders who were at large in the countryside. This in itself suggests that the so-called 'Great Raid' involved a great many relatively small groups of plunderers, rather than a barbarian army. Nevertheless, it was two years before all the barbarians were expelled, and it was even longer before the damage they had done was repaired and the defences strengthened. Indeed, it is quite possible that barbarian attacks were in progress all the time this work of reconstruction was going on.

There is no doubt that the barbarian incursion in 367 was one of the most serious ever to fall on Roman Britain; neither is there any doubt that the achievement of Theodosius in restoring the administration and defence of the island was a considerable one. A year later, the name 'Augusta' was bestowed on London; an honorary title denoting that its citizens had shown outstanding bravery or loyalty during the crisis. Also, Ammianus says that Theodosius: '. . . protected the frontier with lookouts and garrisons, recovering a province that had yielded to enemy control, so restoring it that, as his report advised, it should have a legitimate governor, and be styled Valentia'.

In the past, most historians have taken this to mean that Britain was made up of five provinces, not four; that one of them was called Valentia and that it was taken back by Theodosius after it had been overrun. Nowadays, a new interpretation of what Ammianus is saying has led to a growing belief that Britain's group of four provinces were amalgamated and the whole renamed Valentia in honour of the emperors of east and west, Valens and Valentinian. One important aspect of Theodosius' restoration and reorganisation was that the Roman Army garrisons were withdrawn from the forts north of the Wall and a new kind of 'buffer zone' created, in which Theodosius, using a mixture of intimidation and bribery, persuaded the Caledonian tribes who lived between the Wall and the Firth of Forth to accept Roman prefects and to act as a shield against the Picts of the far north. It was a policy that was to have far-reaching consequences.

Not long after the Theodosius expedition, the Danube frontier of the Roman Empire came under terrible external pressure as that most fierce of all nomadic tribes, the Huns, swept across the Volga. They destroyed the eastern empire of the Goths, and the western Visigoths migrated in terror before their onslaught, seeking to be allowed within the Roman boundaries. Valens, the emperor of the east, permitted them to settle west of the Danube and also allowed them to retain their arms. His officers also supplied the refugees with food—but at appalling black market prices which the Visigoths, who had no coinage system and few commodities with which to barter, could not afford. Unrest spread among the barbarian people like a brush fire and Valens, terrified, tried to have their leaders assassinated. The Goths rebelled, and in 378 they destroyed Valens and his Army of the East at Adrianople.

Valentinian, too, was now dead, and his son Gratian ruled the western provinces in his place. It was Gratian who was instrumental in installing Theodosius I, the son of the Theodosius who had restored Britain, as head of the eastern empire after the death of Valens. In a long and bitter campaign he cleared and secured the eastern provinces, often by using Goth mercenaries to subdue their own kind.

The Goths were a Germanic people and,

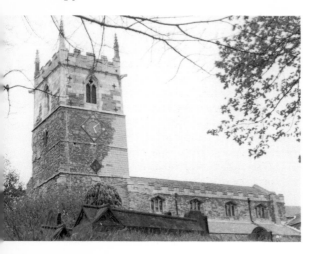

The former Roman town of Caistor was occupied in Anglo-Saxon times, and the late Saxon church of St Peter and St Paul was built within the boundaries of the Roman settlement. Traces of the original Saxon work may still be seen in the lower stages of the tower, which has walls five feet thick—thicker than those of any other pre-conquest church.

although Germans had served in the legions for a very long time—and had proved loyal and reliable fighters—this wholesale 'germanising' of the army by the use of mercenary auxiliaries was viewed with disfavour in influential Roman circles. Gratian's personal bodyguard was made up of Germans, who wielded considerable power; they were a law unto themselves, in much the same way as Hitler's SS were to be 15 centuries later, and anyone who went against them was mercilessly executed.

Part of the problem was that Gratian was a weak man; athletics and pious living appear to have been his main interests in life. What the empire needed was a tough leader who could weed out the corrupt factions, and bring about a situation where Romans once again ruled their own destiny. Dissent against Gratian spread rapidly, and it was in Britain that it first flared into open rebellion. At its centre was an able and well-loved officer named Magnus Maximus, a Spaniard who had campaigned in Britain with Theodosius in 367-8. Maximus' mother was probably British, which would certainly have endeared him to the ordinary British people. In 383 he was back in Britain, probably dealing with another outbreak of trouble caused by the Caledonians and the Scotti in the north. Whether he held the rank of *Dux Britanniarum*—Duke of Britain, the equivalent of commander-in-chief—or was on a special military assignment with the title of *Comes* (Count) we do not know. What is known is that in 383, the Army of the North persuaded him to declare himself emperor at York with the object of overthrowing Gratian and of securing Gaul and Britain against further barbarian inroads.

In this aim, at first, he seems to have been astonishingly successful. He assembled a substantial army and crossed to Gaul, where a few months later he met the young Gratian in battle, destroyed his forces and killed him. He made Gaul secure, probably by negotiating with the German tribes from a position of superior strength, and was acknowledged as emperor by the provinces of Spain, Africa and Italy. For five years, the power of Magnus Maximus brought peace and stability to western Europe. Then, in 388, came the inevitable confrontation with Theodosius, whose campaigns against the barbarians in the Balkans had so far prevented him from taking action. Maximus was killed, and control of the west passed to Valentinian II, the son of the first Valentinian, who had been an infant at the time of his father's death in 375 and who had earlier been favoured instead of Gratian by the Army of the Danube.

Maximus was dead, but neither he nor his exploits would ever be forgotten by the British people. It is believed that when he crossed to Gaul, he was followed by large numbers of civilians, who settled across the Channel in Armorica—the future Brittany. In later centuries, Welsh and Cornish folklore would remember him as 'Prince Macsen', and in telling his legend would give birth to some of Europe's loveliest early prose:

'Seven years did the emperor stay in this island . . . So the men of Rome made a new emperor. So Macsen set forth to Rome, and sat down before the city. A year was the emperor before the city, and no nearer to the taking of it than on the first day. Then came the brothers of Helen from the isle of Britain, with a small army, and better warriors were in that small army than twice as many Romans. They came to the city, and set their ladders against the walls, and came into the city; and none could give it to the emperor but the men of the island of Britain. Then the gates of the city of Rome were opened, and the emperor sat upon his throne.

'Then the emperor said to Kynan and Adeon, "I give you this army to conquer what regions you will". So they conquered lands and castles and cities. Then Kynan said to his brother, "Will you stay in this land, or go home to the land from whence you came?" He chose to go home to his own land, and many with him; but Kynan stayed with the others, and dwelt there, and the men of Armorica are called Britons. This is the dream called the Dream of Macsen, emperor of Rome, and here it ends.'

History has placed the date of the final withdrawal of the regular legions from Britain at the time of Maximus' expedition to Gaul. Large numbers of troops were certainly pulled out of the island, but there is no reason to suppose that the defences were left in a depleted state. It is quite likely that some regular units remained in key positions, in much the same way, for instance, that two battalions of a modern British Army regiment might be sent on overseas service while a third stays at home on garrison duty or in reserve. In fact, there is some evidence to show that the Twentieth Legion was still in Chester 20 years later.

Nevertheless, Maximus seems to have instituted a policy whereby the British regional councils, or *civitates*, were made responsible for their own defence. This was presumably based on the widespread use of territorial and auxiliary forces, supported by deliberately-settled barbarian mercenaries and by small regular units. It was a policy that led, in the course of time, to the rise of regional tyrants who founded their own 'royal' dynasties throughout Britain. Yet, in the later years of the fourth century, the basic Roman defensive structure in Britain still seems to have been intact; there was still a *Dux Britanniarum*, based at York and commanding the turbulent northern defensive zone up to and including the Wall, and there was still a *Comes Litoris Saxonici*, Count of the Saxon Shore, although this command—which had once been responsible for areas on both sides of the Channel—now applied only to the British coastline.

The death of Maximus, the one man who was enough of a leader to have saved the western empire from collapse, opened the floodgates to fresh barbarian onslaughts. The Franks sacked Cologne and extended their settlements around the lower Rhine, and in 393 the German commander of the Rhine Army deposed the young emperor Valentinian II, precipitating a bloody power struggle between himself and Theodosius. It was a bitter mercenary war in which both sides employed large numbers of barbarian troops, the latter offering their services to the highest bidder. In fact, victory only went to Theodosius after a substantial force of his adversary's mercenary soldiers changed sides.

Theodosius was the last sole ruler of the Roman Empire. When he died in 395, the empire was permanently divided between his two sons Arcadius and Honorius, the former ruling in the east and the latter in the west. The year when Theodosius died was a bad one

for Britain, for it marked the resumption of
large-scale pirate raids. This time, the main
assault came from Ireland. According to the
Irish Annals, it was led by the High King of
Ireland, Niall of the Nine Hostages, whose
raiders sacked Deva (Chester) and Isca Silurum
(Caerleon) and also seized some territory in
Wales.

The sharp increase in raiding resulted in a
British plea for help to Honorius, the western
emperor, who in 399 despatched an army
under Stilicho, the son of a Vandal who had
been an officer of high rank in the Roman
Army. Stilicho drove back the barbarians and
tried to strengthen the British defensive
system, then took his forces back to the
continent to repel further barbarian onslaughts,
a task in which he enjoyed some brilliant
successes. His principal adversaries were the
Visigoths, who, under their outstanding
General and ruler Alaric, had grown tired of
being penned up in Rome's eastern Balkan
provinces and were now threatening Italy
itself. Stilicho was able to hold them at bay, but
only at the expense of the empire's western
frontiers, which were stripped of forces. This
included, in 403, what must have been the last
legion to serve in Britain on a regular basis—
probably the Twentieth.

Stilicho's action in saving Italy spelled
disaster for Gaul, which now lay at the mercy
of hordes of barbarians—mainly Vandals,
Suebi and Alans—who flooded across the
Rhine to escape the Huns, still ravaging
central Europe. With the Gallic defences
shattered and the land virtually overrun,
Britain's plight was once again desperate, for
her lines of communication with the rest of the
empire were severed. In 405, however, the
British defences had achieved a morale-boosting
victory of no small proportions. A British fleet,
under unknown circumstances, intercepted an
Irish fleet and destroyed it, killing Niall and for
the time being almost eliminating the threat
from across the Irish Sea.

Much encouraged, the British once again
elected their own emperor, a soldier who
assumed the title of Constantine III. Like his
predecessor, Magnus Maximus, he too was to
have his place in later Welsh legend, where he
appears as Bendigeit Custennin—Blessed
Constantine. Also like Maximus, Constantine

assembled a British army and crossed to Gaul
in 407, where in a vigorous campaign he
smashed the Vandals. Their remnants fled
across the Pyrenees into Spain, where they
settled for a time before moving on to North
Africa, and gave their name to a province:
Andalusia.

Constantine had opened the way to Rome,
and had secured the vital lines of supply and
communication; but his success spelled
disaster for Stilicho, who was seized and
executed on imperial orders in 408. By this
time the Roman administration in the west had
left Rome, now seriously threatened by Alaric's
Visigoths, and had set up a shaky government
in Ravenna.

The empire was dying; and in a frenzy of
anti-barbarian sentiment those who still called
themselves Romans turned on the Germans
who, for years, had been the very core of the
continental armies. The purge began in the
east, when a Gothic general seized Constantinople and was cut to pieces, together with
his men. After Stilicho's death, wholesale
massacres of German garrisons also took place
in the west; but whereas the events in
Constantinople led to a resurgence of Roman-
style integrity that would last under various
guises for a thousand years, the massacres in
the west led only to a further weakening in the
defences and more internal power struggles.

Looming over the problems in the west was
the question of Constantine and his army. In
409 or thereabouts there was a confrontation
between Constantine and forces loyal to the
Ravenna Government. In the ensuing conflict
Constantine's Generals were killed, but were
soon replaced by two more, named as
Ediovinchus, a Frank, and Gerontius, a Briton.
Gerontius, too, seems to have been something
of a hero among the British, who for
generations named their sons after him; his
name is the origin of the later Welsh 'Geraint'.

Constantine and his new Generals launched
fierce counter-attacks, and the western empire
began to dissolve in a chaos of civil war.
Constantine's mission was now seen to be a
failure, and Gerontius eventually led part of his
forces in rebellion against him; both men
perished in the turmoil that followed, Constantine being captured by Honorius and executed

after an abortive attempt to invade Italy in 411.

Meanwhile, a year earlier, events had occurred which rocked the Roman world to its very foundations. On August 24 410, Alaric's Visigoths captured the city of Rome. His forces remained in the city for only a week, departing with a massive amount of booty and large numbers of captives, but the effect of their action was incalculable. The writings of St Jerome record the tragedy:

'The Roman Empire is beheaded. In the one City, the whole world dies. All things born are doomed to die; every work of man is destroyed by age. But who would have believed that Rome would crumble, at once the mother and the tomb of her children? She who enslaved the east is herself a slave.'

The shock effect of Rome's fall was felt in Britain, too, although there is evidence that the British administration, faced with renewed barbarian attacks in 408, had already taken steps to free itself from central Roman authority, expelling senior Roman officials who still remained in the island. It is probable that the British colonies in Armorica did the same. However, it was soon apparent that the regionalised British defences could not hold the barbarians at bay on three fronts, and—piecing together the fragmentary details of the story—it seems that in 410 the *civitates*, the regional council, jointly wrote to Honorius with an appeal for help, promising that they would return to the fold of the empire if troops were send to their aid. The emperor's reply was recorded by the historian Zosimus, one of the primary sources of information about the events of those turbulent years: 'Honorius dealt with the states of Britain by letter, telling them to look to their own defence . . . and remained inactive'. For the first time in three and a half centuries, Britain, chilled by the dark winds that swept across her frontiers, stood alone.

Small and simple—an early Saxon church near Cockley Cley.

Part One:
The British Resistance
410–642 AD

Chapter 1

Britain alone

For the British, the sudden divorce from Rome did not mean an abrupt end to the way of life the people had enjoyed for so long. The economy, administration and the army remained Roman in style for at least a generation, and perhaps much longer. There was doubtless a series of coups in those early years of independence, until one regional leader emerged stronger than the rest and imposed some sort of authority over them; this must have happened, for an unco-ordinated defence could not have achieved results against the enemy. Those results were certainly achieved, as Zosimus tells us: 'The British people took up arms, bore the brunt of the attack, and freed their cities from the barbarian threat'.

As an historian, Zosimus, who was a Greek, was more reliable than the other major source for the events of the fifth century. This is the book *On the Ruin and Conquest of Britain*, written by a monk named Gildas in the 540s. An extremely irritating document, it gives us tantalising glimpses of what *might* have happened, but its historical narrative is wildly inaccurate and much of it may be disregarded. Nevertheless, we shall meet Gildas several times, and try to interpret his meaning.

Other sources for the period include the *Gallic Chronicle*, which was compiled in the middle years of the fifth century and which records a fearful raid by the Saxons on the Channel coasts in 411; the *Irish Annals*, which recorded the death of Niall, the High King; and, to a lesser degree, the *Anglo-Saxon Chronicle*, which was probably compiled in the late ninth century from a lot of other sources

on the orders of Alfred the Great. The Venerable Bede's *Ecclesiastical History of the English People*, written about 700, contains some information on the fifth century, but this is little more than a re-hash of Gildas, with one or two amendments.

The last major source is perhaps the most intriguing of all. Called the *History of the Britons*, it was compiled sometime in the ninth century, supposedly by a Welsh monk known as Nennius, but probably by someone quite different of whom we know nothing. Whoever did compile the document prefaced his work with the apologetic comment, 'I have made a heap of all I could find'. In fact, much of the Nennius text is compiled from other documents which have long since been lost, and although most of it is dubious it represents a valiant attempt to bring the events of the fifth and sixth centuries into some sort of chronological order.

Almost nothing is known about the events in Britain during the 15 years which followed the break with Rome, although an unlikely source, the *Anglo-Saxon Chronicle*, records a Roman expedition to Britain in 418. If this date is correct, it means that the split with the Ravenna Government was by no means final.

In fact, there is some cause to think that Honorius may have appointed, or at least officially recognised, a separate emperor who ruled in Britain alone. The title, really, is not important; what matters is that, during the first part of the fifth century, a Roman style of government was maintained. The governing body was the Council of Britain, which must

The village of Piercebridge, near Darlington, is a fascinating example of a settlement that grew out of a Roman fort during the Dark Age period. The present cottages stand almost exactly around the fort's perimeter, and the road where the cars are parked follows the line of the original Via Principalis. Even the George Hotel, just across the River Tees outside the village boundary, may stand on the site of a Roman hostel.

have been composed of representatives of the *civitates* and doubtless also included leading soldiers and businessmen. The Council, however, probably held sway only over the agricultural lowlands, the Cotswolds, the West Country and what is now Wales, for in the north, circumstances must have created a far different structure.

The north was still a military zone, for the principal threat still came from beyond the Wall and across the Irish Sea. The Wall defences must have been maintained well into the fifth century; not by regular garrisons, certainly, but more probably by settlers who took up arms as it became necessary. Although Roman coinage found in the various Wall excavations dates only to the end of the fourth century, with one or two notable exceptions, pottery is of a much later date. The finds suggest that although continuity of settlement existed in some form, the settlers had no use for money. They were by no means isolated, however, for the late pottery came from kilns in Yorkshire, and it is possible that whoever was settled on or near the Wall in the

early fifth century still received supplies from the military headquarters in York.

Tradition asserts that the last officially appointed *Dux Britanniarum* in the north was a man named Coelius, a name that was transformed into 'Coel Hen'—Coel the Old—in the Celtic tongue, and into legend as Old King Cole. As time went by, and central authority gradually slipped away, Coelius' status as *Dux* assumed a new significance; from a position of absolute power he set himself up as king over the whole of the north, and became the founder of a series of dynasties which, a century later, established themselves in the Pennines and the north-west.

The Military Zone. Maintaining a Roman-style government in northern Britain at the beginning of the Dark Ages depended on secure communications between Eburacum—York—the Wall and the 'buffer zone' beyond it, inhabited by friendly tribes such as the Votadini. The main artery of communication was Dere Street, along which the principal forts and settlements were Aldborough, 16 miles north of York (Roman name: Isurium), Catterick, Piercebridge, Binchester (Vinovia—possibly the Arthurian 'Castle Guinnion' described in Chapter 3), Lanchester (longovicium), Ebchester (Vindomora), Corbridge (Corstopitum), Risingham (Habitancum), High Rochester (Bremenium) and Newstead (Trimontium). Control of Dere Street greatly influenced the outcome of Dark Age campaigns in the north.

Coelius' contemporary in the south was Vortigern. This is not a personal name, but a title; it means 'High King'. Just who Vortigern was is a matter for conjecture. He was certainly powerful, and tradition, supported to some extent by scant information extracted from later genealogies, suggests that he was a wealthy aristocrat from the Gloucester area. No one knows how he came to power, but the circumstances in which it happened are worthy of examination. The ruling class of wealthy magnates to which Vortigern must surely have belonged was a pale shadow of what it had been when Rome's presence was everywhere in the island. It made a pretence of governing after the Roman fashion, still professed itself to be educated in the Roman style, and kept up trade links with the Mediterranean; it was also Christian, although in the early fifth century the British church was in a state of revolution. It all stemmed from the preachings of a British monk called Pelagius, who for some time had been urging radical and somewhat puritanical reforms in some of the established Church's doctrines. He had a huge British following, but the Roman bishops considered his teachings to be heretical, and there was a real danger of a complete split between the two.

Nor was that all. Among the peasant classes, who had always spoken their native Celtic tongue, the spread of Christianity had been painfully slow, and the collapse of Roman rule had brought about a resurgence of the old religions. There was a considerable spread of pagan shrines early in the fifth century, as though the peasantry were turning back to their old gods in the search for security. Or, perhaps, there was another reason. The peasants now were probably better fed than they had been for two centuries, for there was no longer a central Roman authority to enforce the compulsory export of grain to the continent; and it is a full belly, not fasting, that stimulates religious thought. Whatever the reasons for a sweeping return to paganism, the under-currents must have been seen as a substantial threat to those who clung to the Roman way of life. A kind of Celtic nationalism was sweeping the south and west, fostered in part by the regional despots—or their descendants—who had been planted in the troubled frontier areas

of what was to become Wales by Magnus Maximus and, perhaps, Constantine III. It is hardly likely that such men owed allegiance to the Council of Britain and its elected members.

The threat to Britain, then, must have been an internal as well as an external one, and it was probably an internal struggle that brought a strong man—Vortigern—to the forefront in defence of the organised, urban way of life the Romanised upper classes had known for so long. Yet that way of life was even then in rapid decline, not because the people who still lived in the old Roman towns were immediately threatened from outside, but because they were losing the necessary skills—and probably the will—to repair decay. In Verulamium— later St Albans—commerce still flourished, but the formerly splendid Roman theatre, now crumbling into ruin, was used as a rubbish tip. Culture had no place in early fifth century British life.

Whatever the reason for Vortigern's rise to power, he was immediately faced by a major crisis, and it came from the far north. The Picts, held in check for many years by the frontier defences, now circumvented the latter by taking to the sea. Gildas records their coming, saying that they sailed to the former Roman diocese of Britain 'in their coracles', and refers to them by the word *transmarini*, from across the seas. It was probably the Picts who, as a preliminary to further raiding, destroyed the Roman signal towers on the Yorkshire coast.

St Albans (Hertfordshire). Once the leading Roman town of Verulamium, St Albans was occupied well into the Dark Ages; its Saxon name was Uerlamacaestir, and the modern name recalls the saint who was martyred in the third century. There was once a cathedral dedicated to him and also, possibly, a church erected by Offa of Mercia in the late eighth century, but both have long since disappeared. Two Anglo-Saxon churches still exist: the church of St Stephen, near the southern perimeter of the Roman settlement, and the church of St Michael in the centre. The former is built mainly of Roman materials and the latter, although not much of the original Saxon work is now visible, is probably of ninth century date.

A typical house, with sunken floor, at the reconstructed Saxon village of West Stow.

The Picts were always the true enemies of Roman Britain, and serious raiding had probably been going on for some years by the time Vortigern came to power in about 425. Until that time, the Romano-British administration seems to have been uncertain about how to combat the menace. Gildas records what happened next:

'The time drew nigh, when the iniquities of Britain should be fulfilled, as with the Amorites of old. A Council was convened, to decide upon the best and soundest means of withstanding the frequent brutal invasions and raids of the aforesaid peoples.

'All the members of the Council, and the proud tyrant, were struck blind . . . To hold back the northern peoples, they introduced into the island the vile unspeakable Saxons, hated of God and man alike . . . Nothing more frightful has ever happened to this island, nothing more bitter. The utter blindness of their wits! What raw hopeless stupidity! Of their own free will, they invited in under the same roof the enemy they feared worse than death . . . So the brood of cubs burst from the lair of the barbarian lioness, in three "keels" as they call warships in their language. At the orders of the ill-fated tyrant, they first fixed their fearful claws upon the eastern part of the island, as though to defend it . . . Their dam, learning of the success of the first contingent,

sent over a larger draft of satellite dogs . . . Thus were the barbarians introduced, in the guise of soldiers running great risks for their kind "hosts", as the lairs asserted. They demanded "supplies" which were granted and for a long time shut the dog's mouth.'

The 'proud tyrant' referred to by Gildas is almost certainly Vortigern, although the chronicler does not say so. Also, Gildas' historical facts are somewhat confused, for there had already been Saxon settlements in the eastern part of the island, and possibly in the north, too, for years. His diatribe against the action of the 'proud tyrant' in engaging the service of Saxon mercenaries, was hardly fair, for Vortigern was only following a long-accepted practice. Moreover, it was eminently

---

West Stow (Suffolk). This interesting site was discovered in the late 1940s, but it was not until 1972 that the excavation was completed. It seems from the evidence found that the site dates from 400-650 AD.

About 80 buildings were discovered as well as a large number of artefacts. Stanley West, a noted local archaeologist, and a group of Cambridge undergraduates, undertook a reconstruction of part of the site. The intention was, as far as possible, to carry out the work using the same materials and tools which the Saxons used.

To reach West Stow, follow the A1101 from Bury St Edmunds for about 3 miles and you will come across a signpost. As an added bonus there is also a nature reserve for those who enjoy a walk in the country.

sensible to set Saxons, who were excellent seafarers, against Pictish raiders from the sea.

Three ships, then, arrived on the Kentish coast from across the North Sea, probably in 428, bearing a force that probably did not exceed 150 men in number. They were commanded by Hengest, a Danish mercenary who had been fighting for the Jutes in Frisia, and in all probability the men who manned the ships were Jutes, not Saxons.

Vortigern, presumably with the approval of his Council, settled the newcomers as federates in Kent, furnished them with supplies in return for military services. Such a small force of men can hardly have made a useful contribution to campaigns on land; from their base on the Isle of Thanet they were probably employed in patrolling the coastline, and it was only later, with the arrival of more mercenaries from overseas, that the threat so graphically described by Gildas began to materialise.

Meanwhile, in 429, an expeditionary force arrived in Britain from Gaul. Assembled by the bishop of Gaul, it was commanded by Bishop Germanus of Auxerre, who had been an army commander before taking holy orders, and its purpose was to stamp out the Pelagian heresy. There was undoubtedly a 'purge' of some sort, because it is recorded that Germanus destroyed the stronghold of a 'wicked king' and, in his place, set up another who founded a dynasty in Powys. However, the real value of Germanus' expedition to Britain was that it apparently wiped out, or at least subdued to a negligible level, the Irish foothold in Wales. Germanus' biographer, Constantius, says that the fight took place against a mixed force of Saxons and Picts, but it is more likely that the enemies were Irish, for the countryside described by Constantius is typically Welsh. The decisive battle was fought at Easter time, and Constantius tells how Germanus' '. . . light troops thoroughly explored the countryside through which the enemy's advance was expected; choosing a valley set among high hills, he drew up his army in ambush. As the enemy approached, he ordered his whole force to respond with a great shout when he cried out. The bishops cried out thrice together ''Alleluia''; the whole army replied with a single voice, and the great cry rebounded, shut in by the surrounding

---

Where Hengest and Horsa landed: the Isle of Thanet is the peninsula of land that forms the easternmost tip of Kent; the Celts knew it as Ruim. Today, much of it is covered by the urban complexes of Margate, Broadstairs and Ramsgate. To the south of the latter, the Roman fort of Rutupiae (Richborough) may be the site of the battle of 'Ypwinesfleot', mentioned in the Anglo-Saxon Chronicle under the date 449. In the same area, just inland from Sandwich Flats, a battle fought against Danish pirates in 851 is commemorated by the name 'Bloody Point'.

The church of St Mary and St Sexburga at Minster on the Isle of Thanet is well worth a visit. The building was reconstructed in 1027, but the north and south walls of the nave are seventh century, dating from the time when Queen Sexburga founded a convent on the site. There are fragments of four Saxon windows, two in the south wall and two to be seen externally in the north wall.

The 'Alleluia Battle'. The site of this battle in 429, when an expeditionary force under Bishop Germanus smashed what was probably a predominantly Irish army, has never been determined, but it is possible that it was fought in the Vale of Llangollen, where the name of Germanus appears in early Welsh tradition more than anywhere else. It would be a logical spot to encounter an enemy army advancing south from the Dee Estuary and Chester. Llangollen lies on the A5 road that runs north-west from Shrewsbury.

---

hills. The enemy column was terrified; the very frame of heaven and the rocks around seemed to threaten them. They fled in all directions, many drowning in the river they had to cross. The bishops won a bloodless victory, gained by faith, not by the might of men.'

It may be that a force of Picts and Saxons was involved; that they were on their way to reinforce the Irish, and that Germanus smashed them before they could do so. Indeed, the whole campaign may have been part of Vortigern's overall strategy, aimed at securing the whole of the west under Romano-British rule before turning his attention to other threatened areas.

Vortigern's campaign against the Irish may not have ended in Wales. In 432, the *Irish Annals* record the first Saxon raid on the Irish coast, and it is possible that these Saxons were Vortigern's allies. On the religious front, Pope Celestine sent a noted priest, Palladius, to convert the Irish and bring them into the fold of the Roman Church; the Irish virtually threw him out, but he was replaced by another priest who was allowed to preach by the High King of Ireland, Leogaire. The name of this priest was Patrick.

An entry in the Nennius manuscripts describes another step taken by Vortigern to overcome the Irish problem in Wales: 'Cunedag, ancester of Mailcunus, came with his eight sons from the north, from the district called Manau Guotodin, CXLVI years before Mailcunus reigned, and expelled the Irish with enormous slaughter, so that they never came back to live there again'.

'Cunedag' was Cunedda, a chieftain of the Votadini tribe from the area north-east of the Wall, and was the grandson of a Roman-appointed prefect, Paternus. Together with a large portion of the Votadini, he was re-settled in Wales sometime in the 430s (the Nennius dating is incorrect) and embarked on the reconquest of the north. His prowess turned him into a kind of folk hero; his name is the origin of the later 'Kenneth'.

In the meantime, Hengest had been urging Vortigern to call up more reinforcements from across the sea. Vortigern agreed, and shortly afterwards 40 ships arrived with a considerable force of Frisian warriors led by Hengest's son Ochta and his cousin, Ebissa. According to the *Kentish Chronicle*, they raided the very homeland of the Picts and plundered the Orkneys, after which they occupied several regions beyond the Solway Firth. This is historical fact; the name Dumfries means 'Fortress of the Frisians'.

With the settling of these foreign mercenaries north of the Wall, the menace of the Picts was removed forever. Britain's ancient enemies would no longer raid southwards into the former Roman diocese and, although they were still a force to be reckoned with—and occasionally to be confronted in Caledonia—their eventual fate was to be conquered and submerged by the

The church of Barnack, near Stamford, is of late Saxon date. The windows and lower part of the tower are original.

> **Cunedda's kingdom.** In Roman times, and indeed throughout the Dark Age period, the Votadini were the principal Celtic tribe of north-east Britain, their territory extending roughly from the Firth of Forth to the Wall along the coastal strip between the Cheviots and the North Sea. Their name was later corrupted to 'Gododdin', and their territory known as the 'Manau Gododdin'. The language spoken by the Votadini survives today in some place names such as Dunbar (Dynbaer) and Edinburgh (Din Eidyn).

Irish peoples who later settled in the west of what was to become Scotland. Here, an interesting point arises. The movement of Cunedda's Votadini, and the settling of the Germanic mercenaries in the north, implied that in the 430s Vortigern and the Council of Britain held power over most areas of the island which had been occupied by the Romans. There must still have been some sort of collusion between Vortigern and Coelius, if indeed the latter still ruled in the north.

The Frisian settlers north of the Wall filled the gap left by the migration of Cunedda's people. With Hengest and his men still in control of the Saxon Shore, the security of Britain was now perhaps more promising than it had been at any time in the past half-century. But events were to show how tenuous that security really was; it was finally shattered not by external threat, but by civil war.

According to the Nennius texts, Vortigern had a rival named Ambrosius. Who this man was is not known, but it may be that, by birth or other links, he was held by a large faction to be more suited than Vortigern to the position of High King. It may even be that Vortigern was a usurper who had deposed him, the rightful ruler. Whatever the real facts, the two fought one another in the late 430s, possibly as a result of a split in the Council brought about by controversy over the Saxon question. Hengest's forces, and those who came later, had fought hard and bravely in the British cause. Now, in the mid-430s, with the island relatively secure from attack, it was not unnatural that they should expect the supplies that had been promised to them as their reward. This promise had been made by Vortigern; but when the time for payment came, the Council refused to make it, claiming that the Saxon numbers had grown too large. This was probably untrue; it is far more likely that influential members of the Council—possibly landowners from whose granaries the bulk of the supplies would have to come—decided that the Saxon and Frisian

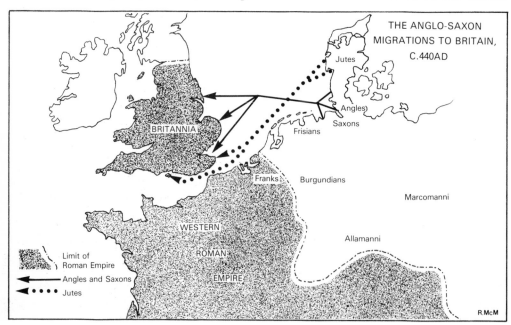

THE ANGLO-SAXON
MIGRATIONS TO BRITAIN,
C.440AD

Jutes

Angles)

Saxons

Frisians

BRITANNIA

Franks

Burgundians

Marcomanni

WESTERN

ROMAN

Allamanni

EMPIRE

Limit of
Roman Empire

Angles and Saxons

Jutes

R.McM

mercenaries were no longer useful, and that they should be expelled from the island forthwith.

It is logical to suppose that this faction supported Ambrosius as Vortigern's rival; and in 437, probably in a bid to overthrow the High King, the row flared into open conflict. The Nennius text records that: 'From the beginning of Vortigern's reign to the quarrel between Vitalinus and Ambrosius are 12 years; which is Guoloppum, that is the battle of Guoloph'.

This entry is interesting, for it perhaps gives a clue to Vortigern's true identity. We shall never know for sure. But 'Guoloppum' is probably Wallop, in Hampshire. It was unlikely to have been a clear-cut battle, for both sides must have relied heavily on mercenary forces. So Briton would have fought Briton, and Saxon fought Saxon. About the outcome, we know nothing except that Vortigern, apparently acting on Hengest's advice, sent for reinforcements from Frisia; they arrived in 19 vessels, and presumably fought in support of Vortigern against his British rival. Vortigern was now 'supping with the devil' with a vengeance, and the story goes that his involvement with Hengest became ever stronger when he fell in love with the Dane's daughter and pleaded for her hand in marriage in exchange even for half his kingdom. This is probably a piece of romantic fiction, but whatever the true facts, the former High King was now little more than a pawn in Hengest's hands, an excuse to infiltrate more immigrants.

Before long, the Saxons appear to have established control over most of East Kent. They were still technically federates, supported by the state in return for military service, and they seem to have co-existed with the Romano-British people of the area; in Canterbury, excavations have turned up early Saxon pottery of the period, as well as pottery of the kind used by the sub-Roman British culture of the early fifth century.

The uneasy status quo could not last. Early in the 440s, Hengest, now with a substantial army behind him, was in a position to threaten both British factions. Resorting to blackmail, he threatened to devastate the whole island unless more provisions were forthcoming.

Saxon and Norman architecture blend in the Church of St Andrew at Brigstock, Northamptonshire. The lower part of the west tower and the nave walls date from the ninth century.

This is according to Gildas; but what probably happened in reality is that adequate supplies had not been available for some time, and that the immigrants were growing desperate.

In about 442, the Saxons rebelled. The uprising was sudden and devastating, as Gildas recorded. He was writing a century later, but still the horror of the disaster is apparent in his words.

'The barbarians were not slow to put their threat into action. The fire of righteous vengeance, kindled by the sins of the past, blazed from sea to sea, its fuel prepared by the arms of the impious in the east. Once lit, it did not die down. When it had wasted town and country in that area, it burnt up almost the whole surface of the island, until its red and savage tongue licked the western ocean . . .

'All the greater towns fell to the enemy's battering rams; all their inhabitants, bishops, priests and people, were mown down together, while swords flashed and flames crackled. Horrible it was to see the foundation stones of towers and high walls thrown down bottom upward in the squares, mixing with holy altars and fragments of human bodies, as though they were covered with a purple crust of clotted blood, as in some fantastic wine-press. There was no burial save in the ruins of the houses, or in the bellies of the beasts and birds.'

The rebellion began in Kent and spread to other areas where Saxons were settled as federates. Gildas was exaggerating; the destruction was by no means universal, but in some areas of the east and south-east the last vestiges of Roman civilisation were wiped out forever, the Romano-British population passing into Saxon slavery. In other threatened areas, terrified people abandoned the smaller, lightly-fortified towns and sought new refuge in what Gildas described as 'the high hills, steep and fortified'; these can only have been the old Iron Age hill forts, which in the mid-fifth century acquired a new lease of life.

The rebellion lasted for years, rather than months. After the initial outburst the Saxons, probably intent at this stage on survival rather than conquest, retired with their plunder to the areas where they were already established, and from these newly-secure bases continued to raid into British territory.

Cissbury (Sussex). The fort of Cissbury—or Cissbury Ring, as it is perhaps better known—lies about five miles north of Worthing. There was a Neolithic settlement here, but the hill fort dates from the Iron Age. It was abandoned during the Roman occupation and the interior cultivated, but was re-occupied in the fifth century and its upper defences strengthened by the addition of a turf wall. To reach Cissbury, take the A24 north from Worthing for four miles and turn right at the village of Findon. *(OS Sheet 198, 138080.)*

Oldbury Camp (Wiltshire). This Iron Age hill fort, which lies half a mile south of the A4 Marlborough-Calne road on Cherhill Down, forms part of the famous Avebury-West Kennet-Silbury Hill complex in 'White Horse' country. Although the visible remains are mostly prehistoric, excavation has revealed objects including a coin of Valentinian I and a bone comb decorated with a ring-and-dot ornament which indicate that the fort was probably occupied during the Dark Ages. *(OS Sheet 173, 150694.)*

Cadbury (Avon). This is the site of an Iron Age fort covering an area of approximately eight and a half acres; it was re-occupied in the fifth century, presumably at the time of the first Saxon revolt, the western portion being cut off from the rest and fortified with rough stone walls. These defences were allowed to fall into disrepair early in the sixth century, probably during the time of peace that followed the British victory of Badon, and the perimeter sheltered a Celtic monastery for a time. To reach the fort on Cadbury Hill, follow the A370 for three-quarters of a mile north-east from Congresbury and turn left. *(OS Sheet 172, 442650.)*

In 446, the Britons sent a desperate appeal to Aegidius, the Roman supreme commander in Gaul: 'The barbarians push us to the sea, the sea pushes us to the barbarians; between the two kinds of death, we are either slain or drowned'. Aegidius could not help, for his armies were fully committed to defending Gaul against the terror of the Huns. But the British rallied and fought back, beginning a series of campaigns which were to last, on and off, for half a century. Some of the battles are recorded by the *Anglo-Saxon Chronicle*, but it reports

Castle Dore (Cornwall). Another Iron Age fort, reoccupied by a local ruler in the early Dark Age period, Castle Dore lies between the B3269 Lostwithiel-Fowey road and the Fowey estuary, and is actually situated on an ancient trackway running from Bodmin to Pridmouth. The earthwork has two defences, each consisting of a bank about 8 ft high with a deep outer ditch, enclosing a space 220 ft in diameter. Excavations have uncovered a stone guard-house by the inner entrance, where the concentric defences diverge, and traces of two rectangular halls, one measuring 90 ft by 40 ft, the other 65 ft by 35 ft. To the south of Castle Dore, about a mile and a half north of Fowey, a grey memorial stone stands at a crossroads. It once stood nearer to Castle Dore itself, and the inscription on it reads: DRUSTANUS HIC IACIT FILIUS CUNOMORI (Tristram lies here, the son of Cunomorus). Cunomorus— or Commorius, or Cynvawr, as the name is variously spelt—was a definite historical figure, and Drustanus is the name which passed into later legend in the tragic romance of Tristram and Yseult. *(Map refs, both OS Sheet 200: Castle Dore 103548, Memorial Stone 110542.)*

Chun Castle (Cornwall). Situated on high moorland at Boshallow Common, south of the B3306 coast road that runs from St Ives to St Just and joins the A30 just before Land's End, Chun Castle has an inner compound 180 ft in diameter, surrounded by two concentric stone walls. It was occupied during the fifth century, and a tin smelting furnace has been discovered there. *(OS Sheet 203, 405339.)*

only Saxon successes and is therefore of only partial value; moreover, its dating is highly suspect. However, it records that in 455: 'Hengest and Horsa fought against Wyrtgeorn (Vortigern), the king, at the place which is called Aegelsthrep; and his brother Horsa was there, slain; and after that Hengest succeeded to the command, and Aesc his son'.

This, too, is interesting, for it reveals that it was Horsa, who had come to Britain with his brother on board the first 'three keels' in 428, who was the army commander. 'Aegelsthrep'

is Aylesford. Other, later sources claim that Vortimer, Vortigern's son, played a prominent part in these early battles and actually drove the Saxons back to the far shores of Kent, but the *Anglo-Saxon Chronicle* makes no mention of him, or of a serious reverse. However, it is hard to understand how Vortigern, having allied himself with Hengest, could suddenly lead the British—who probably regarded the High King as a traitor—in battle against him, unless the plain fact was that Vortigern was the only man with the necessary skill and leadership to save the British from annihilation.

Two years after the Aylsford battle—in 457, according to the *Anglo-Saxon Chronicle*— there was another major battle, and this time the Saxons emerged as clear victors: 'In this year Hengest and Aesc his son fought against the Britons at the place which is called Crecganford (Crayford) and there slew four thousand men; and the Britons then forsook Kent, and in great terror fled to London'.

From this moment on, the *Chronicle* refers to the British sometimes by that name, but more often as the 'Walas', a word that means 'foreigners'; the modern name Welsh is derived from it. The next significant entry, for example, says that in 465: 'Hengest and Aesc fought against the Welsh near Wippedes fleot [possibly Ebbsfleet] and there slew 12 Welsh aldormen; and one of their thanes was there slain, whose name was Wipped'.

According to the Nennius manuscripts, sometime in the midst of this confused period Vortigern tried to arrange a peace treaty with Hengest. The latter agreed to a conference, to which 300 British leaders were invited. But Hengest instructed one of his own men to sit next to each Briton, and, on a given signal, to draw a dagger and kill his neighbour. Only Vortigern was to be spared, for the sake of his wife, Hengest's daughter. If this really happened, then most of Britain's leaders must have been massacred at one blow, and the way opened for more Saxon successes. The *Chronicle* records two more, the first in 473: 'In this year Hengest and Aesc fought against the Welsh and took countless booty; and the Welsh fled from the Angles as fire'.

This is the *Chronicle's* last mention of Hengest. The dating is probably incorrect, because if Hengest had been in his twenties

when he first arrived in Britain he would now
be in his seventies. Nevertheless, it is just
possible that he was still chieftain among his
people.

The second entry, dated 477, says that: 'In
this year Aelle came to Britain, and his three
sons, Cymen, and Wlencing, and Cissa, with
three ships, at the place which is named
Cymensora [possibly Shoreham] and there slew
many Welsh, and drove some in flight into the
wood which is named Andredeslea'.

Andredeslea is the Weald of Kent, and a
strong British presence indicates that the
success story told by the *Anglo-Saxon
Chronicle* had not been all one-sided. Even at
this date, the Saxons were fighting hard to
establish themselves, and it appears from a
further entry in the *Chronicle*, dated a few
years later, that the British were installed in
some key points: 'In this year Aelle and Cissa
besieged Andredescaester, and slew all that
dwelt therein; not even one Briton was there
left'.

Andredescaester is the Roman fortress of
Anderida (Pevensey), which was one of the
Saxon Shore Forts. Reading between the lines,

then, it seems that although the Saxons might
have controlled much of the countryside, it
was the British who held most of the fortified
towns, even in the south-east, and continued
to do so until they were overwhelmed by
Saxon reinforcements. In East Anglia, the
immigrants seem to have established themselves much more quickly and efficiently; there
seems to have been much less fighting among
the federates who were settled in that area, and
although two of the principal Roman towns of
the area, Camulodunum (Colchester) and
Venta Icenorum (Caister by Norwich) both
show signs through excavation of violent
attack, this has never been firmly dated to the
period in question. Somehow, then, Vortigern
seems to have been able to rally the British to
fight back, and to fight back with success, until
the massacre of the 300 British elders. After
that he was a broken man; in the words of
Nennius, '. . . wandering from place to place,
till his heart broke and he died without
honour'. The tragic, misunderstood Vortigern
was gone. But in the 460s, another British
leader rose in his stead; the resistance was only
just beginning.

Chapter 2

Ambrosius Imperator

The Saxon revolt of the mid-fifth century was accompanied by a mass migration of Britons to Armorica. Their coming is still remembered in the places where they settled; a map of present-day Brittany is scattered with a rash of villages called Bretteville, 'the place of the British'. There were those, however, who did not choose to seek refuge in flight, but who felt that their mission was to stay in Britain, and attempt to restore at least in part the old order of things.

'God strengthened the survivors, and our unhappy countrymen gathered around them from all parts, as eagerly as bees rush to the hive when a storm threatens, "burdening the air with prayers unnumbered". To avoid complete destruction they challenged their conquerors to battle, under the leadership of Ambrosius Aurelianus, perhaps the last of the Romans to survive, whose parents had worn the purple before they were killed in the fury of the storm . . .'.

The words of Gildas are the only clue to the identity of the man who led the British resistance after the time of Vortigern. He apparently came to power sometime in the 460s, and therefore cannot be the same Ambrosius who fought against Vortigern 30 years earlier; but he might have been his son, and if his father had indeed 'worn the purple'—that is to say, had held an imperial position in Britain—then Vortigern must indeed have been a usurper.

We know nothing more about Ambrosius Aurelianus, or how he came to lead a British counter-offensive; but Gildas refers to the men

Surviving masonry of the baths basilica, Wroxeter.

Above *The* piscina—*open-air swimming pool—at*
Wroxeter.
Below *New excavation work at Wroxter—in this*
case, of the macellum—*may reveal more secrets of*
Dark Age occupation.

he led as *cives*, which is translated as citizens.
Gildas, in turn, may have been translating a
Celtic word which means the same thing; that
word is Combrogi, the modern Welsh form of
which is Cymru. Those who sought to
preserve Britain had assumed a new identity,
but it may have had older connotations. For in
fifth century Britain, the patriots who banded
together and called themselves 'citizens' may
have been trying vainly to re-establish a link
with the days when all freeborn Britons were
citizens of the Roman Empire. The core of the
resistance movement must have been the
magnates who still held estates and wealth in
the west, and who as yet had been untouched
by the Saxon threat. It must have been clear to
Ambrosius and his officers that, if the Saxons
were to be overcome on the field of battle, new
tactics would have to be devised in order to
give the British some form of superiority, for
the British were probably outnumbered and
would stand little chance of beating the enemy
in a straightforward hand-to-hand struggle.

In this quest for supremacy, the British had
one big advantage. They had horses; the
Saxons did not. The latter had always been an
infantry force. Indeed, the use of cavalry had
been a feature of the Roman Army only from a
relatively late date, but the Romans had
quickly become skilled in the use of light
horse, and at least some of their cavalry tactics

Lincoln. The old Roman legionary fortress city of Lincoln—Lindocolina Civitas, known later by its Saxon name of Lindcylene—continued as an important settlement throughout the Dark Ages, and was probably used as a base for British cavalry forces during the Arthurian campaigns of the late fifth century. There is visible evidence of the Anglo-Saxon occupation in the form of three churches, the first of which, St Mary Wigford, not far from the railway station, bears the Anglo-Saxon inscription 'Eirtig had me built and endowed to the glory of Christ and St Mary' in the west face of the tower. The tower, and the west wall of the nave, are eleventh century. A point of interest inside the church is an animal's head, carved in a stone in the south jamb of the doorway leading to the tower. The church of St Peter-at-Gowts in the High Street also has a Saxon tower and part of the original west wall of the nave; the arch leading from the latter to the tower is Saxon too. The third of the churches in Lincoln, St Benedict's, also has a Saxon tower, although this has been substantially rebuilt.

The City and County Museum in Broadgate has a rich haul of objects from the Anglo-Saxon cemetery on Loveden Hill, including urns, swords, bucket mounts of iron with sheet bronze repousse work, a thin bronze hanging bowl and a ceremonial whetstone. There is also a collection of Viking artefacts.

---

must have survived into fifth century Britain.

So the force commanded by Ambrosius must have been based largely on cavalry, a small but mobile army with the ability to strike quickly—although not necessarily hard, for the use of heavy cavalry would only come after the invention of the stirrup. It would certainly be able to deal with small groups of enemy, and, because of speed in reconnaissance, would also be able to prevent the assembly of small forces into larger armies. Successful encounters would depend on speed and surprise; Saxon foot soldiers, hit suddenly by a cavalry charge, would almost certainly break and flee in panic, and once they were in flight they could be cut down relatively easily by skilled riders. A cavalry force of the kind that was probably raised and led by Ambrosius, however, could hardly go over to the offensive. Cavalry

operations against static defences—even lightly-stockaded villages—would result in substantial losses, and a cavalryman cannot fight effectively on foot. At best, the British cavalry could hope only to seek out and destroy marauding bands of the enemy, and perhaps make them think twice about penetrating more deeply into British-held areas.

The pattern of British activities in the years after 460 may, conjecturally—for there is no evidence whatsoever, and the best one can do is to try and put oneself in the place of a military commander of the time—have been as follows. From a secure base in the west, possibly Gloucester, British cavalry forces began to probe eastwards, destroying the enemy wherever he was to be found. As advanced bases, the cavalry used the fortified towns that were dotted throughout the lowlands, and which presumably had resisted or escaped Saxon attack; alternatively, in less densely populated areas, they might have found refuge in the reconstituted hill forts. The defences of the latter should have been reasonably secure from Saxon assault; after all, they had only been invested by the Roman Army in the early days of the occupation after considerable effort and loss.

Where Ambrosius came from is not known. The Welsh form of his name is Emrys; but whether Dinas Emrys, the craggy hilltop fort in southern Snowdonia, is linked with him in any way remains a mystery. Some scholars, however, think that it is possible to trace the course of some of his campaigns in Britain from place-names that preserve his memory.

These include Amesbury in Wiltshire and

Dinas Emrys (Gwynedd). Perched on a craggy hilltop in Snowdonia, Dinas Emrys was occupied well into the Dark Ages and is traditionally associated with both Vortigern and Ambrosius, from whose name Emrys is derived. Traces of stone walling have been found on both the east and west sides. The fort may be approached either by a tough climb through the triple ramparts to the western entrance, or more easily from the east. It lies just off the A498, a mile and a half north of Beddgelert. *(OS Sheet 115, 606492.)*

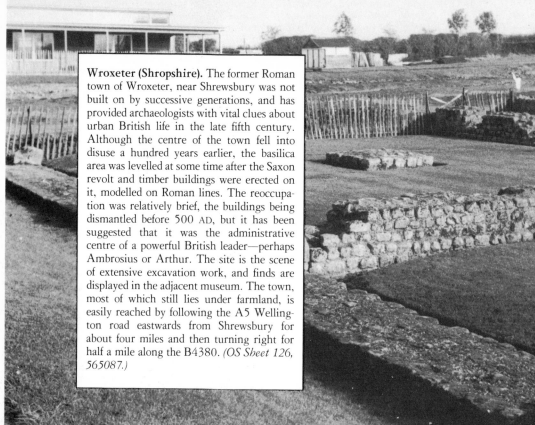

Wroxeter (Shropshire). The former Roman town of Wroxeter, near Shrewsbury was not built on by successive generations, and has provided archaeologists with vital clues about urban British life in the late fifth century. Although the centre of the town fell into disuse a hundred years earlier, the basilica area was levelled at some time after the Saxon revolt and timber buildings were erected on it, modelled on Roman lines. The reoccupation was relatively brief, the buildings being dismantled before 500 AD, but it has been suggested that it was the administrative centre of a powerful British leader—perhaps Ambrosius or Arthur. The site is the scene of extensive excavation work, and finds are displayed in the adjacent museum. The town, most of which still lies under farmland, is easily reached by following the A5 Wellington road eastwards from Shrewsbury for about four miles and then turning right for half a mile along the B4380. *(OS Sheet 126, 565087.)*

several Amberleys, including one in Herefordshire, one in Gloucestershire and one in Sussex. There are, in all, perhaps as many as 20 such derivations, none of which have a connexion with local features; there are, for example, a lot of Amber- names in Derbyshire, but these are derived from the river of that name. The names that may be connected with Ambrosius extend in a broad sweep from the West Country into Hampshire, Kent and East Anglia, with a particularly dense concentration north of the Thames in Essex. Also, archaeology has turned up concentrations of weapons at river crossings, and the remains of warriors dating from the Dark Age period have been found at intervals at the East Anglian end of the Icknield Way, the ancient road running diagonally across Britain from the Cotswolds to the flat lands of the East Coast. Such remains cannot be precisely dated to the time of Ambrosius; they may be the relics of much later Dark Age battles. But the fact that they are distributed along the Icknield Way, the possession of which was strategically important in preventing expansion to the north and west, suggests that the combatants were British and Saxon.

John Morris, in his excellent book *The Age of Arthur* (Weidenfeld & Nicolson, 1973) has done much valuable detective work in an attempt to sort out some fact from the confusion of this period. One extract in particular is intriguing.

'Sometimes the detail suggests an incident. On a Roman farmstead at Dunstable a Saxon warrior was buried beside the upper summer track of the Icknield Way. The underside of his skull was stove in, smashed by a blunt instrument before he was buried; and with him was a broken spear without a point. He was buried hardly later than the fifth century, for by the second half of the sixth century a Saxon village and its cemetery occupied the site, and these

Opposite page and above and below *The baths complex at Wroxeter, which played such an important part in the everyday life of the town's Romano-British citizens, may still have been in use to a limited extent in the Dark Age period.*

Bichamditch (Norfolk). On some maps this is erroneously labelled 'Devil's Dyke'. It cuts across the Downham Market-Swaffham road to the east of Marham Airfield, and probably dates from the time of the British counter-offensive under Ambrosius Aurelianus and Arthur. *(OS Sheet 144, 749129-740064.)*

later burials cut into his grave; it was therefore already forgotten and unrecognisable. A mile away across the Watling Street a spur of the Chilterns rises sharp above the Roman town to a flat defensible top. Halfway down the hillside, a ditch of unknown date is cut into the chalk. It was dug in an unusual place, unlike the ditches of normal earthworks, at the point where the slope suddenly ceases to be sharp and becomes gradual. Above the ditch, the descent is too sharp for horses to be ridden on slippery grass; at the ditch men might mount to charge down the gentle incline. Below the ditch, men on foot might run uphill; above it they could only walk. Nothing dates the ditch; but the site suggests the possibility that a force of British cavalry encamped upon the hill-top, intending to attack the Saxon villages grouped around Dunstable, and took precautions against counter-attack. The injuries to the dead man's skull are those that a horse's hoof could have caused. But if it were so, the result was not a decisive British victory. The villages of the Dunstable Saxons continued uninterrupted, and the survivors were able to carry their dead from the battlefield for decent burial.'

Assuming that something of the sort did in fact happen, then this must have been the kind of skirmish which characterised the campaigns of Ambrosius. His cavalry forces were not large enough to achieve a decisive victory; the best they could hope for was to hold the Saxons in check and to keep them constantly on the defensive with the skilful use of hit-and-run

Above and above right The baths basilica, Wroxeter. From 450 until a date late in the fifth century, this area was fully occupied, and timber houses modelled on classic Roman lines were erected there. These, apparently, were later dismantled and the Romano-British inhabitants moved to a place of greater safety.

tactics. In fact, it is probable that by this time, the state of the former Roman roads was such as to impede the rapid movement of large bodies of men, whether on foot or on horse-back. Roads in the more affluent British-held areas might have remained in repair for some considerable time, but elsewhere, as the need for long-distance communication declined, they must have fallen out of use fairly quickly. Indeed, the native population had probably never used the roads at all to any degree, preferring the ancient tracks and ridgeways used by their ancestors.

Along the roads themselves, the wooden bridges would have been the first to succumb to the combined effect of disrepair and weather; and with the bridges gone, possession of the relatively few fordable crossings would have assumed major importance. Most movement, then, must have taken place along the old tracks, which tends to give the lie to the traditional image of hordes of barbarians flooding out across the land from their Kentish and East Anglian bases to burn and pillage. Movement must have been by small groups of people, settlers seeking new land; fighting

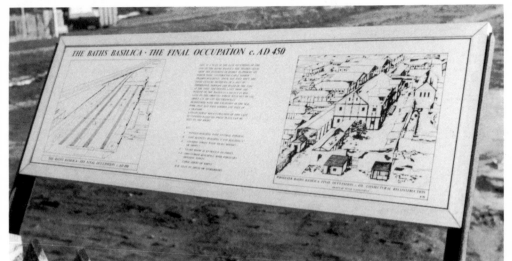

where they had to, but in all probability existing in a kind of uneasy peace with British neighbours and intermarrying with them.

One area where reasonably large movement does seem to have taken place is southern Cambridgeshire, where the broad strip of chalky land that lies between the northern fens and the wooded claylands to the south is intersected by a series of large ditches, the biggest and most famous of which is Devil's Dyke. These lie astride the Icknield Way, and from two of them comes archaeological evidence of fighting involving Saxon warriors. There are two possibilities; the first is that the ditches

Bokerley Dyke (Dorset). An impressive linear earthwork some six miles long, Bokerley Dyke was first built by the Romans across the road to Old Sarum, later dismantled and then rebuilt by the Romano-British as a barrier against the Saxon advances of the fifth and sixth centuries. The ditch runs close to the A354 on the Hampshire–Dorset border, 1¼ miles south-west of Martin Drove End. *(OS Sheet 184, 032199-063168 (best section).)*

Brent Ditch (Cambridge). Designed to cut the Roman road of which the A11 Bishop's Stortford–Newmarket road forms part to the south-east of Cambridge, the Brent Ditch lies a mile south of the A11's junction with the A505 and a little to the east of the main road. It is two miles in length, running in a south-easterly direction. *(OS Sheet 154, 515474.)*

were thrown up by the Saxons as a defensive measure, the second that they were clearly-defined boundaries between Saxon and British territory, and that skirmishing took place in their vicinity. The latter case is probably the correct interpretation, although whether the ditches were erected at the time of Ambrosius, there is no way of telling. They may even have been put up earlier, to form a defensive bulwark against Pictish raiders; a knife-handle with Pictish symbols on it was found near Devil's Dyke, although there is no evidence that a Pict was the owner.

Ambrosius Aurelianus probably remained in command of the British war effort until sometime in the 470s. Nothing is known of the battles he fought, or of his real status; he may have been just a military commander, but it is far more likely that he was greater than that—perhaps even styled Imperator, emperor of the British. There may also be a clue to his seat of government. Recently, excavation has shown that Wroxeter (Viconium, the fourth largest town of Roman Britain and the tribal capital of the Cornovii) near Shrewsbury, which was abandoned and gradually demolished about 350, was rebuilt sometime in the latter part of the fifth century. Where the basilica had stood, a hard core of thousands of tons of rubble was laid, and many timber buildings were erected on it. They included a great hall, 125 ft long and 52 ft wide, with a narrower extension some 80 ft in length. The hall was finished in classical style, as were the buildings

Devil's Dyke (Cambridge). The most impressive of all the East Anglian earthworks, the Devil's Dyke extends for a full seven miles from Reach to Ditton Green. The best way to approach it is to take the B1102 Cambridge–Mildenhall road to a point a mile or so past Swaffham Prior. The origin of the Dyke is in dispute; it may have been built during the British-Saxon partition, or as a defence against Pictish raiders attacking the East Anglian coast. In either event, it controls the Icknield Way, the ancient ridgeway route into East Anglia. It was originally about 30 ft high. *(OS Sheet 154, 567660-653583.)*

that surrounded it; it was as though the architects, with the materials that were available, had sought to recapture the majesty that the empire's builders had wrought in stone and marble.

The rebuilding of Wroxeter must have involved great expenditure, and the kind of skills which are not normally associated with late fifth century life in Britain. The work obviously required careful planning, and it is hard to imagine why it was undertaken in the first place unless those who planned it had meant to turn Wroxeter into a centre of major importance, a seat of government on the lines of those that graced the provincial cities of the

empire. Then, suddenly, towards the end of the fifth century, Wroxeter was abandoned and its structures dismantled. The reason, probably, was that it was under some kind of threat, and was no longer considered to be easily defensible. This implies that the struggle to retain the Romano-British identity was changing course; that the dream of re-establishing an inviolate corner of the empire had died, and that the fight now was solely one of survival.

We shall never know what really happened during the turbulent latter half of the fifth century. But Ambrosius Aurelianus is the only British leader who is named after Vortigern for nearly a century, and the part he played

must have been considerable. He is even said to have built a navy, and this may be true; it is a fact that during the 460s, British emigrants were able to cross the Channel to settle in Brittany without interference from the Saxons, which suggests some form of seaborne protection, and about 470 the last emperor of the west, Anthemius, engaged the services of a British naval force to sail up the Loire to Bourges, where their task was to stem a Gothic invasion until a Roman army arrived. The latter failed to get there in time and the British were defeated; but the action they fought may have been decisive, for the Goths never became masters of the whole of Gaul.

The fact that Ambrosius was prepared to send aid to Gaul is important, for this in itself reveals that Britain, alone of all the nations north of the Alps, was still loyal to the idea of empire. But by 476, Odovacer, the great adventurer whose Germanic mercenaries had taken control of much of northern Italy, had transferred his allegiance to the Empire of the East, and had brought the line of western emperors to an end. The Western Empire was no more. No more, that is, save for what might have been one last outpost. That outpost was Britain; and out of the mists, after Ambrosius, a great and shadowy figure arose to be its leader. His name was Arthur.

Chapter 3

Arthur: the fact and the legend

Traditionally, the legendary hero Arthur finished the task Ambrosius Aurelianus had begun, waging the campaign against the Saxons to a decisive conclusion. Gildas makes no mention of him; the first inkling that such a figure ever existed comes in the Nennius texts, which inform us that there were 'many more noble than he'; in other words, he was not a member of a royal dynasty, which is perhaps why Gildas ignores him. Nennius gives the real clue as to Arthur's status: 'Arthur fought against the Saxons alongside the kings of the Britons, but he himself was *Dux Bellorum*'.

Dux Bellorum is a Roman military title, 'leader of battles'. Specifically, it is applied to a cavalry commander. It is logical to suppose, then, given that Arthur was a true historical figure, that he served as a cavalry leader under Ambrosius Aurelianus, and afterwards, on the latter's death or retirement, assumed command of the whole army of the Britons. This must have been sometime in the mid-470s, a date that probably coincided with the arrival in Britain, according to the *Anglo-Saxon Chronicle*, of Cerdic, who was credited by later historians—probably erroneously—with founding the Kingdom of Wessex. For Cerdic is a British, not a Saxon name, which opens up all kinds of fascinating possibilities—not the least of which is that he was Vortigern's son, Hengest's grandson, returning to the island in maturity to claim his inheritance.

Cerdic may have been Arthur's principal enemy, at least in the south. But if the list of battles fought by Arthur—or Artorius, to give him the more appropriate Romanised form of his name—is anywhere near correct, then his enemies must have been much more varied and widespread. Once again, the list is supplied by Nennius:

'The first battle was at the mouth of the river which is called Glein. The next four were on the banks of another river, which is called Dubglas and is in the region Linnuis. The sixth was upon the river which is called Bassas. The seventh was in the wood of Celidon; that is, Cat Coit Celidon. The eighth was by Castle Guinnion, in which Arthur carried on his shoulders an image of St Mary Ever Virgin, and there was a great slaughter of them, through the strength of Our Lord Jesus Christ and of the holy Mary his maiden-mother. The ninth was in the City of the Legion. The tenth was on the bank of the river that is called Tribruit. The eleventh was on the hill that is called Agned. The twelfth was on Mount Badon, in which, on that one day, there fell in one onslaught of Arthur's 960 men; and none slew them but himself alone, and in all his battles he remained victorious.'

The sites of some of these battles can be located with fair certainty; the big problem is that they might be completely out of context in the Nennius collection, and some of them might not even be Arthur's. For the first battle, on the River Glein, there are two possibilities. There is a River Glen in both Northumberland and Lincolnshire, and if this battle is attributed to Arthur the Lincolnshire site is more probable than the other, considering that his main mission would be to hold the Anglo-Saxons in check.

Tintagel (Cornwall). Tintagel, one of the most spectacular and interesting Dark Age sites in Britain, is the traditional birthplace of 'King' Arthur—although the tradition seems to have been started by Geoffrey of Monmouth in his *History of the Kings of Britain* several centuries later. To reach Tintagel, take the B3263 which forks off the A39 Stratton–Truro road. From the car park in Tintagel village, follow the path which leads across a small stream between precipitous cliffs up to the walls of the castle. This is mediaeval, dating from the twelfth century; the Dark Age remains stand on the exposed headland known as the island, and are reached via a bridge and stone steps. These remains, which are monastic, appear as clusters of low drystone walls and are identified by letters. Excavation in the mid-1930s showed that the monastery dated from the fifth of sixth century, at which time—judging from many pottery fragments—trade with the Mediterranean still flourished. A large porched wooden building which once stood on Site F may have been a library, while a smaller rectangular building nearby was perhaps a school. Site B enclosed several smaller buildings, probably living quarters, grouped around a courtyard, while structures on Sites C and D may have been barns and byres. Site E is mostly obscured by the remains of a mediaeval garden, while hardly anything is visible of Site G. Site A, however, which lies on the edge of the plateau, encloses the religious hub of the monastery, including a possible oratory and a square block of masonry in the courtyard that was probably an open-air shrine. Excavations at Tintagel have proved extremely important when linked with the study of other Dark Age sites in Britain, the study of pottery fragments having led to more accurate dating elsewhere *(OS Sheet 200, 050890.)*

Tintagel, one of the most spectacular and interesting of all Dark Age sites in Britain, is the traditional birthplace of Arthur. It was certainly a very important religious centre, and probably had significant connections with the Mediterranean during the early Dark Age period (L. Woodhouse).

River Glen. The Glen, possibly the same as 'Glein', one of Arthur's battles, flows north-south through the area between Grantham and Stamford, in Lincolnshire, roughly following the line of the B1176 road. Its north-south course may have made it a natural boundary during the period of partition that followed the wars of Ambrosius and Arthur, and as such there may have been frequent skirmishing at crossing-points.

The River Glen near Greatford, Lincolnshire, may have been the site of 'Glein', the Arthurian battle mentioned in the Nennius texts.

The next four battles can also be narrowed down to a specific area. 'Linnuis' is the Lincolnshire district of Lindsey, which would also fit the pattern; the name 'Dubglas' means simply 'Black Water' and could refer to a number of streams, although the only significant river in the Lindsey district is the Witham. These battles were probably fought against an English force, and their object may have been to secure Lincoln against the Middle and East Angles, driving a wedge between them and English settlements farther north, around the Humber.

The sixth site, the river 'Bassas', cannot be identified. But the seventh can; the Wood of Celidon is the forest that once covered most of Strathclyde, north of the Solway Firth. What Arthur's forces were doing there can only be guessed at—if, indeed, Arthur was involved at all. The enemy here may have been Picts, or Irish, or a combination of the two, forestalled from attacking southwards by a timely British intervention.

The eighth battle—'Castle Guinnion'—has

Looking out over the Lindsey district of Lincolnshire from the A631, east of Corringham. Lindsey was the 'Linnuis' mentioned in the Nennius text as the scene of an Arthurian battle.

long puzzled historians. There is, in fact, a possible solution to where it took place, but only if it is lifted out of the Arthurian context and placed a century later, when the sixth century chieftain Urien of Rheged was fighting the Angles for control of the north country. One of Urien's battles was Gwen Ystrad, in which—according to his bard, Taliesin— his forces fought around a place with a low rampart and a river ford called Granwynion. It does not take a great deal of imagination to see how 'Granwynion' might be corrupted into 'Guinnion'. If the two are one and the same, it means that the compiler of the Nennius texts tacked on a later Dark Age battle to the earlier list; either that, or Arthur did indeed fight a battle of 'Granwynion', just as his successor Urien did a hundred years afterwards. This is not an impossibility, for 'Granwynion' has been tentatively identified as Vinovium—the Roman fort of Binchester, which lies north of the present town if Bishop Auckland, County Durham, and which once commanded a vital river crossing on the line of Dere Street, the old strategic road that runs northward from York into Caledonia. Whoever held Dere Street, with its forts, held the north, and more than one Dark Age battle was fought for its possession.

The ninth battle—'Urbs Legionis', the City of Legion—is much easier to identify; it is either Caerleon or Chester, but again it is impossible to guess who Arthur's enemies may have been. Irish sea raiders, however, would seem likely in either case. The tenth

> River 'Dubglas'. This is possibly one and the same as the River Blackwater in Essex, a favourite mooring spot for pirate raiders throughout the Dark Age period; fierce battles were fought around this area at a later date between English and Danes, the battle of Maldon being the most notable. If an Arthurian battle was indeed fought here, it was probably in the form of a British assault on Saxon base camps in the neighbourhood of the estuary.

battle, also, may be fitted fairly snugly into southern Scotland, for Tribruit is a Caledonian name.

The eleventh battle is a mystery—unless it, too, is out of context. 'Mount Agned' appears under different guises in the various copies of Nennius' *Historia*; in one it is named Agned Cat Bregomion, and attempts have been made to identify this with Bremenium, the Roman fort at High Rochester in the Cheviots—again, one of the strongholds that guarded Dere Street. If Arthur fought a battle there, it cannot have been against the Anglo-Saxons, for another half-century was to pass before they penetrated this area. But Urien of Rheged

'The River Ford of Granwynion'—the bend in the River Wear north of Bishop Auckland, with the tree-shrouded ramparts of Binchester ford beyond. Was this the scene of Arthur's 'Castle Guinnion' battle—or a battle fought by Urien of Rheged a century later?

Binchester fort.

fought them here, and his battle is recorded.

Finally there is the most famous and controversial Arthurian battle of all, 'Mons Badonicus'—Mount Badon. It was fought, as nearly as can be established, about 495, and is named by Gildas, writing 40 years or so later when the memory of the British achievement must have been as fresh as the memory of the Battle of Britain is to our own generation. There is no doubt that Badon was a British victory, and a decisive one at that. It may have been an all-out attempt by the English of the south to smash the British by invading their territory; if that is the case, it went disastrously wrong. If the English did succeed in penetrating deeply into British territory, their army must have been of considerable size; a joint force, perhaps, assembled by the rulers of the embryo English kingdoms that were springing up in the south and south-east. The names of three such rulers come to the fore: Aesc of Kent, Cerdic of the West Saxons, and Aelle of the South Saxons, aged now but still with a voice to be heard. Both the *Anglo-Saxon Chronicle* and the Venerable Bede state that Aelle was overking of the southern English at this time.

Let us suppose, then, that an English field army was assembled and marched from the south towards the British strongholds in the west, its primary task being to besiege and

destroy the reconstituted hill-forts which provided secure bases for the British cavalry. With these obstacles out of the way, there would be nothing to stop the Anglo-Saxon army from rolling forward to the Severn, driving a great wedge between the British of Dumnonia—Devon and Cornwall—and those of the Cotswolds. Fifteen centuries later, part of Operation Sealion, the German plan to invade Britain, was to envisage exactly the same thing.

Some historians have tried to identify Badon with Bath, but Gildas states specifically that the site was a 'mons', or hill, which does not fit Bath at all. The battle is much more likely to have been fought on or around one of the major hill-forts that stood in the way of the English advance. Gildas also says that the battle of Badon was a siege; he does not say who was besieging whom, but it seems likely that the cavalry were on the defensive, surrounded by superior numbers of enemy infantry. Of all the places that might fit the description of 'Mons Badonicus', two in particular stand out. The first is Solsbury Hill near Batheaston, which has steep sides and could be readily defended by a small body of dismounted men; but a more likely choice is Liddington Castle, a notable Iron Age hill-fort near Swindon, in Wiltshire. Nearby lies the village of Badbury; the name is Saxon—Baddan-byrig—and the first part of it could have been derived from the Celtic 'Badon'.

Liddington Castle, in about 500 AD, stood squarely between the Anglo-Saxon settlements of the south-east and the British-controlled areas of the west. It was a kind of Dark Age Stalingrad, a mighty obstacle that had to be

The road to Mount Badon? The minor road leading from Badbury village, Wiltshire, to Liddington Castle.

overwhelmed before the advance could continue, for it commanded the strategic road junction between Ermine Street, the main Roman road south, and the Great Ridgeway, the Dark Age artery running across central Britain. Excavation has shown that Liddington Castle was re-fortified and re-occupied late in the fifth century. Anyone manning the defences of Liddington would have the advantage of a superb all-round view, and it would be logical for a British commander to set up his head-quarters here, astride the approach route to the west.

The battle of Mount Badon, then, was a tremendous victory for the British. It is useless to guess at the pattern the struggle might have followed, for battles seldom follow the test-book. The Nennius manuscript, however, makes one significant comment: 'There fell in one onslaught of Arthur's 960 men; and none slew them but himself alone . . .'. This does not, of course, mean that Arthur personally despatched nearly a thousand of the enemy. It means that, for once, his forces were acting independently, with no aid from any of the Romano-British rulers of the west. So the

Solsbury Hill (Avon). Lying two miles north of Bath across the River Avon, Solsbury Hill is another candidate for the battle of Mount Badon. Its sides are steep, making it easily defensible, and from the fort on its summit there is a fine view south-east down the Avon Valley. The best way to reach it, from Bath, is to follow the north bank of the river for two miles via the A4 Chippenham road, then turn sharp left on the outskirts of Batheaston village. *(OS Sheet 172, 768680.)*

Badbury. Its Saxon name, Baddanbyrig, may be derived from an earlier Celtic 'Badon'.

picture gradually emerges of a cavalry force of perhaps a thousand men, not more, under attack on Mount Badon by perhaps three of four times that many infantry; and the cavalry, eventually spotting some enemy weakness, launching a devastating charge that broke the attacking army and put it to flight, inflicting enormous slaughter on it during the pursuit that followed.

Liddington Castle (Wiltshire). According to recent theories, this hill fort near Swindon may be the site of the battle of Mons Badonicus—Mount Badon—where the British under Arthur routed the Saxons. The theory is reinforced by the name of Badbury village, which is situated about a mile to the west and which was known to the early English as Baddan-byrig. The 'Baddan' might be derived from the Celtic 'Badon'. Recent excavation has shown that the impressive ramparts were rebuilt at some stage during the post-Roman period; the logical conclusion is that the British occupied the fort in order to control the Ridge Way that runs past it across the Marlborough Downs, Liddington Castle lies five miles south-east of Swindon; the best way to reach it is to follow the A345 south to Chiseldon and then turn left along the Ridge Way. The fort lies to the right of the road, and the hill on which it stands is easily identifiable from a long way off. *(OS Sheet 174, 209707.)*

The *Anglo-Saxon Chronicle*, predictably, makes no mention of Mount Badon. It does not need to do so. For the next 30 years or more, there is no further record of westward expansion. The Anglo-Saxons in the south had suffered a reverse that was to hold them static for a generation or more; a generation that left the Romano-British free to try to re-create something of their long-lost society. The tragedy was that it was too late. The memory of Roman civilisation was too dim and hazy, although it was not lost altogether. The Britons who had fought to preserve it were themselves slipping inexorably into barbarism; ironically, it would be their enemies, the Anglo-Saxons themselves, who would one day re-create, in Britain, something of the orderly society of Rome.

That was still a long way in the future. In 500 AD, two alien cultures, the Romano-British and the Anglo-Saxon, were sliding into the melting-pot that would remould them both and mingle them in one great new culture; the British nation. The victory of Mount Badon made this possible, for Britain, alone of all the former Roman provinces, suffered no overwhelming onslaught that resulted in the total

Top right *Liddington Castle, near Swindon. An Iron Age hill fort, reconstituted in the late fifth century, this is a likely contender for the site of Arthur's Mons Badonicus battle.*
Centre right and right *These two photographs, taken at the summit of Liddington Castle, give a good impression of the massive nature of the defensive ramparts.*

subjugation of her native races. Badon bought a generation's breathing-space, and when the struggle was eventually renewed, it was from a position of consolidation and strength on both sides.

Elsewhere, it was a different story. By 500, Gaul had ceased to exist, overrun by the armies of Clovis, King of the Franks; the Alemanni of southern Germany also came under the heel, as did Bohemia. In 507 he grasped the kingdom of the Visigoths in Aquitaine—the first mediaeval state, where Alaric's people had settled following the sack of Rome nearly a century earlier, and the unhappy survivors fled across the mountains into Spain. So the land that was to become France was born. In Italy, too, Odovacer, the great military commander who had brought an end to Roman imperial rule in the west, was himself overthrown in 489 by the Ostrogoths, who set their own emperor, Theodoric, upon the Italian throne. Western continental Europe was now one great Germanic confederation, as alien to what remained of the Romano-British culture as the Saxons, and in some cases more so.

The events in Britain that followed Badon are as confused and uncertain as those that led up to it. It is likely that the British followed up their success by wresting back at least some territory from the Anglo-Saxons, and that a strict partition was enforced between the two

Looking west from Liddington Castle towards Swindon. The narrow road is the Ridge Way.

peoples. Gildas refers to a *Lugubri divortio barbarorum*—unfortunate partition with the barbarians—in lamenting that certain Christian shrines could no longer be reached by the British. The years after Badon may have witnessed some kind of peace treaty, with certain areas of territory ceded by both sides—but with the British now presumably holding most of the cards—and clearly defined boundaries separating the two sides. Saxon burial grounds provide evidence of such a partition; some cemeteries contain grave goods from the fifth and later sixth centuries, but from the early sixth century there is nothing—an indication that the area was abandoned by the Saxons for many years.

With the Anglo-Saxons under control, at least for the time being, the resurgent British administration under Arthur may have set itself the task of securing Britain's former Roman frontiers, hence the campaigns in Caledonia. There may also have been more tribal movements about this time, as there had been 70 years earlier, when Cunedda of the Votadini moved to Wales; one genealogy suggests that he was followed in Arthurian times by his grandson, Marianus, who gave his name to Merioneth.

As part of his frontier policy, Arthur may

have set about purging south-west Wales (Demetia, which was later to become Pembrokeshire and part of Carmarthenshire) of Irish colonists. Cunedda had cleared them from the north and his descendants had successfully held them at bay during the succeeding decades, but in Demetia an Irish colony had been well established for more than a century. As evidence of a sudden change, John Morris (*The Age of Arthur*) claims that independent British and Irish lists of the Demetian kings agree on one point; the names are Irish until about 500, when they revert not just to British—but Roman. Morris quotes as one example Agricola, son of Tribunus, which may be a genealogist's mistake for Agricola the Tribune. Agricola was the father of Vortipor, whose tombstone survives to this day, and Morris points out that on it he is styled not 'king', but 'Protector'—a Roman military rank which, in the fifth century, had a kingly connotation. If Arthur did campaign in south Wales, then the battle Nennius calls 'The City of the Legion' may well have been at Caerleon-on-Usk.

It is tempting to suppose that, in the years after Badon, Arthur may have risen to be emperor over the shades of Roman Britain. If so, it is strange that Gildas does not mention him, for Gildas was writing less than half a century after these events. It is possible, however, that the memory of Arthur was still so fresh and vivid that Gildas never even thought of mentioning him by name. In any case, Gildas' diatribe was levelled at the petty kings, the tyrants, who followed Arthur's 'golden age'.

At this point, it is worth digressing to see how the fact of Arthur was turned into legend, and how a British Dark Age warrior became one of the principal heroes—perhaps *the* hero—of the English-speaking world. It took six centuries and a Norman invasion for it to happen, despite the fact that Arthurian stories were current in Wales and Brittany throughout that long period. The Anglo-Saxons

undoubtedly knew of the tales, but they concerned an old enemy; besides, the English had their own folk heroes. So had the French. When the Normans advanced up Senlac hill to meet Harold's English on that day in 1066, William's minstrel Taillefer rode before them, singing the High Song of Charlemagne and Roland, stirring the Normans with the tale of the hero and his host who had died defending the pass at Roncesvalles against the Saracen invader. This was the 'Matter of France', a kind of high-born mystique that elevated French kings to something that seemed larger than life; but there was no equivalent 'Matter of Britain' to strengthen the pedigree of the embryo monarchy that was founded in England by the Duke of Normandy. When the Norman overlords began to have glimpses of the shadowy figure that was Arthur, through

The Ridge Way. Winding across the Marlborough Downs, this road was probably used by the Saxon army advancing into the Romano-British areas of the west, only to be confronted and destroyed by Arthur's forces at Badon.

> **South Cadbury (Somerset).** Another
> isolated hill fort dating to the Iron Age,
> South Cadbury is traditionally associated
> with Camelot, the legendary 'Court of King
> Arthur'. The upper rampart was strengthened
> late in the fifth century with timbers faced in
> stone, and traces have been found of a large
> timber feasting hall and a big timber gateway
> on the south-west side. The 18-acre area of
> the fort was thoroughly fortified, so South
> Cadbury must have been an important
> centre, although there is no proof of any
> association with Arthur. It was abandoned by
> the British after 658, when the Saxons
> conquered Somerset, and has the distinction
> of being the biggest of all the fortified Dark
> Age settlements. It also had a history
> extending over 4,000 years, having been first
> occupied by neolithic settlers and in the end
> by the English in the eleventh century, its
> defences finally being demolished by the
> Danes under Cnut. The fort lies five and a
> half miles south-west of Wincanton and a
> quarter of a mile south of South Cadbury
> village. It can be reached from the A303
> Wincanton–Sparkford road. *(OS Sheet 183,
> 628252.)*

folklore and legend, their intrigue was therefore understandable.

It was the Benedictine monk and historian William of Malmesbury, a literary mind of no mean repute, who was the first to try to crystallise the legend into something more tangible. The story goes that, sometime between 1125 and 1130, he visited Glastonbury Abbey in Somerset, which was believed to have existed as a small church in Arthur's time, and there his fellow Benedictines told him of the hero who had broken the Saxons at Badon and brought peace to the land for a generation. William already knew something of the Welsh legend, and he realised that the central figure in the stories must be one and the same person. Setting down his thoughts afterwards, William summed up the whole question of the Arthurian legend in simple, forthright words: 'This is that Arthur of whom modern Welsh fancy raves. Yet he plainly deserves to be remembered in genuine history rather than in the oblivion of silly fairy tales; for he long preserved his dying country.'

A few years later, the story was taken up and elaborated by another writer, Geoffrey of Monmouth, who produced, in Latin, a work entitled *History of the Kings of Britain*. He dealt at length with Arthur's reign, claiming that his writings were based on an old British manuscript given to him by 'Walter, archdeacon of Oxford'. Such a person certainly existed, but the source remains a mystery; and although Geoffrey undoubtedly drew heavily on Welsh and Cornish legend, his writings were fanciful and inventive. It was he who formulated the Arthurian pedigree that was to be passed down in all successive writings on the subject during the centuries that followed. After dealing with a highly dubious succession of early British kings, who are followed by a Roman 'protectorate', he introduces Constantine as sovereign at the end of the Roman era and gives him two sons, Ambrosius and Uther Pendragon. Arthur enters the scene as the illegitimate child of Uther, his mother being Ygerne and his birthplace Tintagel. Later, when Ygerne's husband is killed in battle, Uther marries her and legitimises his son, who succeeds to the throne as a young man and launches into a war against the Saxons.

It is Geoffrey who introduces all the names which form the core of the Arthurian legend: his sword Caliburn, forged by fairies on the magical isle of Avalon, his wife Ganhumara, his noble lieutenants Kay, Bedevere, Lot and Gawain. Geoffrey has Arthur campaigning in Ireland, the Orkneys, Iceland and Gaul, where he fights the armies of the Emperor Lucius; in this case, Geoffrey appears to have woven in the earlier exploits of Magnus Maximus. He also takes a name that appears briefly in the old Welsh annals—Medraut—and turns him into Modred, Arthur's nephew, who subsequently leads a rebellion against him and is responsible for his downfall.

Top right *Solsbury Hill, Batheaston, on the outskirts of Bath. A reconstituted hill fort, this is another contender for the site of the Mount Badon battle.*
Centre right *The ramparts of Solsbury Hill.*
Right *The view from Solsbury Hill, looking down the valley of the Avon. This photograph gives a good idea of the commanding position enjoyed by the defenders of a hill fort.*

Glastonbury (Somerset). Although Glastonbury is traditionally identified with Avalon, the burial-place of Arthur, this tradition goes back only to the twelfth century and probably has no basis in fact. Nevertheless, Glastonbury—today consisting of a group of hills surrounded by rich meadowland which was once marshland and swamp—is a very old site; excavations have turned up pre-Roman pottery dating from the second or third century BC. The 'island' of Glastonbury was once linked to the mainland by a low narrow causeway which is now followed by the line of the A361 Shepton Mallet road. The highest of the hills that form the island is the Tor, which rises prominently above the surrounding meadows; it is possible that this was the centre of a great pagan sanctuary which was subsequently Christianised. There is, in fact, evidence of a very early Christian foundation at Glastonbury; relics of two Celtic saints, St Indracht and St Patrick, are thought to have been kept here, and the 'island' may have been an important place of Celtic pilgrimage before the Saxon conquest of Somerset in the seventh century. The tower that dominates Glastonbury Tor is all that remains of the mediaeval Church of St Michael, while Glastonbury Abbey, although rich in Arthurian legend, in fact dates from the twelfth and thirteenth centuries—700 years after his reported death.

Geoffrey's fabulous exploits of Arthur received a big boost in 1154, when Henry II came to the throne of England. The Plantagenets saw in the Arthurian saga a unique status symbol, one that would give them an equal—if not superior—standing with the French kings who still basked in the light of Charlemagne, and they went to extraordinary lengths to show that they were the heirs of Arthur. The story has it that Henry, while travelling through Wales, learned that Arthur's body was buried in Glastonbury, which—surrounded as it was my waterlogged marshes—was now thought by many to be the semi-mystical Avalon. The king asked the Glastonbury monks to search for the tomb, but they seem to have resisted his request. Not until 1184, when the abbey burned down, did the quest begin, and Henry did not live to see it. But in 1190, the story runs, the searchers

discovered, seven feet down, a stone slab and a lead cross, on which were inscribed the words *Hic iacet sepultus inclitus Rex Arturius in insola Avalonia*: Here lies buried the renowned King Arthur in the Isle of Avalon. Nine feet further down, the diggers uncovered a great coffin made from a hollow oak log. It contained the skeleton of a tall man, with an injury to his skull, and some smaller bones with a scrap of yellow hair—presumably the remains of Ganhumara.

The Plantagenets were able to announce that Arthur was really dead, and that his heritage was theirs. A year later, Richard I, on his way to the Third Crusade, carried with him a present for Tancred of Sicily; a great broadsword which he claimed was Arthur's Caliburn, or 'Excalibur' as the name had now become in the Norman-French romances.

The whole affair was probably one of history's biggest confidence tricks, and the bones, gathered up and deposited among the abbey's sacred relics, were conveniently lost at a later date. But it served the purpose of the Plantagenet monarchs very well, and as the story spread it altered subtly until Arthur became not so much a warrior king but a figure of wisdom and chivalry, presiding over a Round Table and surrounded by faithful and brave knights who championed just causes and who, in fact, displayed all the qualities that were conspicuously lacking in the mediaeval lords whose minstrels sang of them. Yet some glimmers of truth shone through the tangled web of fabrication. The knights of the Arthurian legend were, for the most part, fictitious or else woven in from other stories; but some had a true Dark Age origin. Tristan, for example, the tragic lover of Yseult, was a fact; he was a petty king who lived at Castle Dore, Cornwall, in the middle of the sixth century. Sir Perceval, too, had his origin in Peredur of York, who died in 580 and was one of the heirs of the Coel dynasty of the Pennines.

Successive ages twisted the legend and stamped it with their own imprint, granting gallantry and power beyond belief to Arthur and his knights and bringing them to the rescue of Britain in her hour of need. Subsequently, every landmark in British history was to be followed by a resurgence of Arthurian legend, altered each time to fit the needs of the age. At the end of the Wars of the Roses, for example, Sir Thomas Malory produced his *Morte d'Arthur*; Caxton edited it and printed it in 1485, and in its English text the legend achieved fame as never before. The story was resurrected under the auspices of the Tudor and Stuart monarchs, and in the great days of Victorian empire the members of Tennyson's Round Table became a race of hardy but benevolent adventurers, admired by lesser breeds and prepared to stand firm to the end in their defence. And in 1940, with Britain in the direst peril she had known for a thousand years, Francis Brett Young recalled the Arthurian legend with these beautiful lines:

Arthur is gone . . . But he will come again
Riding to Camelot on a May morning
When hawthorn-buds are swollen, and the dykes
Golden with water-blobs and fringed with spears
Of yellow marsh-flags; and a glittering host
Will ride behind him—Tristram and Lancelot
And Gawain—to give back freedom to the earth
And Britain to her own . . . .

Such was, and still is, the legend. But in older writings, there are disconcerting hints that Arthur may not in reality have been the all-wise, much-loved saviour the legend would have us believe. In some early Welsh tales he was cast in the mould of an oppressor, holding down Britain's frontier territories with a ruthless and iron hand, scorning God and the Devil alike. It may have been so; ordinary folk seldom have any great love for those in supreme authority, especially if foraging troops demand part of their meagre sustenance. But weaklings do not hold kingdoms together, particularly if those kingdoms are under constant threat; and a strong man will use force if necessary to feed his army, just as Hengest had done years earlier.

As to Arthur's eventual end we have only one clue. It comes in the *Annals of Wales*, which was written in the early twelfth century and now forms part of the same manuscript collection as Nennius' History of the Britons. At a date that lies somewhere between 511 and 537, the Annals record: 'The fight at Camlann, in which Arthur and Medraut fell'. Attempts have been made to fit Camlann into numerous locations all over Britain, but one

fits better than all the others. Philologists today think that Camlann is a corrupted form of Camboglanna—the Roman fort at Birdoswald on Hadrian's Wall, described in the introduction to this book. Later legend turns Medraut—'Sir Mordred'—into Arthur's implacable enemy, yet in the *Annals* there is nothing to suggest that they were on different sides. It is impossible to tell what the fight was about; it may have been a struggle between rivals, or an attempt to crush a rebellion, or simply a skirmish between British and Irish or Caledonians. It is interesting to note, however, that whereas the *Annals* use the Latin word *bellum*—battle—in recording Mount Badon a few years earlier, the word used to describe Camlann is the Celtic *gueith*, which literally means 'a fight'—in other words, something less than a full-scale battle.

There is another interesting point, too. After the last battle, according to the legend, the mortally-wounded Arthur was taken to Avalon, the 'Place of Apples'. A few miles west of Camboglanna, on the line of the Wall

Camboglanna (Birdoswald). A visit to the Roman Wall fort of Camboglanna, known also by its English name of Birdoswald, is a 'must' for any addict of the Arthurian period. The fort is described in the introduction to this book, and further information on its history may be obtained by visiting the Roman Army Museum at Carvoran, near Greenhead, and Tullie House Museum in Carlisle. Here, two inscriptions record the fort's history and the units responsible for rebuilding it at various stages. When visiting the fort, it is also worthwhile inspecting the church at Over Denton, in the valley half a mile to the south, whose chancel arch is built of Roman stone.

Llangian (Gwynedd). Llangian lies on the Lleyn Peninsula in Wales; Lleyn is a corrupted Irish name, recalling the immigrants from Leinster who settled there early in the sixth century. In the old churchyard at Llangian there is a very interesting pillar, standing near the church wall; it is of sixth century date, and bears the inscription MELI MEDICI FILI MARTINI IACIT (The stone of Melus the Doctor, son of Martinus). *(OS Sheet 123, 296290.)*

at Burgh-by-Sands, on the other side of Carlisle, there is a fort whose Roman name was Aballava—the Apple Orchard. Did the names of Avalon and Aballava somehow become intertwined—and if so, is the Roman fort the true Avalon? The question is just as intriguing as all the other Arthurian enigmas that have perplexed historians since they first tried to give Arthur his correct status. At the end of it all, the fact still remains that there is only just enough evidence—and that of a tenuous nature—to show that Arthur existed at all. Yet the name does not matter. What matters is that, at the close of the fifth century, a British leader—Arthur or someone else—fought to assure the continuity of the Romano-British way of life, and for a time succeeded. The success was destined to be short-lived, but the impact it made sent ripples down the centuries, and the pride of the achievement embedded itself forever in the soul of the British race.

Left and below left *The fort of Camboglanna, on Hadrian's Wall, which has been identified as 'Camlann, where Arthur and Medraut fell'.*
Below *The Crooked Glen, the tree-shrouded valley of the River Irthing, seen from the ramparts of the fort that takes its name from this view.*

Llanaelhaearn (Gwynedd). There are two interesting memorial stones, both dating from the sixth century, in the churchyard of this Welsh village, which is on the A499 near the centre of the Lleyn Peninsula. The first, near the patch by the lych-gate, bears the name MELITU (Melitus), and the second, set in a wall of the north transept, carries the inscription ALIORTUS ELMETIACO HIC IACET, indicating that the Aliortus who was originally buried under it came from the north British kingdom of Elmet. *(OS Sheet 123, 387448.)*

Llangybi (Gwynedd). This is another interesting site on the Lleyn Peninsula; parts of the church there, which stands in the middle of the village and is surrounded by a circular churchyard, may date from the seventh century. From the churchyard, a path leads to a roofless stone building housing a well dedicated to St Gybi, a sixth century ecclesiastic. *(OS Sheet 123, 429412.)*

Bryncir (Gwynedd). Here, by the A487 some seven miles north-west of Portmadoc, there is a stone set in a wall in the yard of Llystyngwyn Farm. It bears an inscription in both ogham and Latin, which reads 'Icorix, son of Potentinus'. It may be that the present farm stands at the centre of what was once an important Dark Age estate. *(OS Sheet 123, 483455.)*

There are about 200 memorial stones—most of them in Wales and Cornwall—dating from the Dark Age period. Their inscriptions are either in Latin or the Irish script known as ogham, and it was probably Irish settlers in the south-west who first raised them. Many examples can be seen in museums; the Brecknock Museum in Brecon, Powys, for example, has a fine collection of early Christian monuments gathered from the surrounding villages.

Caratacus Stone (Somerset). A curious stone, about 5 ft high and standing on isolated moorland beside the B3223 Exford–Dulverton road at Spire Cross, two miles west of Winsford, this monument bears an inscription dedicating it to 'Caraaci nepus', a descendant of Caratacus—although not the Silurian chieftain who fought the Romans. Excavation has shown that there is no grave in the vicinity, so why it was put up remains a mystery. *(OS Sheet 181, 889335.)*

Chapter 4

The British collapse

After Arthur's death, the end of the peace he had imposed on a large part of Britain came swiftly. He had held Britain's enemies at bay, but the men who had served him knew no trade other than fighting, and the outcome was predictable, as Gildas explained: 'Kings Britain has, but they are tyrants; judges, but wicked ones. They terrorise and plunder the innocent; they protect and defend criminals and robbers.'

Law and order broke down. The petty kings of the west, most of whom were military tyrants, fought one another now that the steadying hand of a single leader had gone. Gildas named five of them, all holding territory in the west country. The first was Constantine of Dumnonia, described by Gildas as a 'holy abbot'; a position which had not prevented him from murdering two 'royal youths' in a church in front of their mother. Gildas' next victim was Aurelius Caninus, also known as Conan, whose main trade seems to have been civil war and plunder. Then comes Vortipor of Demetia, growing old now, whom Gildas accuses of violating his daughter after the death of his wife; next it is Cuneglassus of north Wales, who had cast aside his legal wife in favour of her sister.

The bitter monk, however, saves up his biggest tirade for Cuneglassus' cousin, Maelgwn of Gwynedd: '. . . Last on my list, but the first in evil, mightier than many, and mightier still in malice, profuse in gifts and in sin, strong in arms, but stronger still in what destroys the soul; greater than almost all the leaders of the British in the size of your kingdom, as of your physical stature'.

Gildas calls Maelgwn 'Dragon of the Island', which is a noble title, dating back to the time of Vortigern or perhaps even earlier. He describes how Maelgwn killed a royal uncle and crushed his army with 'fire and spear and sword'. Who the uncle was is not known, but Maelgwn came to power about 520, so it is possible that the man was a contemporary of the late Arthur. Maelgwn afterwards renounced his throne and became a monk, but his religious calling did not endure long. He returned to the world, and Gildas laments that his second reign was even bloodier than the first, and considerably more wicked. One can imagine the monk throwing up his hands in horror as he reports that Maelgwn, on renouncing his wife, sought to replace her not with a strange woman, but with his nephew's wife. According to Gildas, he married the woman after murdering her husband and his own estranged wife.

Maelgwn rose to power in early sixth century Wales through a succession of murders and intrigues. In this he was no different from any other of Gildas' 'tyrants', so it seems strange that the monk dealt particularly harshly with him. Yet the harsh prose is tinted throughout with an air of regret, as though

> **Cubert Church (Cornwall).** In the church at Cubert, lying west of the B3075 Newquay–Redruth road, there is a seventh century stone bearing the Latin inscription 'Conetocus, son of Tegernomalus'. *(OS Sheet 200, 786578.)*

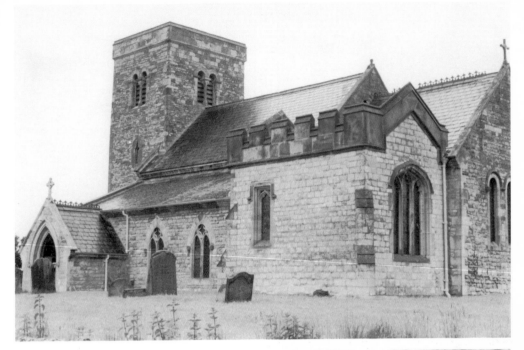

Above *The church of St Lawrence and St George at Springthorpe, Lincolnshire, has an original Saxon window set high in the west face. The belfry windows appear to be Saxon, but are in fact of later date.*

Right *This blocked-up doorway in the tower of Springthorpe church appears to feature reconstructed Saxon stonework.*

Gildas had once thought a great deal of Maelgwn, only to have his liking destroyed by the king's excesses. It may have been so. Gildas tells us that Maelgwn had been taught in his youth by 'the finest teacher of almost the whole of Britain'; this can only have been the great monastic scholar Illtud, who had founded a school at Llanilltud Fawr—now Llantwit, in Glamorgan—early in the sixth century. Illtud had been Gildas' mentor too, so the two men might well have known one another in their early days.

Whatever his faults, Maelgwn seems to have been the only one of the early sixth century kings of the south and west who might have filled the vacuum created by the death of Arthur. He was an immensely powerful man, and his sons Bridei and Rhun were to found powerful kingdoms in their turn. Like that of

The Anglian Tower, York. Excavated in 1971, this is the only substantial remaining part of the city's defensive stonework built by the Anglo-Saxon occupants. Its crudeness contrasts sharply with the refinement of the Roman masonry in the lower walls around it.

Arthur, his name passed down into legend; the fact that it did not gain the same kind of foothold as the Arthurian tale may have been due in some measure to Gildas' portrayal of him as a wicked man.

Maelgwn's fortress may have been Degannwy Castle, near Llandudno. Henry III had a castle here centuries later; this was destroyed in 1263 by Llywelyn ap Griffyd, and archaeology in recent years has discovered earlier levels of occupation, beginning with a Roman fort of third century date. A few sherds of pottery from the eastern Mediterranean, datable to the late fifth or early sixth centuries, may indicate the import of wine during Maelgwn's time, and inscribed memorial stones from his dynasty indicate that a degree of Romanisation still existed. Maelgwn's kingdom of Gwynedd emerged more or less intact from the old *civitas* state of Venedotia, and was one of the few sub-Roman states to survive in this way. Most of the others were dismembered, either in Arthur's time or afterwards. Of the others which did survive, one was Demetia, ruled by Vortipor's dynasty; it eventually became Dyfed. In south Wales,

Eglwys-Cymmyn (Dyfed). In the churchyard at Eglwys-Cymmyn, north of Pendine in south Wales, there is a stone whose inscription, in both Latin and Ogham, carries the bare words 'Avitoria, daughter of Cunigos'. The church stands on the north side of the B4314.

Men Scryfa Down (Cornwall). On the common that lies north-east of the minor road running from Morvah to Madron there is a stone, probably of early sixth century date, bearing the Latin inscription 'Rialobranus, son of Cunovalus'. *(OS Sheet 203, 427353.)*

Brecon (Powys). The Brecknock Museum here, although small, has a good collection of stones gathered from the surrounding villages. They include a fifth century memorial to one Maccutrenus Salicidunus, with inscriptions in ogham and Latin, and a sixth century stone commemorating Nennius, son of Victorinus (no connexion with the historian Nennius, who came along three centuries later). *(OS Sheet 160, 045285.)*

St Just (Cornwall). Inside the western end of St Just Church there is a memorial known as the Selus Stone which, on one side, bears the chi-ro monogram and on the other an inscription saying that the stone marked the burial place of one Selus. The memorial is of fifth or sixth century date. To reach St Just, take the A3071 from Penzance. *(OS Sheet 203, 372315.)*

Lewannick (Cornwall). Lewannick lies to the left of the A30, five miles south-west of Launceston, as you travel towards Bodmin. In both church and churchyard there are stones with ogham inscriptions *(OS Sheet 201, 276807.)*

Llanerfyl (Powys). To reach Llanerfyl, follow the A458 westwards from Welshpool for ten miles. In the churchyard there is a stone bearing the poignant inscription, probably of sixth century date: 'Here in a tomb lies Rustica, aged thirteen. In peace'. On the way to Llanerfyl, incidentally, look out for Castell Caereinion, which has been proposed as a possible site for the Arthurian 'Castle Guinnion' battle. *(Llanerfyl ref: OS Sheet 125, 034097.)*

however, the territory of the Silures was reduced to a narrow strip of land between the Usk and the Wye; known as Gwent, derived from the name of the Silurian capital of Caerwent (Venta Silurum), it was ruled in the early sixth century by one Honorius, whose name was translated into Welsh as Ynyr. Other territories in Wales also degenerated into a spattering of small kingdoms, ruled in the main by force of arms by men who sometimes preserved old Roman family names and who still lived on their ancestors' estates, the latter now crumbling and in disrepair.

John Morris' researches turned up one item of information which, in itself, forms a sad epitaph to the shreds of Roman civilisation that still lingered in sixth century Wales. The owner of an estate near Chepstow kept the baths of his villa in repair—but as a rule used them only on Saturdays.

Dumnonia—today's Devon and Cornwall—preserved its British integrity for a long time and possibly also maintained substantial contact with Brittany. At some point in the sixth century the defenders of Dumnonia erected the great earthwork known as Wansdyke; its name—Woden's Dyke—was bestowed upon it later by the English, and implies that they did not know its origin. North of the Thames, the British continued to hold territory until well into the second half of the sixth century; under an entry dated 577, the *Anglo-Saxon Chronicle* records that: 'Cuthwin and Caewlin fought with the British and slew three of their kings, Coinmagil, Candidan and Farinmagil, in the place that is called Deorham, and took three chesters: Gloucester, Cirencester and Bath'.

The use of the word 'chester' means that the English captured three cities that were still fortified behind their defensive walls. Here, too, the former Romano-British *civitas* appears to have been divided into small kingdoms. Elsewhere, there seems to have been more cohesion; in 571, a British army was destroyed by the English near Bedford, after which the victors pushed on down the Vale of Aylesbury to the Thames. On the eastern fringe of the island, Briton and Saxon appear to have lived in harmony during much of the sixth century; archaeology has shown no trace of permanent English settlement in either Verulamium (St

---

Llangadwaladr (Anglesey). A little off the beaten track, but well worth a trip to see, is a solitary stone erected in Llangadwaladr churchyard. Dating from about 630, it bears an inscription in a mixture of Latin and rounded Irish 'uncial' script, reading 'Cadfan king, wisest and most famous of all kings'. *(OS Sheet 114, 383692.)*

Maen Madoc (Powys). To reach this stone, follow the A4067 Swansea-Brecon road and turn off to Capel Coelbren, from where you can pick up the course of Sarn Helen, the Roman road that winds its way up to the Brecon Beacons. The stone stands in the Roman metalling and carries the inscription 'Dervacus, son of Justus, lies here'. *(OS Sheet 160, 918157.)*

Nevern (Dyfed). In the church at Nevern, seven miles south-west of Cardigan on the B4582, there are two notable sixth century stones, one commemorating Vitalianus Emeretos (could this have been the 'Vitalinus' who is sometimes identified with Vortigern?) and the other Maglocunus, son of Clutorius. There is also a finely ornamented tenth century free-standing cross in the churchyard. *(OS Sheet 145, 083401.)*

St David's (Dyfed). Traditionally, St David, the patron saint of Wales, founded a religious house here in the sixth century. Nothing of it remains today; the present cathedral belongs, in its earliest phase, to the twelfth century. However, there are several stones dating from the Dark Ages in the cathedral, including a ninth century monogram cross slab bearing the monogram IHS XPC (IESOS CHRISTOS) and another of Irish wheel-headed type with an inscription that seems to indicate that someone named Gurmarc erected it. A third cross-slab fragment in the cathedral has interlace work with a pair of animal heads holding a human head, with a six-winged seraph above. *(OS Sheet 157, 751254.)*

Albans), London or Colchester for a hundred years after Arthur's time.

After half a century of stagnation, the English began to push westwards again about 570, breaking the boundaries that had been imposed upon them after Arthur's wars. They were enabled to do so not because the British

Penmachno (Gwynedd). To reach Penmachno, take the A5 Bangor road and turn down the B4406, 2½ miles before you reach Betws-y-Coed. There is a group of stones in the church, and one of them is very interesting because it can be precisely dated to 540, as its inscription implies that it was erected 'in the time of Justinus the Consul'. Another cross in the group carries the Christian chi-ro symbol, while others bear the word 'magistratus'—indicating that some form of Romanised administration still existed in Maelgwn's Gwynedd in the mid-sixth century. *(OS Sheet 115, 789505.)*

had grown militarily weak, but because the British areas were devastated by plague. Its effects were not felt by the English, which in itself is proof that partition existed; there was no contact between the two sides and therefore no spread of the disease. The plague was bubonic, and reached Constantinople from Egypt in 543. From there is spread rapidly throughout the whole of the former Roman Empire, striking Britain and Ireland in about 544. This in itself is a revealing fact, for it shows that Britain's trade routes with the eastern Empire were still open. The transference between Britain and Ireland may have been due to the movements of the clergy, which formed by far the heaviest traffic between the islands at this time. The ravages of the plague must have been apparent to the English, and encouraged them to attempt

Sourton (Devon). About four miles south of Okehampton, at the junction of the A30 and B3219 at Sourton, there stands what is known as Sourton Cross—in fact, a memorial stone bearing the chi-ro symbol, indicating its Christian origin. *(OS Sheet 191, 918548.)*

Tavistock (Devon). There is a group of stones in the vicarage garden here, all of them inscribed. The one bearing the inscription 'Nepranus, son of Conbevus' is of local origin, but the other two—'Sabinus, son of Maccodechtus' and 'Dobunnus the Smith, son of Enabarrus'—were moved to Tavistock from their original locations at Buckland Monachorum.

further conquest. In 552, the *Anglo-Saxon Chronicle* informs us, Cynric fought the British at Salisbury and defeated them, and four years later he fought them again at Barbury (Beranbyrig) near Swindon. For a time after that the English seem to have been involved in wars amongst themselves; in 568, for example, Ceawlin and Cuthwulf fought against Aethelbert, the ruler of Kent, at a place called Wibbandune, which might be Wimbledon. Aethelbert, apparently, had tried to break out of his territory, and had failed in the attempt.

Three years later, in 571, Cuthwulf routed the British near Bedford, and then in 577 Ceawlin launched a campaign against the British in the Severn Valley, culminating in the great battle of Deorham (Dyrham, near Bath) and the capture of the three fortified cities mentioned earlier. For the first time since their arrival in Britain, the Anglo-Saxons now had a foothold in the fertile Cotswolds. More serious still for the Britons, the English advance had driven a wedge between the British of Dumnonia and those of Wales and the Midlands. Ceawlin renewed his campaign in the early 580s, capturing more British territory and fighting a major battle in 584 at a place called 'Fethanleag' in the *Anglo-Saxon Chronicle*. Some historians have identified this place with a wood near Stoke Lyne in the north east of Oxfordshire; twelfth century documents refer to the location as 'Fethelee'. This entry in the *Chronicle* ends with the enigmatic statement that afterwards, Caewlin 'returned in wrath to his own', which may imply that he was forced to quell an insurrection among his people. Certainly, in 592, the *Chronicle* mentions a battle at 'Woden's Barrow'—a neolithic long barrow now called Adam's Grave, at Alton Priors in the Vale of Pewsey—in which Caewlin was 'driven out'. He died the following year, and his kingship passed to Aethelbert of Kent.

It is a curious fact that, once the British collapse had begun, the former states of the south—where Roman tradition and culture had been so firmly rooted for four centuries—succumbed far more readily to English conquest than did the Celts of the north. Within the space of very few generations, the Celts of the south had absorbed the language and the culture of their conquerors; and when their native language died, so did the tales that held the memory of the battles and the triumphs and the ultimate defeats that had gone before. It was left to the Britons of Wales and Cornwall to preserve the old tales in song and legend.

In the north, following the Saxon revolt of the mid-fifth century, two English kingdoms had taken shape. The first was Deira, which sprawled across the Yorkshire Wolds and perhaps owed its origin to German mercenary troops who were settled there as federates in late Roman times. The second, and more powerful state was Bernicia, founded by a small number of Anglian invaders on the Northumbrian coast north of Alnwick in the 'Manau Gododdin'—the territory of the Votadini. In the middle of the sixth century the king of the Bernicians was Ida, who was said to have begun his reign in 547. At some point during his rule he fought against a British leader named Outigirn and annexed 'Din Guayrdi', which is Bamburgh; he subsequently fortified it and turned it into a Bernician stronghold.

It was the Bernicians under Ida who began the English conquest of the north, and the resistance they encountered was fierce. Their opponents were no levies from the softer lands of the south, but warriors born of warriors, who had fought to hold the former Roman Military Zone against invasion for generations. Tradition, supported by some evidence, tells us that there were 13 British kings in the north, ruling sections of what had been the Military Zone, the territory of the *Dux Britanniarum*, in the sixth century. Some are named; they include Eleutherius of York, known also as 'Eleuther of the Great Army', who was of the dynasty founded by Coel in the fifty century, and his son Peredur Steel Arm, who ruled after him.

The most important of the sixth century kingdoms to emerge from the splitting up of the Military Zone was Rheged, which was divided into two portions, the southern covering what is now the north of Lancashire and the northern extending south of the Wall across Cumbria. The name 'Cumbria' itself means land of the Combrogi, the Citizens.

Up to the middle of the sixth century, the British kingdoms of the north, not yet faced with any substantial English threat, seem to have fought consistently amongst themselves. Nothing is known of these wars, although it is reported that in the 560s Maelgwn's son Rhun, who had succeeded him as ruler of Gwynedd, fought against a king of Rheged

Urien's kingdom: the tree-shrouded town of Carlisle, seen from the heights of the north-west, above the River Eden.

Tucked away at the end of a sunken lane at Brisco, south of Carlisle, this attractive little 'well' is said to have been used by the fourth century monk St Ninian, of Whithorn in Galloway, for baptism ceremonies. The stonework is actually of a much later date, but baptism may have been carried out here during the Dark Ages. The site is worth visiting for its atmosphere alone (OS Sheet 85, 423520). There are no baptisms there now, but children fish for tadpoles in its murky waters; St Ninian, one is tempted to feel, would have liked that.

named Elidyr. Then, about 570, a new and powerful leader emerged on the British scene in the north. His name was Urien of Rheged, and the campaigns he fought came close to expelling the English from the north. Urien's power must have been far-reaching, his armies reaching out across the Pennine lands from his base at Carlisle. From what is known of him, it is likely that he led some sort of federation of British kingdoms. One of his many titles was 'Llyw Catraeth', Lord of Catterick, and this is highly significant, for Catterick—the Roman town on Dere Street—commanded the Stainmore route across the Pennines to Carlisle. Only by holding Catterick could communications be kept open between the British kingdoms of the west and the Yorkshire kingdom of Elmet, which existed like an island in Deiran territory.

Nennius' *History of the Britons* states that Urien, together with three other British chieftains, Rhydderch, Gaullauc and Morcant, fought against Mussa, the son of Ida of Bernicia, and that Urien and his sons also besieged a Bernician force led by Deodric (Theodoric), who was another son of Ida's, in 'Metcaud' for three days and nights. Metcaud is the Island of Lindisfarne, so Urien must have carried the war right into the enemy's territory. Other battles are attributed to him at High Rochester and possible Binchester, in County Durham; these, as mentioned earlier, may be confused in the Nennius manuscripts with Arthur's battles.

The vigorous British response to Bernician expansion in the north might have been the result of the destruction of a British army at an unknown site called 'Caer Greu', which was probably an old Roman fort, in 580. The army was led by Peredur of York, who was killed; he may have marched north in an attempt to crush the Bernicians, only to meet defeat himself. It was probably at this time that York, now undefended, was occupied by the Deiran English under their leader, Aelle. The Bernicians rallied and fought back, but were defeated by Urien and his son, Owain, in the battle of 'Argoed Llwyfein', which translates as Leven Forest. The site is not known, but there are a number of Leven names north of the western end of Hadrian's Wall in the Carlisle area. The story of warfare under Urien is one of constant British victory. Urien himself was assassinated in about 590 following an intrigue by a rival king, Morcant, whose territory in the north was adjacent to that of the Bernicians and who may have made common cause with them; there are interesting parallels here with the story of the conflict between Arthur and Medraut. Encouraged by Urien's death, the English rallied and went over to the offensive, led by Aethelric, whom the British knew as Fflamddwyn—the Firebrand. Once again the English were broken, and their defeat was recorded in a poem, *The Death Song of Owain*, by the greatest bard of the day, Taliesin:

When Owain slew Fflamddwyn
It was no more than sleeping.
Sleeps now the wide host of England
With the light upon their eyes . . ..

This battle was probably fought in 593. The British triumph, however, was short-lived, for Owain was killed soon afterwards, and his death left Rheged without a leader. His lieutenants fought amongst themselves, and the military power of the Cumbrian kingdom was shattered almost overnight. The collapse of Rheged left the English of the north free to consolidate their position and to push westwards through the Pennines. Yet the British made one last attempt to secure the strategic roads that were the key to the domination of the whole area.

In 598, a British cavalry force led by two noblemen, Mynydawc and Cynan, assembled in the Manau Gododdin—the ancient territory of the Votadini, near the Firth of Forth—and rode south, probably skirting Bernician territory by riding to Carlisle and then across the Pennines by way of the Bowes pass; they may have envisaged some sort of joint operation against the Bernicians in concert with Aelle, king of Deira, who had as much to fear from the aggressive intentions of his northern neighbours as did the British themselves. In any event, the British force confronted the Bernicians as Catraeth—Catterick—and was annihilated. The battle may not have been fought at Catterick itself, but a little further north; a possible site is Stanwick, near Aldbrough-St-John in north Yorkshire. This is the site of a huge Iron Age fortress, long

Above *The defensive ditch of the old Brigantean fortress of Stanwick, near Aldbrough St John, North Yorkshire. Covering an impressive area, this may have been the site of the last battle between the British of the 'Manau Gododdin' and the English under Aethelferth. Catterick—'Catraeth'—is a few miles to the south.*

Below *The great defensive rampart at Stanwick. The name Stanwick is derived from the Anglo-Saxon 'stein wegges', or stone walls; the name of nearby Aldbrough means 'old fort'.*

thought to have been the scene of the Brigantes' last stand against the invading Roman army in 71 AD (a theory that is now seriously disputed). The great revetments of the fort were still prominent at the time of the first English settlement in the area; the name 'Stanwick' is derived from *stein wegges*, stone walls, while Aldbrough means 'Old Fort'.

The disaster was described by the bard Aneirin, who rode with the British and was one of the few to escape death. Parts were added to his elegy by other poets at a later date, but the core is substantially his.

'The men went to Catraeth, strong was their army, the pale mead was their feast, and it was their poison; 300 men battling in array, and after the glad war-cry there was silence. Though they went to the churches to do penance, the inevitable meeting with death overtook them.

'The men went to Catraeth with the dawn, their high courage shortened their lives. They drank the sweet yellow enticing mead, and for a year the bard made merry. Red were their swords—may the blades never be cleansed— and white shields and square-tipped spears.

'The men went to Catraeth, they were renowned, wine and mead from gold cups was their drink for a year, in accordance with the honoured custom. Three men and three score and three hundred, wearing gold necklets. Of all that hastened after the flowing drink none escaped but three, through feats of sword-play; the two war-dogs of Aeron, and proud Cynan, and I too, streaming with blood, by grace of my blessed poetry.

'The men went to Catraeth in column, raising the war-cry, a force with steeds and blue armour and shields, javelins aloft and keen lances, and bright mail-coat and swords. He led, he burst through the armies, and there fell five times fifty before his blades; Rhufawn the Tall, who gave gold to the altar and gifts and fine presents to the minstrel.

'The warriors arose together, together they met, together they attacked, with a single purpose; short were their lives, long the mourning left to their kinsmen. Seven times as many English they slew; in fight they made women widows, and many a mother with tears at her eyelids.

'It is grief to me that after the toil of battle they suffered the agony of death in torment, and a second heavy grief it is to me to have seen our men falling headlong; and continual moaning it is, and anguish. After the battle,

Remains of earthworks inside the great horseshoe-shaped perimeter of Stanwick. The fort must have been an impressive sight in the sixth century, and may have provided regular shelter for British cavalry forces in Urien's time.

may their souls find welcome in the land of heaven, the dwelling-place of plenty.'

The Bernician leader, Aethelferth, may have tried to exploit this success by marching north-west to attack the British of Dal Riada, on the Clyde, where British, Irish settlers and the descendants of German federates had intermingled to form a kingdom of growing power. In 603, the king of Dal Riada was a man of Irish lineage, Aedan, and in a bid to crush the Bernicians he enlisted the help of Mael Uma, brother of the Irish High King. A decisive battle was fought at Degsastan, the site of which has not been determined but which might lie in English terrtitory well to the north of Hadrian's Wall. If this is so, it would indicate that the forces of Dal Riada marched south to meet Aethelferth, who inflicted a severe defeat upon them. 'From that time on,' Bede wrote later, 'no king of the Scots dared face the English in the field'. Aethelferth now swung south once more. In 604 he occupied York and annexed Deira, although the children of Aelle, the Deiran king, escaped and found refuge with the British of the west.

Aethelferth was now master of the whole of the north-east; the Kingdom of Northumbria was born. In the decade that followed, its power increased to such an extent that Aethelferth felt sufficiently confident to attack north Wales, where Aelle's son Edwin was reportedly being sheltered by the king of Gwynedd. In 614, the Northumbrian army marched to Chester, where they confronted an alliance of the British of Gwynedd, Powys and the Cornovii; the British were accompanied by a huge body of monks and priests, most of them from the monastery of Bangor-is-Coed, who had fasted for three days and were now standing in what they believed to be a safe place and chanting prayers for a British victory. On seeing them, Aethelferth decided that prayers were just as powerful as more normal weapons of war, and ordered his forces to attack the clergymen first. Some accounts claim that 1,000 were massacred; others put the figure as high as 2,000. The sight must have had a demoralising effect on the British forces, who were heavily defeated in the battle that followed.

The decisive battle of Chester effectively cut off the British kingdoms of Wales from those

---

Degsastan. The site where Aethelferth of Bernicia decisively defeated the forces of Dal Riada has never been accurately determined, but it is possible that it lies just to the north of the Kielder Forest in Northumberland, at the apex of an area bounded by Liddesdale on the west and the North Tyne on the east. To explore this area, follow the B6357 north from Newcastleton for about nine miles and look for Dawston Burn where that stream follows the line of the road on the left; the name Dawston may be a corruption of 'Dagsastan'.

Yeavering Bell (Northumberland). One of the royal palaces—perhaps the principal seat—of King Edwin of Northumbria, Yeavering lies five miles west of Wooler and south of the B6396. The site was first revealed by air photography, and subsequent excavation unearthed traces of several timber buildings, including a royal hall, what might have been a church and a wedge-shaped timber grandstand built on the lines of a Roman theatre. Yeavering was occupied from late in the sixth century for about 100 years; one of its main points of importance is that it shows how early English kings appear to have adopted Roman-style methods. (OS Sheet 74, 928293.)

---

that still existed in Cumbria and the Pennines. However, Aethelferth had no opportunity to exploit his success further, for warlike rumblings were coming from the southern English, under their leader Aethelbert of Kent. Aethelbert may have contemplated going to war against the Northumbrians in an attempt to bring the whole of the island under his own rule, but he died in 616, and supremacy over the southern English passed to Redwald of East Anglia.

Edwin of Deira had now sought shelter with Redwald, and strong pressure was brought to bear on the East Anglian king to hand the fugitive over, or to kill him. Redwald refused, and Aethelferth assembled an army to march on him. Before the preparations were completed, however, Redwald struck first, attacking the Northumbrian king and killing him in a battle on the east bank of the River Idle. The young Edwin was now accepted as rightful king by both the Bernicians and the

Deirans, and it was the turn of Aethelferth's sons to flee into exile.

Edwin quickly proved himself to be an able and talented ruler; during his reign the embryo English kingdoms were consolidated as never before. He overran Elmet, the last British Pennine kingdom, and expelled its king, Cerdic; then in 626 he led an expedition against the West Saxons and killed five members of their royal house. Edwin's exile among the British of Wales had brought him into close contact with Christianity, and customs and traditions that still lingered from the days of Rome. His royal seat was at Yeavering, in Northumberland, and brilliant excavation work there has revealed, among other buildings, an assembly place with seating arrangements modelled on those of a Roman theatre. His armies carried banners and insignia that were reminiscent of the trappings of the legions, and when he travelled around his domains a signifer carried his personal standard before him. He was the most powerful English monarch the island had ever known. All the southern English kingdoms except one owed allegiance to him; the exception was Kent, and even then he had close links through his marriage to Aethelburh, daughter of the Kentish King Aethelbert.

Sometime towards the end of his reign, Edwin invaded Gwynedd and subdued the islands of Anglesey and Man, forcing the British ruler of Gwynedd, Catwallaun (Cadwallon) to seek refuge in Ireland. However, he did not leave an occupation force in the territory he had conquered; he withdrew, leaving Catwallaun free to return and raise a large army composed of Britons and Mercians, with whose king, Penda, he had formed an alliance. His forces met those of Edwin somewhere near Hatfield in 634, and in the battle which followed Edwin and his eldest son were killed. The Northumbrians were scattered, and for a year Catwallaun's armies ranged over the English kingdom. Had

Although much obscured by later work, traces of the original Saxon structure may still be seen in the nave, chancel and axial tower of the church at Newton by Castleacre, Norfolk.

Celtic areas

Approximate territorial
boundaries

THE KINGDOMS OF BRITAIN,
C.620AD

PICTS

PICTS

SCOTS

Bernicia

Rheged

Northumbria

Deira

Elmet

Lindsey

GWYNEDD

Mid-Angles

East
Angles

POWYS

Mercians

Magon-
saetan

DYFED

East
Saxons

Hwicce

Kent

West Saxons

South
Saxons

DUMNONIA

R McM

Above *The old Roman road of Dere Street, leading from Catterick to Corbridge, runs two miles to the east of Stanwick. Control of it was vital to the Romano-British of the north in the sixth century. The monument is 'Legs Cross'; it is probably Anglo-Saxon in origin, but may be on the site of an earlier Roman milestone. One suggestion is that the name 'Legs' derives from 'Legio X', the Tenth Legion.*

Below *Rowley Burn, south of Hexham, Northumberland. It was here that Oswald, son of Aethelferth, destroyed the British leader Catwallaun, Penda's ally, in 635.*

Catwallaun been a different kind of leader he might have also subdued Kent and reimposed a British kingship on the whole of the island; but his armies came as plunderers, and Penda's pagan Mercians brought death and horror to people who, under Edwin, had known at least a measure of peace and security.

Catwallaun's end came swiftly. In 635, Oswald, one of the exiled sons of Aethelferth of Northumbria, returned from Ireland and raised an army to challenge the British. After assembling his forces at Hallington (originally Halidene—the Holy Valley) a few miles north of Hadrian's Wall, Oswald met Catwallaun in battle near Rowley Burn, south of Hexham, and inflicted a crushing defeat on him. Oswald's victory made him supreme over all the English, and destroyed forever the British capacity for organised resistance to English conquest. There remained, however, one thorn in his side: the formidable Penda, King of Mercia and ally of the Welsh. It was inevitable that, sooner or later, the two should confront one another in battle; it happened in 642 at Maes Cogwy, in north Wales, and the result was a disaster for the English. Oswald was killed, and Penda ordered his head and hands to be cut off and nailed to a tree at the site of the Mercian victory. The place became known as Oswald's Tree—Oswestry.

Penda's victory was achieved with the help of his Welsh allies. Foremost among them, perhaps, was Cynddylan of the Cornovii, whose people still held their old territory in what is now Shropshire and Staffordshire, on the north-west boundary of Penda's kingdom; his capital may have been Wroxeter. Sometime in the years after Maes Cogwy, Cynddylan fought the English. Whether his enemies were Northumbrians or Mercians is not known, but he was the last British king to challenge

Wansdyke (Wiltshire and Avon). Much more impressive than the earthworks of East Anglia, the Wansdyke marks the northern frontier of Wessex. It is thought to have been built by the Anglo-Saxons of Wessex in the sixth and seventh centuries as a defence against Mercia, but the name bestowed on it by the English—Woden's Dyke—implies that they did not know who had constructed it, and it may therefore have been built by the Romano-British to defend the territory of what had once been three Roman states in the south-west. The Wansdyke is in fact built in two separate sections; the eastern part is larger and more easy to follow, running for 12 miles from Morgan's Hill near Devizes across the Marlborough Downs to a point just to the west of Severnake. The best access to it is by following the Swindon-Devizes road (A361) to where the Wansdyke crosses it at Shperherd's Shore (OS Sheet 173, 044663) and then exploring it eastwards. Alternatively, you can join it on the minor road that runs from Lockeridge to Alton Priors (OS Sheet 173, 126653). The western section of the Wansdyke is about ten miles long, starting just west of the A37 Shepton Mallet-Bristol road at Maes Knoll (OS Sheet 172, 600660) and running eastwards to Horsecombe on the southern outskirts of Bath. The western section is only partially intact, and is best reached from a point north of Norton Malreward (OS Sheet 172, 605658).

English supremacy. He was killed, and his lands, which had remained intact for so long, came under English domination. Later, an unknown Welsh poet wrote his elegy, and added a postscript which, perhaps, is a fittingly poignant epitaph to Celtic British rule: 'The dykes endure. He who dug them is no more.'

Caedmon's Cross, which stands in St Mary's churchyard at Whitby, is a reconstruction of an original monument commemorating Caedmon, the humble cowherd who composed and sang the first great English hymn and who later became a monk in St Hilda's abbey.

Part Two:
The Anglo-Saxon kingdoms
642–800 AD

Chapter 5

Northumbria and Mercia: the power struggle

The death of Oswald in 642 and the triumph of the Welsh-Mercian Alliance did nothing to lessen the implacable hostility that continued to exist between Northumbria and Mercia. In a series of campaigns lasting 30 years, King Penda made Mercia supreme over central England, fighting always on the side of the Welsh; a family feud provoked a war against the king of Wessex, Cenwalh, who had married Penda's sister and then cast her aside, with the result that even Wessex fell under Mercian domination for a time. Shrewdly, Penda made his boundaries secure. On the south-west frontier, the small English principality—it was scarcely a kingdom—of the Hwicce, which comprised Worcestershire, south-west Warwickshire and Gloucestershire east of the Severn, was ruled by a dynasty that depended on him; one of his sons, Peada, was installed as king of the Middle Angles south of

the Trent, providing a useful buffer zone between Lindsey and East Anglia; while another son, Merewalh, ruled over the land bordering Wales, from Wroxeter to the Wye.

Penda's armies also made two large-scale raids into Northumbria in the years that followed Oswald's death, and one of them may have penetrated as far as Bamburgh. Oswald had been succeeded by his brother, Oswy, and in 656 Penda assembled a huge army of Mercians and Welsh and marched north, intent on his destruction and on bringing Northumbria under the Mercian heel for good. In desperation, Oswy—having tried vainly to sue for peace on promise of payment of a considerable fortune to his enemies—assembled a scratch force of warriors and marched to confront them. The two armies confronted one another somewhere near Leeds, and an unexpected turn of events came to the rescue of the Northumbrians. During the night before the battle, Penda's Welsh ally, Cadafael of Gwynedd, suddenly withdrew his army and headed back to Wales, leaving the Mercians supported only by a contingent of East Angles

---

Taplow (Berkshire). At Taplow, a mile and a half north-west of Maidenhead, there is a Saxon burial mound, or barrow, standing on high ground overlooking the Thames in the old churchyard at Taplow Court. The person buried here can be identified, for Taplow means 'Taeppa's tumulus'. The barrow was excavated in 1883 and yielded many objects which are now in the British Museum. They include a Coptic bowl from Egypt, glass beakers, bone counters, a gold buckle and drinking horn mounts. To reach Taplow, take the A4 eastbound out of Maidenhead and then turn north on to the B476.

Above right *Seen here shrouded in the early-morning smoke from its many chimneys, the harbour town of Whitby, on the Yorkshire coast, was the scene of the famous Synod convened by King Oswy in 663. It was also one of the first Danish settlements in Britain.*
Right *The ruins of the abbey which stands high above Whitby harbour date from the thirteenth century, but the site has been hallowed since 657 AD, when St Hilda founded a community there.*

The church of St Martin at Kirkleavington, Cleveland, is Norman and early English, but contains a large collection of fragments of pre-conquest sculptures.

Reculver (Kent). In 669, King Egbert gave a plot of land to a priest named Bassa for the building of a church. The land in question lay within the perimeter of the old Saxon Shore Fort of Regulbium, and the church built by Bassa stood intact until 1802, when workmen pulled it down under circumstances described by the parish clerk:

'October 13 1802. The Chapel house fell down. Mr C.C. Nailor been vicar of the parish, his mother fancied that the church was kept for a poppet show, and she persuaded her son to take it down, so he took it in consideration and named it to the farmers in the parish about taking it down; sum was for it and sum was against it, then Mr Nailor wrote to the bishop to know if he might have the church took down and his answer was it must be dun by a majority of the people in the parish, so hafter a long time he got a majority of one, so down come the church.'

So a piece of English history was destroyed for ever. The stones from the church went to Margate for the foundation of a new pier. Only the foundations are left, and may be reached by taking the A28 Margate-Herne Bay road. The site is constantly threatened by the sea, which has washed away half the shore fort. *(OS Sheet 179, 228694.)*

Bakewell: cross shaft. At Bakewell, on the A6 Matlock-Buxton road in Derbyshire, look in the churchyard for the lower part of an eighth century Mercian cross shaft, decorated with animals and figures but unfortunately vandalised.

under their king, Aethelhere. In the ensuing fight the Mercians and their allies were completely routed, leaving both Penda and Aethelhere dead behind them.

With the death of Penda, Oswy annexed most of Mercia, although it appears that he did not disturb the reigns of Penda's sons over the adjacent territories. Peada, however, was murdered late in 656, leaving the throne of the Middle Angles vacant, and it was then that the Mercian ealdormen played their trump card. They produced another of Penda's sons, Wulfhere, who had been kept in hiding, and proclaimed him king of all Mercia. The southern English appear to have respected Wulfhere's right to kingship, just as they had respected his father's, largely because Penda's dynasty claimed direct descent from the Iclingas, who were said to have ruled all the Angles of Europe. There was, however, another reason; the Mercian kings did not rule with the ruthless dictatorship exercised by their Northumbrian counterparts. Instead, they exercised their power with a curious mixture of British and Irish methods, giving gifts to subordinate rulers in the manner of the British overlords and exacting hostages and tribute after the manner of the Irish.

Under Wulfhere, the Mercian dynasty

slowly regained its stability and strength. The campaigns he fought were directed principally against the West Saxons, whose kingdom was divided and held in subjugation by force of arms. But the West Saxons were a continual thorn in the Mercians' side, and continued to resist fiercely. Not only that; their king, Cenwalh, reinstated after Penda's death, seems to have waged a vigorous campaign against the British of the south-west. In 658, the *Anglo-Saxon Chronicle* records that Cenwalh fought at 'Peonna' against the Welsh, and drove them in flight as far as the Parrett; Peonna is possibly Penselwood in Wessex. Three years later, he fought at 'Posentesburgh'—perhaps Posbury, near Crediton—and opened the way for the English colonisation of south Devon. However, it was to be more than two centuries before the last British ruler of Dumnonia was defeated, and the last of the Romano-British states fell to the English invaders.

In 661, while Cenwalh was busy with the British of Dumnonia, Wulfhere of Mercia siezed his opportunity and overran Wessex, severing the South Saxons and the Isle of Wight from it to form a separate kingdom. The British of Wales seem to have taken advantage of the resulting confusion to launch a new offensive; the *Cambrian Annals* note that in 665: 'Easter was celebrated among the Saxons for the first time. The second battle of Badon. Morcant died.' Morcant was ruler of the British kingdom of Glevissig, in south Wales, and may have been the leader of a British force that crossed the Severn in strength to attack the West Saxons. The site of the second battle of Badon is just as mysterious as the first, in Arthur's time, and there is no record of who won; but the British never again attempted to invade western Wessex, so a West Saxon victory seems likely. However, the West Saxons were in no position to launch a counter-offensive; there was no central administration any longer, and Cenwalh was left to preside gloomily over the dismembered remnants of his kingdom from Winchester. He died in 672, and for a decade the West Saxons were ruled by underkings; the dynasty founded, according to tradition at least, by Cerdic was at an end.

Wulfhere's Mercia was now undisputed mistress of the south. Wulfhere himself died in

Bewcastle Cross (Cumbria). This magnificent cross, probably dating from the late seventh century, may be reached by taking the B6318 westbound from either Greenhead or Gilsland and then turning right at *OS Sheet 86, 550675*. A drive of just over three miles across moorland (with the Ministry of Defence danger area at Spadeadam on your right) brings you to the cluster of farms which constitute Bewcastle. The cross stands in the churchyard and is fashioned from a single stone block. The head is missing, but the shaft is decorated with panels depicting Christ, John the Baptist and John the Evangelist. It also bears many runic inscriptions, with a reference to King Oswy and possible one to Alcfrith of Deira. It may have been erected by St Wilfrid sometime in the 680s. Its site is magnificently bleak, overlooking the old Roman outpost fort which was built at the same time as the Wall. Incidentally, it is a good plan to visit Bewcastle and Camboglanna—the Camlann of the Arthurian story—on the same trip, as they are only a few miles apart.

Little Bardfield (Essex). The church of St Katherine in this village, about six miles north-east of Great Dunmow, shows Saxon work in parts of the tower and nave and is especially noteworthy because of the extensive use of flint in the original construction *(OS Sheet 167, 656307)*.

675; he left a son who was not old enough to rule, so he was succeeded by his brother Aethelred, who carried on Wulfhere's policies—including one of hostility towards Northumbria. The Northumbrian king, Oswy, had died in his bed in 671, to be succeeded by his son Egferth (Ecgfrith). The latter enjoyed some early success against the Mercians; in what must have been one of Wulfhere's last campaigns before his death, a Mercian invasion was checked and thrown back by Egferth, who then detached Lindsey from the Mercian sphere of influence. In 679, however, Aethelred defeated Egferth in a battle near the Trent, and took over Lindsey once more. It was the last time that the Northumbrians attempted to recover a measure of supremacy in the south. Compelled by the powerful Mercians to accept the river Trent as a

Langford (Oxfordshire). The tower of the church at Langford, three miles north-east of Lechlade, was originally Saxon, and traces of the original building may be seen in the tower. There are two fine windows with sculptured imposts in each side of the belfry, and the lower part of the tower, visible inside the church, has two Saxon arches with square-headed windows above them. Two roods, probably of late Saxon date, depicting Christ, St Mary and St John, are built into the mediaeval porch. *(OS Sheet 163, 249025.)*

Somerford Keynes (Gloucestershire). The church of All Saints at Somerford Keynes is mainly interesting because the blocked door north of the nave may date from the time of Bishop Anselm, who received a grant of land here in 685. The door jambs are in the style of the church at Escomb, Co Durham. The village lies some four miles north of Cirencester. *(OS Sheet 163, 016955.)*

permanent frontier, Egferth turned his attentions north and west. The Northumbrian kingdom already extended as far as the Firth of Forth, but Egferth planned expeditions beyond it with the intention of subduing the Picts—something that the might of the Roman Army had been unable to achieve. His primary objective, however, seems to have been to establish supremacy over the British of Strathclyde and Dalriada, whose territory still extended as far east as Dere Street, the old Roman road north through the Cheviots. As a preliminary to this, and possibly to forestall Irish intervention in support of the Dalriada Scots, he launched a fierce attack on Meath, at the heart of which lay Tara, seat of the High Kings, and caused great devastation; the attack was carried out in the face of strong opposition from the Northumbrian clergy and it was later deplored by Bede, who made the point that the Irish had always been very friendly towards the English.

That raid took place in 684. In the following year, again acting against advice, Egferth led a sizeable force into Pictland, and learned the same bitter lesson the Romans had learned several centuries earlier. The Picts let the Northumbrian army come on, luring it across the River Tay and probably harrassing it all the while; and then, at Dunnichen Moss near Forfar, they turned on it and utterly destroyed it. Egferth was killed in the disaster, and on his death it was the Northumbrian clergy who influenced the choice of his successor, his elderly half-brother Aldfrith, a scholar and a pacifist. Aldfrith's mother was Irish; he had been raised in Ireland and educated in the monastic circles of Iona. During his 20-year rule, Northumbrian art and learning were to rise to a level of glory that outshone any in the British Isles, except perhaps Ireland. The tragedy was that there was no ruler wise enough or powerful enough to hold Northumbria intact after his death in 705; from then on, the Bernician dynasty was doomed to totter to extinction amid a confusion of civil wars. Northumbria, Mercia, Wessex and Kent all left written records of their kings, their wars and to some extent their way of life. The other major seventh century English kingdom, East Anglia, did not; yet twentieth century archaeology has given us an unrivalled insight into the splendour of the early East Anglian royal household. The findings are worth examining at this point, for they probably had parallels in the other English kingdoms too; and they show, beyond all doubt, that Rome still exercised a great and lasting influence on the peoples that had helped to destroy her power.

In 1938–9, archaeologists examined a group of 11 East Anglian burial mounds, or barrows, situated to the west of the B1083 road that runs south from Woodbridge, in Suffolk. When they had completed their work in August 1939, they knew that they had made discoveries that rivalled the world's greatest; discoveries that dramatically elevated our English forebears from the level of barbarians to an undreamed-of state of culture. In one of the barrows, the archaeologists found the 'ghost' of a ship. No material traces of the wooden parts of the vessel remained, but its imprint was still there in the ground. The ship had been constructed of 15-inch-wide planks, lashed to the ribs; there was no seating for a mast, but on the port gunwale there were traces of a rowlock. The vessel was over 80 ft long, with a beam of 14 ft and a depth of 5 ft, although it drew only two feet of water. It was an elegant, streamlined craft, but an interesting point was that it was not new; there was evidence that it had been repaired in places. It bore all the hallmarks of a well-loved, well-worn royal barge, designed to be rowed rather than sailed along the East Anglian waterways. In the centre of the vessel, where there had been a wooden chamber, the excavators found an astonishing range of objects, ranging from domestic utensils to royal regalia, some of it from far-off lands. Personal accoutrements included a magnificent iron helmet with bronze decoration, owing much to Roman design, a body harness with gold and garnet fittings—superbly worked jewellery that had probably been produced locally—a stone sceptre about two feet long, a 5 ft iron rod with a spike at its foot and a stag at its head, together with four projections that probably served to support some kind of royal standard, and some spears. There was a shield inlaid with bird and dragon figures, two huge drinking horns, 3½ ft long and each capable of holding six quarts, made from the horns of the aurochs and mounted in silver. There were ten shallow bowls made of silver, inlaid with cross patterns, a great silver bowl from Byzantium, bearing the stamp of the Emperor Anastasius, a large fluted classical bowl, three bronze hanging bowls, a pair of silver spoons bearing the inscriptions 'Saulos' and 'Paulos', referring to the conversion of St Paul, a six-stringed lyre in a bag of beaver skin, 19 pieces of exquisite jewellery, including a gold buckle weighing nearly a pound, and forty Merovingian coins from Gaul.

In fact, there was just about everything but a body, and before long the question arose whether there had ever been a body at all—especially when it was discovered that parts of the helmet were missing, as though the head-piece had been smashed in battle and only the fragments brought to Sutton Hoo. Perhaps the grave was not a grave at all, but a memorial, bearing the personal effects of someone killed in action a long way away. The theory was reinforced by the complete absence of body ornaments such as rings, or of fragments of clothing. However, it was agreed that the acid nature of the sand in which the ship lay might have eliminated all traces of a body, including teeth; and in 1979, when British Museum experts re-examined the copious notes made by

the archaeologists 40 years earlier, they discovered a vital fact that had somehow been overlooked. The excavators had found a complete set of iron coffin fittings, and their position indicated that they had once formed part of a rectangular wooden coffin. The latter had long since vanished, but the items discovered in the grave fitted neatly into its area—just as if they had been laid around a body. The assumption, then, is that there once was a body in the Sutton Hoo barrow. The question is, whose was it?

There are a number of clues. First of all, the coins found in the barrow are dated between 620 and 640; then there is a suggestion that the 2 ft sceptre might denote royal rank, as also might the mysterious iron rod with its four projections, assuming that this really was used to hold a standard. However, the 'sceptre' is an elaborately-decorated whetstone, adorned at either end with head-figures and surmounted by a ring and a stag figurine; it is admittedly unused and may indeed have been a king's symbol of power, but there is no proof that this was so. Also, the iron rod seems a little on the short side to have held a royal standard, and its design owes nothing to the Romans, on whose artefacts the English kings

---

Stow (Lincolnshire). The church of St Mary's at Stow, eight miles north-west of Lincoln, is a fascinating 'must' for any student of the Anglo-Saxon era. Said to have been the cathedral church of Lindsey, established by King Ecgfrith of Northumbria in 674, it is cruciform in plan and still displays a great deal of original Saxon work. This includes a central crossing under the tower, supported by four very fine arches, and transepts. The door leading through the west wall into the north transept is also original, with jambs in the Escomb style. (OS Sheet 121, 882820.)

Swansea. The Swansea Museum in Victoria Road has a collection of Dark Age stones and other objects from excavations in the area. One interesting exhibit is a Roman altar from the fort at Laughor; it carries an ogham inscription, which indicates that the fort was occupied in the Dark Ages, probably by Irish settlers.

Left *The first Christian church of York, the Church of St Peter, a timber building constructed in the early seventh century, may have stood here, between the west end of the present Minster and High Petergate.*

Below left and this photograph *Hexham Abbey, Northumberland. The abbey stands on the site of the original church built by St Wilfrid in 674. It was later razed by the Danes, but the original crypt survives.*

Skipwith (East Yorkshire). The lower part of the tower, and some portions of the nave of the church of St Mary in Skipwith, three miles north-east of Selby, are thought to be of seventh century date, although the rest of the tower was added in the eleventh century. *(OS Sheet 105, 657385.)*

Hackness (North Yorkshire). Hackness, about four miles north-east of Scarborough, is the site of a monastery built by the abbess Hilda of Whitby in 680. Nothing now remains of this, but the church of St Peter is of ninth century date and may incorporate some of the stones from the earlier building. The chancel arch is Saxon, with some intricate carvings of interlaced creatures. *(OS Sheet 101, 969905.)*

Masham (North Yorkshire). Eight miles north of Ripon on the A6108, the church of St Mary is Saxon and may originally be of seventh century date. There are some interesting sculptures in the churchyard, including a ninth century cross shaft showing Mercian influence and bearing rows of carved animal figures. *(OS Sheet 99, 226806.)*

based their military trappings. Nevertheless, the Sutton Hoo burial undoubtedly held a person of high rank and importance. Learned opinion tends to favour Redwald, who in the 620s—for a brief period—had held the title of Bretwalda, Ruler of Britain. The title was first bestowed on Aelle of Sussex, who may have been the English commander at Badon; it then passed to Ceawlin, then to Aethelbert of Kent, and after him to Redwald. The next holder of the title was Edwin of Northumbria, who had been sheltered by Redwald during his exile. The title may have passed to him by some process of election when he achieved supremacy; there is nothing to indicate that he succeeded to it only on Redwald's death. Redwald, therefore, may have lived on into the 640s, a date that would fit nicely with the later coins found in the Sutton Hoo barrow, even though the generally accepted date for his

death is around 624. Equally, however, the grave might have belonged to any one of several kings who followed Redwald.

It does not really matter. What is important is that the items found in the Sutton Hoo grave seem to indicate that the culture imposed on Europe by Rome for centuries was by no means dead. Quite the contrary; the Germanic peoples who had come within the boundaries of the empire had always thirsted after the ways of Rome, and had longed to share in its civilisation; and here, at Sutton Hoo, was a kind of proof that in the seventh century, in the depths of the time erroneously called the Dark Ages, a 'barbarian' king or lord had surrounded himself with objects that might have graced the home and person of one of Rome's high-ranking servants. Not only that; their very presence at Sutton Hoo indicated that a flourishing trade must have existed between East Anglia and the continent. Indeed, East Anglia might well have been the principal trade gateway between the English kingdoms and the rest of the world, with Ipswich as the principal port. The view is supported by the discovery of many early settlements in the Ipswich area.

In Redwald's time, East Anglia was one of the seven Anglo-Saxon kingdoms known collectively as the Heptarchy. After Redwald, however, there was never another East Anglian Bretwalda; and when King Aethelhere fell in battle alongside his ally Penda of Mercia, in the final confrontation with Northumbria, the east coast kingdom fell into deepening obscurity. Sussex and Kent were also left behind in the struggle for supremacy, so that by the end of the seventh century, in terms of real power, the Heptarchy had been reduced to the trinity of Mercia, Northumbria and Wessex. The ascendancy of one over the others was no longer, however, a matter of simple force of arms, for a powerful new factor had intervened in the affairs of the English kingdoms. That factor was Christianity, which in the seventh century burst across the island in a bright flame to keep alight the torch of Roman culture and learning—and, in time, to make or destroy kings.

Chapter 6

The conversion of the English

Christianity had come slowly to Britain, even after Constantine the Great had declared it to be the official religion of the empire. Yet in the time of Ambrosius and Arthur, Celtic Britain was predominantly Christian, and was to remain so, even though some of those who professed to worship Christ may have returned in secret to the worship of older and darker gods.

In large tracts of the island, however, Christianity died with the first Saxon revolt of the fifth century. Although there is no evidence at all that the Germanic people tried to force the Celtic British in their midst into the worship of their own pagan gods, they plundered the Roman churches that had sprung up in the principal towns of the south and east—such as the Church of St Martin in Canterbury, which according to Bede was built 'While the Romans yet inhabited Britain'— and forced the wealthy and educated into flight. Partition, too, imposed after Badon, must have played its part in destroying what remained of the cohesion of the British church. What remained of it in the west slipped steadily backwards, bereft of communication with its more progressive counterparts in the rest of the Roman world, and in many areas must have come close to complete extinction in the civil wars that flared up after the years of peace under Arthur.

It was perhaps appropriate that Christianity should return to Britain from Ireland, where it had been implanted by Patrick and nurtured in the monasteries that grew after his time. There were Celtic monasteries in Britain, too, but they lacked the vitality of their Irish counterparts, and the violent and divided climate of Britain in the early sixth century did not encourage settled monastic life. Even the earliest of the great British monastic scholars, Samson and David, had close links with Ireland; both came from areas heavily settled by Irish colonists, and both had Irish teachers. But it was Columba, nobleman and later saint, who re-kindled the flame of Christianity in Britain. He founded the second generation of Irish monasteries, the first of them at Derry, and appears also to have commanded an army of considerable size; in 561 it confronted the forces of the high king, Diarmait, at Cuil Dremhni, as a result of a bitter quarrel over the rights of an independent church, and Columba's army won, the victory being attributed to the power of his prayer.

However, the victory had unexpected consequences. Sensing the danger that Columba might become all-powerful, head of both church and state, if his career were allowed to continue unchecked, the holy men of Ireland convened a meeting at which Columba was condemned for bringing about such great slaughter through his prayers; he was therefore ordered to spend the rest of his life abroad, where he might win more souls for Christ than he had caused to die in battle. The alternative was excommunication, and Columba accepted his exile voluntarily. Whether this story is entirely true, or whether there were more complex reasons for Columba's exile, the fact remains that he settled in the island of Iona, off the west coast of Scotland, and was there

A fine example of a Celtic cross in the Dumnonian style, this one, dating perhaps from the tenth century, stands near St Piram's church at Perranporth, Cornwall (L. Woodhouse).

Dacre (Cumbria). At Dacre *(OS Sheet 90, 456267)* south-west of Penrith, there are two cross fragments, one showing Adam and Eve and the other an animal. There are also other cross fragments at Penrith, Burton in Kendal, south of Appleby, Heversham, on the A6 south of Kendal, and Kirby Stephen near Brough, where a fragment depicts the devil in chains. All these may be visited on a Cumbrian expedition.

---

welcomed by a group of Irish colonists who had come under the heel of the pagan Picts. Such was Columba's standing and power of leadership that he might easily have rallied the Irish settlers of Scotland's western lands and fought a holy war against their pagan enemies; but his exile had wrought a profound change in him, and he set out alone to convert the Picts. He began the process of evangelisation that was to transform the north; when it was completed, many years after his death, it was to exercise a profound influence in removing the divisions that had traditionally separated the Picts from the British and Irish of the west, and so form the basis of a Scottish nation.

The date of Columba's crossing to Iona was 563. In the years that followed, until his death in 597, his ministry was responsible, to a great extent, for the slow spread of peace throughout the north. It was a ministry of simple faith and discipline, and as such it moved kings; and in the hands of his followers, it brought the beginnings of Christianity to the northern English. In the year of Columba's death another missionary arrived in the Island with the object of spreading the Gospel to the southern English. He was a Roman, Augustine, and he came on the initiative of Pope Gregory the Great, one of whose ideals was to win over the pagan English to Christianity. The story of how Gregory became inspired with the idea of converting the English is well known; it is said that on seeing some English slaves in Rome, and on being told that they were Angli from the kingdom of Deira, then ruled by Aelle, he made the comment that they should be *angeli* (angels) saved from the wrath (*de ira*) and singing alleluia. The story may be apocryphal, but something spurred Gregory to despatch Augustine, together with 40 monks, to Kent in 597. They were well received by Aethelbert, who, although refusing to forsake the pagan religion of his ancestors, gave the monks permission to preach their faith in the church of St Martin, Canterbury.

By Christmas time, Augustine was able to report to the Pope that he had made large numbers of converts—a task in which he was undoubtedly assisted by having the blessing of Aethelbert, for the Kentish king was Bretwalda. After a discreet interval, Aethelbert himself became a Christian; his wife, Bertha, had already been baptised. He also influenced his nephew Saeberht, king of Essex, and Redwald of East Anglia to adopt the faith, but Redwald's adherence to it was never more than skin deep, for back at home he kept a Christian altar side-by-side with a pagan one, worshipping at either with impartiality.

Augustine's early success encouraged Pope Gregory to draw up plans for organising the church in Britain. The country was to be divided into two provinces, each served by 12 bishops, with their sees at London and York. He had, however, overestimated Aethelbert's authority, which in reality did not extend much beyond the boundaries of Kent and Essex, and although a church of St Paul was built in London, it was Canterbury that became the metropolitan see. Another church was built in Rochester, and one of Augustine's assistants, Justus, installed there as bishop. Another assistant, Mellitus, was enthroned at St Paul's in London.

The way in which Augustine and his clergy went about converting the pagan English was extremely clever, and missionaries of later centuries might have done well to follow their example. Instead of destroying heathen temples, they consecrated them as Christian churches, destroying only the idols; ancient pagan festivals now became Christian feasts, the days unaltered. So the winter festival of Yule became the Mass of Christ's Nativity, while the adoration of the Goddess Eostre, the spring festival of rebirth, became Easter. Such had long been the practice throughout the Christian world, since the time of Constantine.

The aim of both Gregory and Augustine was now to form a united Christian church throughout Britain. To this end, representatives of Aethelbert, the Bretwalda, made contact with the ecclesiastics of an unnamed British province. The British appear to have approached the idea of unity with a certain reserve; the story, according to Bede, is that they decided to put Augustine to the test. They arranged a second meeting, which was attended by seven British bishops and many religious scholars, probably from Bangor-is-Coed monastery in Wales, and this time the British made a point of arriving last. The idea was that if Augustine rose courteously to meet

---

Canterbury (Kent). The city of Canterbury boasts four very early churches, the oldest of which is the Church of St Martin, which stands on a rise half a mile to the east of the cathedral on the left-hand side of the A257 Sandwich road. The western part of the chancel is original, and according to Bede the church was built 'while the Romans still inhabited Britain'. He also says that St Augustine first officiated here, and that it was used by Bertha, Aethelbert's queen. The western, and earliest, part of the church was built of flat Roman tiles laid in courses. Whether the church was constructed when Britain was still part of the empire or not—and this cannot be proved or disproved—there is no doubt that it was one of the first centres of Roman Christianity in Britain.

The other three churches, dating from the early post-Augustinian period, form a complicated series of ruins on the site of St Augustine's Abbey in Monastery Street. Extensive excavation work was carried out here early this century, and the most important building uncovered was St Augustine's own church, dedicated to Saints Peter and Paul and built between 578-613. It once consisted of a nave 40 ft long, with chapels on its north and south sides. You can still see the concrete sarcophogi which held the bodies of three of Canterbury's first archbishops, who were buried in the northern chapel; the southern chapel was reserved for members of the royal family of Kent. The eastern end of the church was dismantled in 1050 by Archbishop Wulfric, the idea being to construct an octagonal rotunda joining the church to the next building, the Church of St Mary. This was built in 620 and only the west wall now remains.

Walking eastwards past this wall you come to the third building, the Church of St Pancras, which also dates from the seventh century. Visible remains include the ruined chancel arch, the nave, the western porch and a south side chapel. The church is partly constructed of Roman brick, and is said to stand on the site of a pagan temple that was used by King Aethelbert before his conversion to Christianity. Archaeological finds from all three sites may be seen close at hand in the museum of St Augustine's Abbey.

Eyam (Derbyshire). Situated six miles north of Chesterfield, Eyam is the site of a good cross showing figures on both the shaft and the cross-head, which is original. Eyam, incidentally, is famous as the village that tried to seal itself off from the outside world during the great plague of 1665.

Sandbach (Cheshire). There are two good crosses standing side by side in the town square here; both date from the seventh century and both were smashed by religious fanatics in the seventeenth, but the fragments were recovered and restored. The shorter of the two depicts scenes that purport to show King Penda's conversion to Christianity, but this is clearly a figment of someone's imagination.

Lyminge (Kent). At Lyminge, on the B2065 about six miles north of Hythe, there are the remains of a nunnery founded in 633 by Aethelburh, the daughter of Aethelbert of Kent. When her husband, Edwin of Northumbria, was killed by the joint forces of Catwallaun and Penda she escaped and returned to her own people. The visible remains of her church are the foundations of the nave and apse, built of Roman materials.

Christianity. As a consequence, Eadbald recalled the two bishops from Gaul and restored Justus to Rochester. His power, however, did not extend to Essex, and Mellitus was not able to return to London.

With Kentish Christianity once more secure, at least for the time being, Archbishop Laurence made further approaches to the leaders of the British Church, deploring the rift that existed and inviting further contact. But the battle of Chester in 613, accompanied by the wholesale slaughter of Welsh monks by an English army, had served to widen the division even further; and in the years that followed the Roman brand of Christianity that now had a foothold in Kent was destined to spread north, instead of west.

In 619, Edwin of Northumbria had married Aethelburh, daughter of Aethelbert of Kent. She was a Christian, and when she travelled north to celebrate her marriage she was accompanied by a Kentish bishop, Paulinus. Edwin permitted his wife freedom of worship, promising her that he would consider the Christian doctrine, but like Aethelbert he approached the idea with considerable hesitation, fearful no doubt of the reaction of his pagan followers. However, when his daughter was born at Easter he allowed her to be baptised, together with 11 of her attendants. Bede tells how, soon after Edwin's return from his successful expedition against the West Saxons, the king called a meeting of his council at York to discuss the merits of the new

them it would show him to be a true servant of Christ. The tale is probably allegorical, and intended to portray the initial distrust that must have existed between the two factions. In any event, Augustine remained seated, and the British rejected him. He died in 604, his mission only partially completed. The influence of his teachings had certainly made a lasting impact in Kent and Essex, but had not been felt to any extent beyond their boundaries.

Then Aethelbert died in 618, and his death was followed by a violent anti-Christian reaction. It was started by his son, Eadbald, who had consistently remained true to his pagan beliefs. When his cousin Saeberht died, the whole of Essex was swept by a pagan revival that caused Bishops Mellitus and Justus to seek sanctuary in Gaul, in fear of their lives. Only Archbishop Laurence, who had succeeded Augustine in Canterbury, clung on precariously, and after many endeavours—supported, we are led to believe, by some supernatural assistance—eventually won the heathen Eadbald over to

Above right *Catterick village in North Yorkshire, takes its name from the Roman town of Cataracta, which lay near the present racecourse. Bishop Paulinus, who converted Edwin of Northumbria, carried out baptisms in the River Swale here.*
Right *The church of St Anne at Catterick is mediaeval, but replaces an earlier building. Bede stated that there was no church at Catterick, so the original structure must have been after his time. The only tangible evidence that it existed is part of an Anglian cross head dating from the tenth century, although the present church incorporates stones that probably came from the earlier one.*
Far right *The church of the Holy Trinity at Stone-grave, North Yorkshire, contains several interesting pre-conquest sculptures, including a tenth century Anglo-Danish cross.*

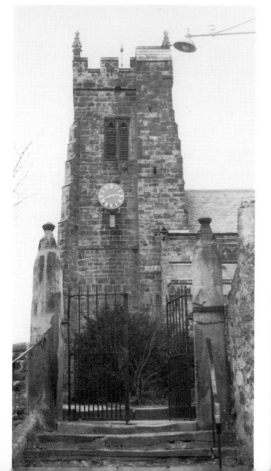

religion against the old. Coifi, the pagan high priest in Northumbria, was strangely unhesitating in telling the assembly that the old religion had never done him much personal good, and that the king had bestowed far more favours on others; therefore, if the new teachings were found to be more effectual, the gathering should not hesitate to accept them. Coifi, no doubt, was looking for better rewards in the future; but another of the king's counsellors summed up the whole question with an appealing allegory.

'When we compare the present life of man with that time of which we have no knowledge, it seems to me like the swift flight of a sparrow through the banqueting hall where you sit in the winter months to dine with your thanes and cousellors. Inside there is a comforting fire to warm the room; outside, the wintry storms of snow and rain are raging. This sparrow flies swiftly in through one door of the hall, and out through another. While he is inside, he is safe from the winter storms; but after a few moments of comfort, he vanishes from sight into the darkness from whence he came. Similarly, man appears on earth for a little while, but we know nothing of what went before his life, and what follows. Therefore if this new teaching can reveal any more certain knowledge, it seems only right that we should follow it.'

At the request of Coifi, Bishop Paulinus spoke at length about the Christian teachings, and when he had finished the high priest dramatically announced that he would abjure heathenism, submitting that all pagan temples and altars be desecrated and burned. According to Bede, he even led the way by borrowing a spear, sword and stallion from Edwin and riding the 12 miles to the old pagan capital of Goodmanham by Sancton, in the East Riding. He threw his spear into the temple, destroyed the idols he had once worshipped and then ordered the temple to be razed.

So, on Easter Day in the year 627, Edwin of Northumbria, with all his nobility and many lesser mortals, were baptised in the church of St Peter the Apostle, York, which had been built of timber. Paulinus remained in York with Edwin and travelled widely throughout Northumbria, baptising converts and preaching. Bede tells us that he accompanied the king and queen to 'Adgefrin', which is Yeavering, baptising people in the nearby River Glen; he also carried out baptisms in the River Swale at Catterick. There was no church here, Bede says, but one was built at 'Campodunum', which is possibly Doncaster; but this was later burnt by pagans, and another was eventually built at Leeds. Paulinus also carried his ministry into Lindsey, where he converted several of the nobility and built a stone church in Lincoln, consecrating Bishop Honorius there.

Edwin, too, had not been idle. Under his influence, King Eorpwald of East Anglia, the son of Redwald, became a Christian, but he was killed soon afterwards by a pagan named Ricberht, who ruled East Anglia for three years until he was ousted by Sigebert, Eorpwald's brother. Sigebert had come a Christian during his period of exile in Gaul, and he was determined to throw the pagan shackles off East Anglia once and for all. He was assisted by a Burgundian bishop named Felix, who had been consecrated in Italy and was now sent to East Anglia by Honorius, who had now moved from Lincoln to become the new Archbishop of Canterbury. Felix established his see at Dulwich, and worked there for 17 years.

It was Edwin's wish, too, that Paulinus should receive the pallium, the vestment blessed by the Pope and worn by an archbishop. Pope Honorius sent two, one for Canterbury and the other for York; it would have made Paulinus the first archbishop of that city, but by the time it arrived Edwin was dead, slain by the combined forces of Penda and Catwallaun.

Burgh Castle (Suffolk). In 631, or thereabouts, King Sigeberht of East Anglia gave the site of the Roman Saxon Shore Fort of Gariannonum to St Fursa, an Irish monk, who established a church there. Traces of it were found during excavation work in 1960-61, when archaeologists found a Christian cemetery, some coloured plaster and the post-holes of some oval huts which might have been cells or workshops. Burgh Castle lies west of the A143, about two miles from Yarmouth. (OS Sheet 134, 475046.)

Above *The church of All Saints at Hovingham, North Yorkshire, has a Late Saxon tower. In the south chapel there is a large sculptured stone, perhaps of ninth-century date, which once served as an altar frontal, and there are also some Anglo-Saxon cross fragments.*

Below *The church of St Gregory at Kirkdale, North Yorkshire, is famous for its Scandinavian sundial in the south porch. It is framed by an inscription which reads, 'Orm, son of Gamal, bought St Gregory's church when it was all broken and fallen down and he had it made new from the foundations for Christ and St Gregory in the days of King Edward and the Earl Tostig'.*

Above left *The church of St Andrew at Middleton, North Yorkshire, has Saxon work in the tower and contains an excellent collection of pre-conquest sculpture.*

Above *The tomb of St Withburga at East Dereham.*

Left *Doorway in the tower of St Andrew's church, Middleton, shows traces of Saxon work.*

Right *The church of St Peter at Hackness, North Yorkshire, has a late Saxon chancel arch and contains two excellent fragments of an Anglo-Saxon cross, linked by their inscriptions to a convent founded here by St Hilda of Whitby.*

The church of St Mary at Wharram le Street, East Yorkshire, is of late Saxon origin, and original work is still to be seen in the nave and chancel as well as in the belfry windows.

With the help of one of Edwin's thegns, Paulinus escaped by ship to Kent, taking with him the widowed queen, the royal children and a good deal of Edwin's treasure. Paulinus was offered the see of Rochester by Archbishop Honorius and the Kentish king, and there he ended his days twelve years later, in 645.

The year-long ravages of Catwallaun's armies throughout Northumbria after Edwin's death did not destroy Christiantiy in the kingdom; however, they brought about profound changes in its future form. When Oswald, the son of Aethelferth, returned from exile in Scotland to defeat Catwallaun and take over the Northumbrian throne, he brought with him the Celtic Christianity of Iona, not that of Rome; and it was natural that he should turn to Iona for a bishop. In 635, a company of monks under a leader named Aedan (sometimes spelt Aidan) came to Northumbria and settled on the island of Lindisfarne, there to establish a community second only to Iona and to give the place its enduring name of Holy Island. Aedan's simple faith and austere discipline contrasted sharply with the monks of Wales, hungry for land and wealth, and with the proud dignity of the Roman church's priests. Bede telle us:

'. . . He gave his clergy an inspiring example of self-discipline and continence, and the highest recommendation of his teaching to all was that he and his followers lived as they taught. He never sought or cared for any worldy possessions, and loved to give away to the poor whatever he received from kings or wealthy folk. Whether in town or country, he always travelled on foot unless compelled by necessity to ride, and whenever he met anyone, whether high or low, he stopped and spoke to them. If they were heathen, he urged them to be baptised; and if they were Christians, he strengthened their faith, and inspired them by word and deed to live a good life and to be generous to others.'

He must have been a gentle, dignified man, yet one who was not afraid to air his views outspokenly, to kings and commoners alike.

He brought with him the best attributes of the British and Irish churches; the authority of Columba, yet unmarred by the violence of Columba's early years; the wisdom of Illtud, without the millstone of wealth; the austerity of David, without the arrogance that had been one of the Welsh monk's greatest failings. Throughout his early ministry he was supported unfailingly by Oswald, the Bretwalda, who also used his power to assist others in the conversion of the southern English, and in particular the West Saxons. Pope Honorius I had sent a missionary named Birinus to preach among the Saxons of the Thames Valley; when their king, Kynegils, was baptised, Oswald stood godfather for him, and the two kings then installed Birinus as bishop in the Roman town of Dorchester.

Oswald was killed in battle against Penda near Oswestry in 643, but his brother and successor, Oswy, maintained the Christian tradition. During his rule, monasteries modelled on Iona were established in the south and midlands, as well as in the north, and churches sprang up in the central squares of the old Roman towns where, one day, there would be cathedrals. Nobles converted in the south travelled to Northumbria for their baptism ceremonies, as Bede testifies; even Peada, son of the heathen Penda the king of the Middle Angles, travelled to a spot known as 'At-Wall', which could be any one of several locations, to be baptised by the Irish Bishop Finan, who had succeeded Aedan at

Penda's kingdom. The view south-east into Shrop-shire from Selattyn.

Lindisfarne. Peada subsequently married one of Oswy's daughters, and Christianity thereupon became the official faith of the Middle Angles.

King Penda himself, in fact, though a pagan to the last, never forbade the preaching of the Christian faith to any of his people who were willing to listen. But, says Bede, 'He hated and despised any whom he knew to be insincere in their practice of Christianity once they had accepted it, and said that any who failed to obey the God in whom they professed to believe were despicable wretches'.

The Celtic form of Christianity, brought to Britain by Columba and his followers and spread by the armies of Northumbria, persisted for a long time; but on some matters, Celtic and Roman Christianity could not be reconciled, and it was inevitable that in the long run there should be a confrontation between the two. The bone of contention that brought matters to a head was the different method used by both schools in calculating the date of Easter. For generations, successive Popes had been reminding the Irish that their stubborn insistence in using the 'old' method—which recalled the Pelagian 'heresy' of two centuries earlier—threatened the unity of the Christian church. Both sides agreed that Easter should be celebrated on the Sunday of the third week of the month in which the full moon fell on or after the Spring equinox. Whereas the Roman Church took the equinox to be the 21st of March, however, the Celts placed it on the 25th, which meant that in some years, depending on the moon's phases, there might be a discrepancy of up to four weeks between the two feasts. The problem made itself felt

inside the Northumbrian royal household, because although King Oswy followed the Celtic tradition, his Kentish-born queen followed the custom of the Roman Church—which meant that while he was feasting on Easter Sunday, she was still observing the Lenten fast, along with half the court. It was a situation that could hardly have fostered domestic harmony, and Oswy determined to

---

Corbridge (Northumberland). The Church of St Andrew, which stands beside the tiny square in the historic town of Corbridge (the former Roman Corstopitum) partly dates from the seventh century, although the upper part of the tower is late Saxon work of the eleventh century. On the north side of the nave there are two very early small windows, now filled in. Corbridge may be reached easily either by the A69 Newcastle–Carlisle road, or (perhaps more interestingly) by the A68, the old Roman Dere Street. In the tenth century, the Viking Raegnald thrashed the Northumbrians at Corbridge before moving on to capture York.

Hexham (Northumberland). The original church, on the site of the present Hexham Abbey, was founded by St Wilfrid in 674. It was a splendid structure, with spiral stair-cases, a colonnaded nave and crypts of well-dressed stone. Ennius, Wilfrid's biographer, said that he 'knew of no other house on this side of the Alps built on such a scale', and yet the building was probably not more than 100 ft in length. The Church was razed by the Danes in 876, and only the original crypt remains; the rest dates from the twelfth and thirteenth centuries. The original building incorporated a good deal of Roman stonework, some of it already carved and including a slab dedicated to the Emperor Severus. A stone 'throne' in the abbey may have been used by Wilfrid for the coronation of Northumbrian kings; later known as the Frith Stool, it was used by fugitives as a sanctuary seat. In a niche in the south wall there is a chalice, dating from about 850. Hexham lies beside the A69, about three miles west of Corbridge; while visiting the area, be sure to explore the countryside to the south, where King Oswald of Northumbria defeated Catwallaun somewhere near Rowley Burn.

---

resolve it. In the autumn of 663 or the spring of 664—the date is in some dispute—he summoned the most learned spokesmen of both churches to Whitby to debate the issue.

The spokesman for the Celtic church was the gentle, mild-mannered Colman, Bishop of Lindisfarne, who was no match for the Roman church's representative, Wilfred. Colman stated his case, quoting the authority of Columba and other Irish bishops before him, but Wilfred destroyed his arguments one by one.

'Even if your Columba,' Bede quotes him as saying, 'was a Saint potent in miracles, can he take precedence before the most blessed Prince of the Apostles, to whom our Lord said: "Thou art Peter, and upon this rock I will build my Church, and the gates of hell shall not prevail against it, and to thee I will give the keys of the kingdom of heaven"?'

The argument impressed King Oswy deeply. 'Who am I,' he said, 'to quarrel with such a doorkeeper?'

Defeated, Colman retired to Iona and then to Ireland. Wilfred's fight, however, was by no means finished. Not only was he striving to create an English church that conformed in all respects with that of Rome, but also to elevate its bishops to new heights of power from which they might be political as well as spiritual counsellors for Kings. His own way of life was different in every respect from the austere simplicity of the Celtic bishops; he travelled accompanied by a retinue of 120 armed men, and on ceremonial occasions was carried on a golden throne by nine bishops.

When Colman departed for Ireland, his place as bishop of the Northumbrians was taken by Tuda, who had been schooled and consecrated in Scotland. Late in 664, however, he fell victim to a plague which ravaged southern England and spread into Northumbria, and it was Wilfred who stepped into his place. With the agreement of Alfrid, underking of Deira, he fixed his see in York; Alfrid sent him to Gaul to be consecrated, but in his absence Oswy, who was Alfrid's father, took control of York and installed Chad of Lastingham, a pupil of Aedan. When Wilfred returned Oswy refused to accept him as Bishop of York, so he retired to Ripon and there built his church.

Part of it survives to this day, in the crypt of Ripon Cathedral.

Meanwhile the see of Canterbury had also become vacant, so Oswy and the king of Kent jointly sent an English priest named Wighard to Rome for consecration. Wighard, however, died soon after his arrival, so the Pope, Vitalian, made his own appointment to the Canterbury see; an elderly scholar named Theodore, a Greek from Tarsus in Asia Minor. Theodore was 70 years old when he arrived in Britain in 669, and on the face of it seemed a most unlikely choice for the exacting position of Archbishop of Canterbury, but he was a shrewd and tactful man, and by the time of his death at the ripe old age of 88 he had succeeded in placing the English church on new and lasting foundations. His first task was to fill the vacant sees of Rochester, Dunwich and Winchester; he also moved Wilfred to York and sent Chad to Mercia, where he established his see at Lichfield. Wilfred therefore achieved his long-standing ambition; but it was not long before his pride and lust for power brought him down. After 671, he found powerful support for a time in the person of King Egferth, who had succeeded his father Oswy to the Northumbrian throne; Wilfred supported him in his rash campaigns against the Picts, against the advice of fellow churchmen. Egferth, however, eventually came to resent ever-increasing status, his '. . . worldly glory and wealth . . . his vast army of retainers, equipped with royal livery and weapons'.

In 678, Egferth sent Wilfred into exile. He stayed for a time in Mercia and Wessex, then spent five years preaching in Sussex, where the king, Aethelwalh, gave him a bishopric at Selsey. Then in 685 Egferth was killed in the last of his disastrous campaigns against the Picts, and Wilfred's fortunes turned once again. An early quarrel with Theodore was patched up and, before the end of the year, he was back at Ripon. His position, however, was by no means secure, as future events were to show.

The church at St Mary at Stow, Lincolnshire, is said to have been the cathedral church of Lindsey, established by King Egferth (or Ecgfrith) of Northumbria in 674. Cruciform in plan, it displays a great deal of original Saxon workmanship.

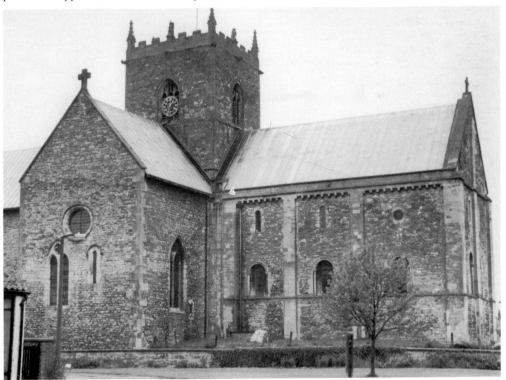

Bradwell-on-Sea (Essex). According to Bede, the Church of St Peter-on-the-Wall was built in 654 by St Cedd, who had been sent from Northumbria to become bishop of the East Saxons. The church stands alone on the coast east of Chelmsford and two miles north-east of Bradwell-on-Sea village, astride the west wall of the Roman fort of Othona. One of the interesting features of the barn-like building (in fact, it was used as a barn until 1920) is the arrangement of its porticus, which were not used for burials but as chapels for the receipt of offerings. This is a Syrian style, for the church was built at a time when numbers of Syrian monks and craftsmen arrived in Europe after their own civilisation was overwhelmed by the Persians. A good deal of Roman building materials were used in the church's construction. *(OS Sheet 168, 031082.)*

Theodore died in 690, by which time England comprised one ecclesiastical province under 14 bishops, all answerable to the Archbishop of Canterbury. Theodore's achievement, in fact, was little short of remarkable, for he had succeeded in creating a united church in a land that was still divided; not for centuries more would England become one nation. But he achieved much more than that. He brought literacy to the English church, and made Canterbury a centre of learning which attracted scholars from all over the Christian world. As the number of monasteries grew and flourished in the English province, so books began to proliferate, copied and illustrated laboriously by hand in cold, poorly-lit cells by monks who drew their light from love and faith. Many of those early works of art were sadly destroyed or lost in later centuries, but some survived; perhaps the best-known of them all is the Lindisfarne Gospels, compiled by Eadfrith, bishop of Lindisfarne from 698 to 721, and now in the British Museum.

Theodore's wish had been that Wilfred should succeed him as Archbishop of Canterbury, but Wilfred's ambitions were still centred on Northumbria, and he made repeated attempts to consolidate his status there. The outcome, once again, was exile, this time on the orders of Aldfrith, who had succeeded his brother Egferth as king. Wilfred returned to Mercia, where during the next ten years he founded several monasteries under the patronage of King Aethelred, and in the meantime appealed to Pope Sergius I in an attempt to redress his grievances. In 702 an English synod was convened at Austerfield, near Bawtry, to hear Wilfred's case; it was attended by King Aldfrith and Archbishop Berthwald, who had been appointed to the see of Canterbury by the Pope.

Wilfred's stand was simple enough. Some years earlier, during his previous exile and his rift with Theodore—caused when the latter divided Northumbria and replaced Wilfred—he had travelled to Rome and appeared before the then Pope, Agatho, and a council of 53 bishops. The council had decided that, although Theodore had been right in his action of dividing Northumbria, Wilfred should be restored to York. He had returned to Britain armed with copies of the decree, but his aspirations had been destroyed by Egferth, who had exiled him. Now, at this new hearing, Wilfred claimed that the original papal decree was still valid. Aldfrith, Berthwald and the others, however, insisted that before they could consider any such claim, Wilfred would have to surrender all his lands and monasteries in both Northumbria and Mercia, a demand which they had no power to enforce and with which Wilfred had no intention of complying. He therefore stood condemned, and once more took himself off to Rome to appeal in person to the Pope, now John VI. After four months of pleading, the Pope sent a letter to Bertwald, instructing him to call another synod and settle the affair for good. He also asked Kings Aldfrith and Aethelred to intervene, and although Aldfrith went on opposing Wilfred to the bitter end, the Northumbrian king's death in 705 removed the last obstacle to a settlement and saw the restoration of Wilfred to his two principal monasteries in the north, Ripon and Hexham. It was in a sense a hollow victory, and did little more than permit Wilfred to live out the last four years of his life in peace. Ironically, his death occurred not in Northumbria, but in the monastery at Oundle, in Mercia.

Wilfred's materialistic outlook, and the decisions taken by the Synod of Whitby, had

Whitby (Yorkshire). The ruins of the abbey which stands high above the harbour of Whitby date from the thirteenth century, but the site has been hallowed since 657 AD, when Hilda, a kinswoman of the Northumbrian King Oswy, founded a community there; and, of course, a few years later Whitby was the scene of the famous synod which led to the ascendancy of the Roman over the Celtic Church in Britain. One of the loveliest stories connected with Dark Age Whitby is that of Caedmon, the humble cowherd who composed and sang the first great English hymn and later became a monk in St Hilda's Abbey.

Breedon-on-the-Hill (Leicestershire). Breedon lies on the A453 Tamworth-Nottingham road, about 18 miles south-west of Nottingham. A monastery was originally founded here in 675, but this was later destroyed by the Danes in the ninth century. However, some of the early sculptures are built into the fabric of the later church, which stands inside the ramparts of an Iron Age fort above a quarry face, dominating the surrounding countryside. In the body of the church, running round the inside, there are the remains of stone friezes 60 ft in length and six to eight inches wide—a kind of cartoon strip depicting birds and animals, and men and animals in combat. The friezes show a definite Frankish influence. Other monumental sculptures in the church include a Celtic-style Madonna, in the south aisle, and a Byzantine-style angel in the bell tower.

Brixworth (Northamptonshire). A very imposing seventh century building, the Church of All Saints at Brixworth—seven miles north of Northampton on the A508 Market Harborough road—was originally built as a monastery in about 670. This was destroyed by the Danes in the ninth century and restored in the tenth, but the present nave is part of the original structure and is 120 ft long, large for the period in which it was built. The blocked arches which once led to the porticus, or side chapels, are of Roman brick, as are the arches of the clerestory windows; the whole produces a fine contrast between the harsh hues of the Roman materials and the softer colours of the Northamptonshire sandstone.

Ripon (Yorkshire). Built by Wilfrid, who was buried there in 709, Ripon Cathedral has a crypt which is over 1,300 years old, and even some of the plaster is unchanged since St Wilfrid dedicated the church on St Peter's Day, 672. The crypt was almost certainly designed as a Reliquary, to display relics of the saints brought back by Wilfrid from Rome. It was illuminated by oil lights set in the five 'light holes' in the walls, in one of which the hollowed-out bowl where the oil was placed is still to be seen in the stonework. At the east end, now filled in, there is a small tunnel or 'squint' probably designed to enable pilgrims to view the relics from the floor of St Wilfrid's church without entering the crypt. The original building was burned to the ground by the Danes in 948.

Monkwearmouth (Tyne and Wear). Situated in a grey, depressing area of northeast Sunderland, the Church of St Peter with St Cuthbert was originally founded as a monastery in 674 by Benedict Biscop, on land donated by King Ecgfrith of Northumbria. The original building had a great library which was stocked with books, relics and paintings which Benedict brought back from Rome on five separate journeys. It was here that Bede spent his formative years before moving to the neighbouring house at Jarrow. Visible seventh century remains at Monkwearmouth include the west wall of the nave and the lower stages of the tower, together with many fragments of carved stonework. The church stands to the north of the River Wear, beside the A183.

Repton (Derbyshire). The church of St Wystan at Repton, which lies on the B5008 north-east of Burton upon Trent, is a Mercian building dating from the eighth century. King Aethelbald, who built Wat's Dyke, was buried here, as was a later Mercian king, Wyglaf and St Wystan himself, who was Wyglaf's grandson. Excavations have revealed what is believed to be an eighth century mausoleum, which was later incorporated as a crypt below the chancel of a new church built by Wyglaf. The building was destroyed by the Danes in 874 and rebuilt in the eleventh century.

by no means stifled the Celtic influences in the church. They were personified in the life of Cuthbert, perhaps the most revered of all the northern saints after Columba. He was appointed to the see of Lindisfarne by King Egferth in 685, the year of the latter's death, and in fact had spent many years in seclusion on one of the Farne Islands, a few miles off the coast, before successively serving as Prior of Lindisfarne and Bishop of Hexham. An ascetic and a great lover of solitude, Cuthbert found even his beloved Lindisfarne less remote from the world than he would have wished; he returned to the Farne Islands and remained there as a hermit until his death in 687, living in a hut 25 feet in diameter. He was buried at Lindisfarne, but in 793, when the north-east coast was threatened by Norse raiders, his coffin and relics were removed by the monks and, after a series of wanderings across the north country, were re-buried, first at Chester-le-Street in 882 and finally at Durham in 995. Nor was that the end of the story, for centuries later his tomb was violated at the time of the Reformation. Amazingly, however, his coffin and other relics survived, and may be seen today in the Library of Durham Cathedral.

St Cuthbert's life was thoroughly documented by Bede, the first and the greatest of the early English historians. Born at Monkton in Durham about 671, he was sent to the monastery of Monkwearmouth at the age of seven, dividing the remainder of his life between this house and its neighbour at Jarrow. Although he never travelled widely, perhaps not even venturing farther afield than York during the whole of his life, Bede must have been able to draw on numerous sources in compiling his works. The two monasteries of Jarrow and Monkwearmouth together held some 600 monks, many of whom would have travelled in the Christian world and perhaps beyond it, and there is evidence that they had access to a considerable library; Bede's writings contain references to more than 80 different authorities. He doubtless received much inspiration in his formative years from Benedict Biscop, the man who founded and ruled both Wearmouth and Jarrow. A nobleman of wide learning and culture, he had come to Britain with Theodore in 669. A second source of inspiration would have been

> **Jarrow (Tyne and Wear).** St Paul's Church, sited on the banks of the River Don that runs south from the Tyne estuary, was where Bede spent his later years and wrote his major works. The chancel of the present church was probably the first building to be erected on the present site, in 681, and contains many interesting features, including three single splayed Saxon windows. Part of the foundations of the original western Saxon church can be seen below the present floor level. The original dedicated stone dating from 685 survives, and can be seen in this part of the church. The tower dates from the eleventh century and surmounts the original porch between the two separate Saxon churches. Finds from excavations of the Saxon monastery are to be seen in nearby Jarrow Hall.

Abbot Ceolfrid of Jarrow, under whose care Bede matured. When the plague of 686 decimated the monks of the two monasteries, Ceolfrid and the boy Bede maintained the regular services almost single-handed until other monks were trained to fill the places of those who had died. Bede wrote on many topics, but the work for which he is best remembered is his *Ecclesiastical History of the English Nation*, which covers the story of the Island from Roman times, relying heavily on the works of earlier writers such as Gildas for the first few centuries—and repeating their inaccuracies—while concentrating subsequently on the development of the church after the arrival of St Augustine. The 'History' was completed in 731, just four years before his death. He was buried at Jarrow, but his bones were later removed by a monk and re-interred in the Galilee porch of Durham Cathedral, where they lay undisturbed until they were scattered during the Reformation.

It was Bede, more than any other, who lifted the early English church out of the darkness. He recorded the exploits of its clergy not as legend, but as fact; and he recorded them not in the dry, day-to-day style of the annalist nor the flowery prose of someone who imagined miracles at every turning, but in the lively, readable fashion of a true author and historian. English history owes a great debt to him.

Chapter 7

'A dyke from sea to sea'

'In modern times in Mercia there ruled a mighty king called Offa, who struck all the kings and regions around him with terror. He it was who ordered the Great Dyke to be constructed between Wales and Mercia, stretching from sea to sea.' So wrote Bishop Asser, the ninth century historian, in his work *On the Deeds of King Alfred*. Curiously, he was the first to mention Offa, of whom there is no contemporary record; yet this mighty and powerful king, who became Bretwalda in his turn, dominated the events of eighth century England. His leadership might have produced a united nation; instead, his arrogance destroyed any such hope, and left English kings warring with one another at a time when the island was under dire threat from over the sea.

For most of the eighth century, the kings of Mercia were the effective overlords of the English south of the Humber. Northumbria, fragmented by disorder after the death of Aldfrith in 705, was no longer a threat; its internal decay was checked for a time by King Eadberht, who reigned for 20 years and waged a successful campaign against the British Strathclyde in 750, but he and his son, Oswulf, were killed by their own bodyguard soon afterwards, and after their death Northumbria slipped more and more into the background of English politics. The architect of Mercia's victory over Northumbria on the Trent, King Aethelred, was a staunch upholder of Christianity and a close friend of Wilfred during the latter's exile from the north. He ruled Mercia for 29 years, and no other king was more powerful; yet he abdicated

---

Offa's Dyke. This landmark, running for 80 miles from the Severn to the Dee, is preserved as one of Britain's national footpaths. To walk the whole length of it is definitely a leisure exercise for the summer holidays, but a day's walking along selected parts gives a good idea of the sheer magnitude of this impressive earthwork. From its starting point near Prestatyn in north Wales, its southward course takes it to the west of Wrexham and Oswestry and on to reach the Severn near Welshpool. In this sector it can be best reached by taking one of three east-west roads, the B4500, B4579 and B4580, all of which cut through it at references *OS Sheet 126, 264374, 252349* and *256310*. The central sector, however, is probably the best,

for the Dyke can be followed almost continuously for some 20 miles from the point where it leaves the Severn at Buttington *(OS Sheet 126 249084)* to Knighton, on the A488. The seven-mile stretch north of Knighton (where there is an information centre) is particularly good, for here the Dyke rises more than 1,000 ft above sea level, descending only to cross river valleys. South of Knighton the Dyke is broken, for when it was built the area was heavily forested and the earthwork was constructed only in places where an open valley or a track needed to be blocked. The last section of the Dyke, where it joins the Bristol Channel east of Chepstow, may be seen where the B4228 cuts through it at *OS Sheet 172 548931.*

Wat's Dyke. Overshadowed by its bigger counterpart, Wat's Dyke, built by Aethelbald of Mercia, nevertheless played a vital part in protecting that kingdom's western flank from the attentions of the British of Wales. It ran for some 40 miles from Basingwerk, on the Dee estuary in Cheshire, to Morda Brook, south of Oswestry. The best starting-point for its exploration is where the B5426 cuts it south of Wrexham. There is also a good half-mile stretch starting at Pentreclawdd *(OS Sheet 126 297320)* leading to Old Oswestry. One tip here; I found that a chat with the local farming folk in the neighbourhood of both Offa's and Wat's Dykes was most illuminating. They will point out features and tell old stories not to be found in the official guides, and provided you shut their gates and do not frighten their livestock their willingness to help is quite amazing. Only once, in my travels through Britain, did I find a farmer who was a little on the irate side, and that was only because some tourists had stupidly taken an uncontrolled dog into a field full of sheep a few days earlier.

The course of Wat's Dyke at Pentreclawydd, north of Oswestry. Built by Aethelbald of Mercia, the earthwork was later overshadowed by Offa's Dyke, constructed a couple of miles further to the west.

in favour of his nephew, Coenred, and spent the last 14 years of his life in a monastery at Bardney in Lindsey.

His abdication almost caused his kingdom to collapse, for his nephew was not strong enough to resist the pressures that began to mount against its frontiers from outside; even the Welsh, Mercia's traditional allies since the days of Penda, launched a series of devastating raids across the frontier, and following a battle at an unidentified spot called Wodensbeorg in 715 between the armies of Mercia and those of Ine, king of Wessex, it seems that Wessex may have recovered some of its northern territory, overrun by the Mercians years earlier.

It needed a powerful ruler to redress the situation. That man was Aethelbald, the grandson of Penda's brother, who came to the Mercian throne in 716. The circumstances in which he came to power are not known, but in his early days he appears to have been something of an adventurer, if not a bandit; he had no estates, and lived in the Fens with his warband. He quickly established himself as a tyrant with a fair reputation for wickedness, but by 731, as Bede records, he had himself master of all the provinces south of the Humber. In 733 his armies made a foray into Wessex and occupied territory in Somerset, forcing Cuthred, the king of Wessex, to support him in a campaign against the Welsh. Aethelbald is credited with the construction of Wat's Dyke, which ran for about 40 miles from the estuary of the Dee in Cheshire to Morda Brook, south of Oswestry in Shropshire and was designed to safeguard the north-west flank of Mercia from Wales. An impressive feat of engineering, it was nevertheless superseded and overshadowed by Offa's Dyke, built further to the west. Aethelbald ruled for 41 years and never married, preferring, we are led to believe, to satisfy his appetite with a succession of women. He was murdered one night by members of his own bodyguard at Seckington, near Tamworth; the year was 756.

The assassination was followed by a brief civil war in which Aethelbald's heir, Beornred, took the Mercian throne, only to be ousted by Offa, another descendant of Penda's brother. Offa subsequently claimed that Beornred was a usurper, legitimately overthrown by force of arms; it was a necessary piece of propaganda, for Beornred survived in exile for a further 12 years, and remained a threat until he was killed in Northumbria.

Offa does not appear to have been recognised as the legitimate successor by the rulers of Mercia's neighbouring kingdoms, all of whom had acknowledged Aethelbald as Bretwalda. Yet he was secure enough in Mercia; from the royal centre at Tamworth he travelled widely and frequently among the peoples of the 30 or so different tribes that made up his kingdom, exacting taxes from them and generally asserting his authority. It was a necessary procedure for a king of Offa's time, for somewhere in the kingdom there must always have been undercurrents of rebellion and

---

Bradford-on-Avon (Wiltshire). One of the loveliest of all Anglo-Saxon churches, the Church of St Lawrence at Bradford-on-Avon was built by St Aldhelm, who was friend and counsellor to both Mercian and West Saxon kings, in 700. The chancel is tiny, measuring only 13 ft by 10, and its 18 ft of height seem somehow disproportionate. Two small chapels were originally attached to north and south, but only the northern one survives. The four doorways and the windows all date from the original building, which was substantially rebuilt during the late Saxon period. Bradford-on-Avon lies five miles south-east of Bath, on the A363.

Deerhurst (Gloucestershire). The Church of St Mary here is a most interesting building, with nave, west porch and the side chapels dating from the eighth century. The building was partly destroyed by the Danes in the ninth century but was rebuilt in the tenth, when a polygonal apse was added. In the apse there is a winged angel, which appears to show a certain Byzantine influence; there are similar angels in the nave of the church at Bradford-on-Avon. The font is the stone base of a cross shaft and is probably of ninth century date. To the south-west of St Mary's is Earl Odda's chapel, dating from 1056; it was used as a farmhouse kitchen for centuries before being rediscovered in 1885. Deerhurst lies two miles west of the A38 Gloucester–Tewkesbury road. *(OS Sheet 150, 870299.)*

> **Newent (Gloucestershire).** Standing eight miles north-west of Gloucester, the church of St Mary in the village of Newent displays two interesting sculptures: one a memorial slab bearing an inscription referring to a man named Edred, and the other a cross-shaft in the porch, possibly of ninth century date. This has carvings depicting Adam and Eve and a beast known as the 'Carolingian Lion'. *(OS Sheet 162, 723259.)*

unrest. So he made his presence felt constantly, making sure that his subject estates were carrying out their obligations to the full. Such obligations included the provision of labour to repair roads and bridges, to build fortifications and of course the mobilizing of men for military service.

Catering for Offa and his retinue must have been something of a nightmare for the ealdormen they visited. A list of the food and drink necessary to keep a king and his court for one night has been preserved; it applies to King Ine of Wessex, but Offa's requirements can not have been much different. The list itemises 10 jars of honey, 300 loaves, 12 casks of Welsh ale, 30 of clear ale, 2 old oxen, 10 geese, 20 hens, 10 cheeses, a cask of butter, 5 salmon, 100 eels, and 20 pounds of fodder. To raise such provisions, perhaps often at short notice, implies a very efficient food gathering system, but it becomes more understandable when one realises that no ealdorman was likely to receive futher grants of land unless he was in a position to provide shelter and a feast for the royal party.

Travelling in Offa's time, with a large retinue and all the necessary baggage, cannot have been an easy matter. The old Roman road network would have long since fallen into disrepair, and well-beaten roads must have existed only around the centres of food distribution that were eventually to become the principal market towns. It is hard to imagine that there can have been much travelling between the autumn rains and the spring thaw; indeed, it is on record that the winter of 763 was exceptionally severe, and that travel ceased altogether for four months. The snow and ice lay in a thick carpet all across Europe; food supplies ran out and people died of starvation. Fires swept all across densely-packed wooden towns such as York, Winchester and London, and doubtless many others too, adding to the misery.

Nothing remains today of Offa's royal hall at Tamworth, although excavation has revealed traces of the eighth century ditch and palisade that must have formed part of the outer defensive perimeter. In 1971, archaeologists also discovered the intact timbers of a two-storey Anglo-Saxon watermill in the south-west corner of the defences, by the River Anker. Its degree of craftsmanship was quite extraordinary, with windows of leaded

Below and top right *Offa's Dyke at Carreg-y-Big, north-west of Oswestry.*

Centre right *An interesting feature of Offa's Dyke is that settlements were built in the shadow of its defences. Some survive in modern form today, such as the farm at Carreg-y-Big, built astride the remains of the earthwork.*

Right *Cross-section of the dyke at Carreg-y-Big, where the road cuts through it.*

glass, a steel main bearing and querns of lava from the Rhineland. The mill dates from the middle of the eighth century, and quite probably served Offa's household. The royal hall itself may have stood on raised ground by the church in the present town centre but, since this is now the graveyard, excavation is not possible. Archaeologists are of the opinion that the hall may have been built on a huge rectangular platform, elevating it even more over the surrounding area; it may have been anything between 80 and 160 feet long, but as one later writer, possibly drawing on a contemporary source, says that 'for its magnificence it was the wonder and marvel of the age', it was probably very large indeed. Without doubt it lay at the centre of a large farming complex, all contained within the defensive ditches.

By 770, Offa must have felt that his domination of the Mercian people was secure enough to permit expansion into neighbouring territories. In the following year, he crossed the Thames with a large cavalry force and defeated the 'Haestingas', the men of West Sussex, in a move that may have been designed to provide him with a springboard for an invasion of Kent, the oldest and most civilised of all the English kingdoms. He attacked in 775, but the men of Kent resisted fiercely and a savage battle was fought at Otford, near Sevenoaks. There is no record of who won, but it does not seem to have been Offa; in the years that followed, coins minted in Kent and recorded land grants bore no reference to him, as they surely would have done had he annexed the kingdom.

Nevertheless, if Offa was indeed defeated by the men of Kent, it did not discourage him from launching a campaign against the Welsh in 778. His cavalry stormed over the border, burning and destroying and returning home with great quantities of loot, from cattle to gold and silver. In 779 it was the turn of Wessex. Offa's army, and a host commanded by King Cynewulf, battled it out at Benson on the north bank of the Thames; Mercia's army emerged victorious, and Offa annexed a large slice of Wessex territory in what is now Berkshire. The victory made him all-powerful in the south; whether neighbouring kings liked the idea or not, his military prowess had made

him Bretwalda, and his position was further consolidated when, in 785, he took control of Kent. Whether this happened because he invaded successfully, or whether some internal strife made a Mercian takeover simple, is not known. However, control of Kent marked a new phase in Offa's career. In the space of a few short years, he was transformed from barbarian warrior into a statesman of great standing. Kent opened the door to Europe and its culture; and in the late eighth century this was the Europe of Charlemagne, the Holy Roman Empire, with its attempts at recreating the culture and the administrative structure of that other Rome.

In 786, at Offa's invitation, two papal legates arrived in England, ostensibly to review the state of the church. There seems, however, to have been a political reason, stemming from a dispute beween Offa and Archbishop Jaenberht of Canterbury. The two were enemies, and to have an enemy as head of the church in England was something Offa was not prepared to tolerate. He doubtless went out of his way to impress the legates from Rome; in any event, shortly after their return Offa received papal authority to create a new archbishopric in Mercia, at Lichfield, effectively depriving Jaenberht of a large part of his jurisdiction.

Offa also enlisted Rome's help in a bid to ensure that the Mercian monarchy remained with his own branch of the dynasty. Charlemagne had done the same; in 781 his sons Pippin and Louis had both been anointed as kings by the Pope, this assuring their succession. Offa secured papal approval, and in 787 his son Ecgfrith was duly consecrated, either by the Archbishop of Lichfield or by papal legates. The ceremony was accompanied by the first issue of coins bearing Offa's profile. The English penny had been in circulation since the seventh century, minted with other coinage in Canterbury, but it was Offa who

Opposite page *The oldest church in Canterbury, and one of the oldest in Britain, St Martin's was first built, according to Bede, 'while the Romans still inhabited Britain'. It was one of the first centres of Roman Christianity in the British Isles. Photos show tower under restoration, 1982; north side of church; and south side.*

made it the standard coin of southern England, causing it to be refined and characterised by a degree of workmanship that made coins minted on the Continent appear crude by comparison. He also ordered gold coins to be struck, each of them worth 30 silver pennies. Some of the coins bear the words 'Offa Rex', and the bust that appears on many of them is almost certainly a reasonably faithful representation of the king himself, sometimes attired in the fashion of a Roman emperor, with his hair dressed and curled. The resemblance to Roman coinage, in fact, is quite startling; whether this was a deliberate plan on Offa's part to cast himself in the image of an emperor, or flattery by the moneyer, we shall never know.

Offa died on July 26 796. Behind him he left a lasting monument: the great dyke that 'stretched from sea to sea'. It was the greatest engineering achievement seen in Britain since the building of Hadrian's Wall, and there is still some dispute over why it was constructed in the first place. For a long time, it was believed that the dyke represented an agreed boundary between Mercia and Wales, with gaps at intervals to allow traders to pass through. But the story of Mercia and Wales during Offa's last years was one of continual warfare, so it is far more likely that the dyke was a fortified barrier—a steep bank with a ditch in front, measuring 25 feet from top to bottom, surmounted by a wooden palisade and in places by a stone breastwork. It is possible that there were watchtowers at frequent intervals. Excavations around the gaps in the dyke have shown that the frontal ditch runs across them, below the surface; if there were indeed gateways here, they must have been fortified structures, designed primarily to allow cavalry forays into enemy territory. In fact, the more we learn about Offa's Dyke, the more we come to realise that it bears an astonishing resemblance not the earlier Anglo-Saxon defensive dykes that appeared in Britain, but to Hadrian's Wall itself, with readily-available turf and wood used in place of stone. Offa may even have seen Hadrian's Wall in all its majesty at some point in his life; what is much more likely, however, is that he was inspired by an extract from Bede's 'History', a copy of which he is known to have possessed.

Above Remains of the Chapel of St Pancras, Canterbury, dating from the seventh century.
Below Remains of the Church of St Mary, Canterbury. The original building dates from 620.

'After many critical and hard-fought battles, he [Severus] decided to separate that portion of the island under his control from the remaining unconquered peoples, and he did this not with a wall, as some imagine, but with an earthwork. For a wall is built of stone, but an earthwork, which protects a camp from enemy attack, is constructed with sods cut from the earth and raised high above ground level, fronted by the ditch from which the sods were cut, and surmounted by a strong palisade of logs. Severus built a rampart and ditch of this type from sea to sea, and fortified it by a series of towers.'

Bede's error in thinking that Severus had been the actual builder of the Wall was understandable, for it was during his reign as emperor that extensive repair work was undertaken on the fortifications following massive barbarian attacks in the late second

Right *The west wall of the Church of St Mary, built into the ruins of St Augustine's abbey, Canterbury.*
Below *The Church of St Peter and St Paul, the first Saxon church in Canterbury, built between 578 and 613, is now little more than a grassy area submerged by the later ruins of St Augustine's abbey.*

Wansdyke (Wiltshire and Avon). Much more impressive than the earthworks of East Anglia, the Wansdyke marks the northern frontier of Wessex. It is thought to have been built by the Anglo-Saxons of Wessex in the sixth and seventh centuries as a defence against Mercia, but the name bestowed on it by the English—Woden's Dyke—implies that they did not know who had constructed it, and it may therefore have been built by the Romano-British to defend the territory of what had once been three Roman states in the south-west. The Wansdyke is in fact built in two separate sections; the eastern part is larger and more easy to follow, running for 12 miles from Morgan's Hill near Devizes across the Marlborough Downs to a point just to the west of Severnake. The best access to it is by following the Swindon-Devizes road (A361) to where the Wansdyke crosses it at Shperherd's Shore *(OS Sheet 173, 044663)* and then exploring it eastwards; alternatively, you can join it on the minor road that runs from Lockeridge to Alton Priors *(OS Sheet 173, 126653)*. The western section of the Wansdyke is about ten miles long, starting just west of the A37 Shepton Mallet-Bristol road at Maes Knoll *(OS Sheet 172, 600660)* and running eastwards to Horsecombe on the southern outskirts of Bath. The western section is only partially intact, and is best reached from a point north of Norton Malreward *(OS Sheet 172, 605658.)*

century. Bede's description also referred to the earlier turf wall that was constructed west of the River Irthing, where local materials were used instead of stone, but the general principles were the same, and the monk's brief account would certainly have given Offa the information he needed.

Raising the manpower to build the dyke would have presented no problem; the obligation of all the smaller kingdoms controlled by Mercia to provide levies for military service and construction work would have seen to that. The likelihood is that several thousand men were conscripted for the task and formed into units, each of which would have been responsible for a section of the 80-mile-long barrier; in this way it would have been possible to build it in a single season,

although the effort and energy expended by the builders must have been tremendous. Before construction work could start, there would be forest to be felled and scrub to be burned; beacons to be set up on the hills for purposes of alignment, and furrows to be ploughed to mark out the lines of ditch would follow.

According to a late version of the *Cambrian Annals*, the Welsh devastated a large part of Mercia in the summer of 787, and it was as a result of this that the dyke was built. It was originally thought that the northern sector ran through Flintshire to the Irish Sea near Prestatyn, but this seems to have been a wrong impression; it runs due north to the River Dee. The confusion arose because the northern end of Offa's Dyke was erroneously thought to be part of Wat's Dyke. We do not know if the dyke was permanently garrisoned; future excavation might provide some clues. What is probable, however, is that the dyke was patrolled by units of Offa's subjects doing their national service; if trouble was encountered, they would light a beacon in the appropriate sector so that other defensive forces could converge on it. For the first time, Mercia had a secure defence along her western frontier.

In his last years Offa appears to have become deeply religious. In 792 he travelled to Rome for a personal meeting with the Pope, but the audience does not seem to have cleansed him of all his old barbarism. Shortly afterwards, he ordered the last king of the East Angles, Aethelberht, to be beheaded, probably as the result of an uprising in which a vain attempt was made to break away from Mercian domination. Such treatment of subject kings was the rule rather than the exception during

Towyn (Gwynedd). Towyn (or Tywyn) lies in the old district of Merioneth, which is named after Marianus, the grandson of Cunedda. There is a remarkable memorial stone in Towyn church—remarkable because it bears an inscription in early Welsh at a time when most inscriptions were in Latin. The stone possibly dates from the seventh century and the true meaning of the inscription is now known, although one word—ARTR—may be an abbreviation of Artorius, or Arthur. *(OS Sheet 135, 588009.)*

Offa's reign, and was to have dramatic consequences following his death.

While Offa lived, however, his power was unquestioned. At Whitsuntide in 795 there is a record of him presiding over a huge court in London, through whose ports much of Mercia's wealth now came, and in that same year his army launched a punitive expedition into Wales and ravaged Dyfed. Shortly before his death in the summer of 796, he received messengers from Charlemagne, with whom he had quarrelled earlier over the Frankish king's request that his son, Charles, should become betrothed to Offa's daughter Aelflaed. Offa had refused unless his son Ecgfrith was permitted to marry Charlemagne's daughter Bertha, whereupon Charlemagne had immediately broken off diplomatic relations with Mercia and closed the Frankish seaports to Mercian trade.

Now, in their failing years, the two elderly rulers were reconciled, Charlemagne terming Offa 'my dear brother' in his letters and expressing an eagerness to 'preserve the bond of holy love and the law of friendship formed in the unity between kings'. Whether Charlemagne was expressing true sincerity, or whether his words might have caused Offa to raise a sardonic eyebrow, we have no means of telling; but his gifts on that occasion were real enough, including a sword taken from the Avars during one of Charlemagne's campaigns in Hungary.

Offa died at Offley in Hertfordshire, and the Bretwaldaship passed at once to his son, Ecgfrith. But he too died on November 17, to be succeeded by Cenwulf, one of Offa's distant cousins. His first task was to suppress a rebellion by the men of Kent and East Anglia, and this he did with appalling brutality. The leader of the Kentish rebels, a renegade monk named Eadberht Praen, was brought to Mercia in chains, there to have his eyes gouged out and his hands cut off.

Cenwulf renewed Offa's old campaigns agains the Welsh. In 818 he attacked Dyfed in strength, and may have been preparing for a further offensive in 821 when he died at Basingwerk. In the following year his brother, Ceolwulf I, captured Degannwy and almost wiped out the old kingdom of Powys, but Ceolwulf was deposed two years later, and with him the dynasty founded by Penda came to an

Liskeard (Cornwall). Three miles north-west of Liskeard there is a fragment of a ninth-century cross shaft known as King Doniert's Stone. It is inscribed DONIERT ROGAVIT PRO ANIMA (Doniert has prayed for his soul) and may be a memorial to King Durngarth, a ninth century Cornish ruler. To reach the stone, follow the minor road from Liskeard to St Cleer, then to Commonmoor, and finally turn west towards Redgate. The stone is to the south of the road. *(OS Sheet 201, 236688.)*

Wing (Buckinghamshire). Most of the church at Wing, which stands on the A418 Aylesbury-Leighton Buzzard road, is tenth century, but the north wall of the aisle and the crypt are much earlier. There are doorways set high up in the north and south walls of the nave, probably indicating that the building once featured a western gallery. *(OS Sheet 165, 880226.)*

Penally (Dyfed). There is an interesting group of stones in the churchyard at Penally, which is a mile and a half south of Tenby on the A4139. One is an intact free-standing cross with a Northumbrian-style wheel-head, and the decoration shows both Northumbrian and Irish influence. A second stone, a cross shaft, has an interesting carving depicting two animals devouring a pair of dragons. *(OS Sheet 158, 118991.)*

end. The kingdom was to preserve its independence for 50 years more, but its kings were of unknown ancestry, unloved by those of neighbouring states but, unlike Offa, unable to impose their authority. The old glory of Mercia was gone for ever.

Yet Offa had left his stamp on England for all time, leaving behind him not only a strong central kingdom whose name would echo down the ages, but also the concept of a single, unified nation. If his only son had not died childless, perhaps Mercia would have remained the dominant power in England; as it was, that position was to be filled in due course by Wessex. The real tragedy was that the decline of Mercia's power came at a time when the shores of Britain were once more threatened from across the seas. On January 8

Escomb (Durham). Claimed to be the most complete Anglo-Saxon church in existence, the church of St John the Evangelist lies about a mile to the west of Bishop Auckland in County Durham. To reach it, take the B6282 westbound and then turn right down the minor road into the village. The chancel arch is built of Roman stone from the fort at Binchester, to the north of Bishop Auckland; it measures 15 ft high by 5 ft wide, and the chancel beyond it is only 10 ft square. Apart from a very short four-year break in the nineteenth century, Escomb church has been in continuous use since the eighth century. The custodian, who lives in a bungalow across the road and from whom one obtains the church keys, told me that a party of wealthy Americans were so impressed by the church that they wanted to buy it and re-assemble it in the United States! Incidentally, while you are in the area, explore Binchester Fort, which may have been the site of a Dark Age battle fought by either Arthur or Urien. *References, OS Sheet 92 (Church): 189301, OS Sheet 93 (Binchester) 210314.*

793, three ships had suddenly descended on the Northumbrian coast, disembarking a band of fierce warriors who had destroyed the church of Lindisfarne before sailing away again. The raiders were Norwegians, and the attack was a foretaste of the terror that was to come. It was the foremost statesman and scholar of Europe, Alcuin of York, who issued the dire warning of the tragedy that was about to overwhelm the Island.

'An immense threat hangs over this island and its people. It is a novelty without precedent that the pirate raids of a heathen people can regularly waste our shores. Yet the English people are divided, and king fights against king. Saddest of all, scarcely any heir of the ancient royal houses survives, and the origin of kings is as dubious as their courage. Study Gildas, the wisest of the British, and examine the reasons why the ancestors of the British lost their kingdom and their fatherland; then look upon yourselves, and you will find amongst you almost identical causes.'

Slowly, the wheel of Dark Age history was turning full circle.

Chapter 8

The rise of Wessex

The growing ascendancy of Wessex on the English scene really dates from 802, when Egbert became king of the West Saxons. During the ten years that followed he not only strengthened his position among his own people but also embarked on a programme of expansion in the south-west. In 815 his armies invaded Cornwall; this was not a concerted attack aimed at conquest, but rather a series of major raids in which the West Saxons roved over Cornish territory, burning and looting before withdrawing to their own homeland. The Cornishmen tried to retaliate a decade later, but the West Saxons were ready for them and their attack was repulsed. Then, in 838, Egbert's forces confronted a mixed army of Britons and Scandinavian mercenaries on high ground at Hingston Down, west of the lower Tamar, and inflicted a decisive defeat on them. It was a victory that left Wessex in a position to dominate the whole of Cornwall, and in its aftermath Egbert annexed large areas of Cornish territory, at the same time compelling the Bishop of Cornwall to acknowledge the Archbishop of Canterbury as his superior.

Egbert's standing among his contemporaries seems to have been finally assured when his forces soundly defeated an invasion by the hated Mercians at Wroughton, south of Swindon, in 825. The kings of Kent, Surrey, Sussex and Essex all submitted to him immediately afterwards, and the king of East Anglia placed his people under the protection of Wessex. With this powerful federation behind him, Egbert felt that it was time to deal

with the question of Mercia once and for all. In 829 he invaded the northern kingdom and overran it, forcing Wiglaf, who was then king, to flee. Egbert's army then marched on to the Northumbrian border; at Dore, near Sheffield, he met with several Northumbrian leaders and forced them to recognize him as Bretwalda. Egbert installed his son, Aethelwulf, as overlord of the kingdoms in the east, with the title of King of Kent, while he contented himself with ruling Wessex. His elevation to the Bretwaldaship coincided, unfortunately, with a renewal of Scandinavian pirate attacks after a period of calm, and the savage seafarers were to remain his principal enemies throughout his reign.

The earliest raids had been carried out by Norwegians, a fragmented, impoverished people who found little sustenance amid the

---

Seaham (County Durham). The Saxon church at Seaham stands on the northern edge of the town, only 200 yards or so from the cliff edge. The nave is seventh century and is narrow, as is the chancel; the two are of equal breadth and are separated from each other by the segment of a lofty round arch, which seems to indicate that the building was once much larger in extent towards the north. The tower at the west end of the nave is square and low. The east window in the nave consists of two round-headed lights under an ornament of Saxon zigzag or nail-head. The font is a plain stone basin, its rim ornamented with tracery. (OS Sheet 88, 406573.)

Opposite page and above These photographs show the remains of the Saxon cathedral at North Elmham, Norfolk, which lies in a lovely setting behind the church. The cathedral was destroyed by the Danes, but was rebuilt in the tenth century.

black-walled fjords of their homeland and who consequently looked to the sea to provide their living. As their shipbuilding techniques improved, so did their capability to cross the sea and seek plunder in the British Isles. However, after a series of early raids on the English coast, the Norwegians for the most part concentrated on the western seaboard, eventually founding colonies in Shetland, Orkney, Caithness, Sutherland and Ireland, where they established the Norse kingdom of Dublin.

The seafarers who harried England's eastern and southern coasts in the ninth century were not Norwegian, but Danish; equally as formidable, and geographically much closer to the rich pickings of the Anglo-Saxon kingdoms. Taking the route the Saxons had taken 400 years earlier, from the mouth of Rhine, they struck without warning at points on the coasts of both England and Gaul, debouching from their long ships and

plundering inland on stolen horses until they came into contact with the local defence forces, at which point they either made a speedy escape or stood and fought, depending on the strength of the opposition. No one knows for certain why the Danes suddenly started raiding after generations of fighting amongst themselves; it may be that the movement of populations stirred up by the creation of Charlemagne's Frankish Empire had something to do with it. At any rate, from the 830s onwards they were a constant menace to the security of Britain.

Our main source of information on the early Scandinavian pirate raids is the *Anglo-Saxon Chronicle*, which was compiled in the form that we know in the 890s, within living memory of the turbulent events of the earlier part of the century. It tells us that, in 835, there was a heavy Danish raid on the Isle of Sheppey, and that in the following year King Egbert personally led an army against the crews of 35 Danish ships at Carhampton, between Watchet and Minehead on the north coast of Devon. Egbert died in 839, by which time Danish raids on the English coast had become an annual occurrence—although the Danes had not yet come to settle. He was

Ledsham (West Yorkshire). The nave of the church of All Saints at Ledsham, off the A63 about seven miles west of Leeds, dates from the seventh and eighth centuries, as do some parts of the tower. Four miles further west, the church of St Wilfrid at Monk Fryston on the A63, has a tower that was built in the years immediately before the Conquest. *(OS Sheet 105, 456298.)*

Kirk Hammerton (North Yorkshire). In the village of Kirk Hammerton, which lies just south of the A59 Harrogate–York road, the nave and chancel of the church of St John the Baptist are of seventh or eighth century date, and there is also a tenth century tower. Much damage was done to the original fabric of the building during nineteenth century reconstruction, but original Saxon work survives in some of the doors and windows. *(OS Sheet 105, 465555.)*

succeeded by his son Aethelwulf, who carried on his father's tradition of tough kingship; he had first of all to contend with a brief surge of Mercian aggression under King Wiglaf, who had been ousted by Egbert but who had now returned and annexed Berkshire to his kingdom. Berkshire was recovered and returned to the Wessex sphere of influence by Aethelwulf, although it is not known whether this was achieved by force or by treaty. Aethelwulf was on good terms with Mercia a few years later, however, because in 835 his army and Mercia's carried out a joint expedition against the Welsh.

Aethelwulf does not seem to have been as plagued by the Danes as was his father. He is reported as having defeated a large Danish force in 851, inflicting on it 'the greatest slaughter of a heathen army that was ever heard of to this present day', according to the *Anglo-Saxon Chronicle*. This reverse may have made the Danes proceed with caution in attacking lands belonging to Wessex—or it may be that Aethelwulf made some arrangement with them under which they were permitted to spend the winter on the Wessex coast in exchange for their help in defending the territory against other pirates. What is known is that, from 850 onwards, Danish war hosts made a practice of wintering

in the south-east of England, mainly in the Isle of Thanet and in Sheppey. There was, however, still no attempt at permanent colonisation; the Danes seemed content to plunder and to probe the English defences. With the next generation, it would be different.

One interesting point comes to light about these early engagements between Danes and English. Following the battle in Devon, the *Anglo-Saxon Chronicle* records that: 'The same year (851) King Athelstan and Ealdorman Elchere fought in their ships and slew a large army at Sandwich in Kent, taking nine ships and dispersing the rest'.

Athelstan was king of Kent under both Egbert and Aethelwulf, and this is the first recorded instance of the English engaging the enemy at sea. Although the credit for founding an English navy has always gone to Alfred, later in the ninth century, perhaps it was Egbert or his son who first assembled a defensive war-fleet to meet the raiders and destroy them before they could establish themselves ashore. It would be fascinating to know how the English ships compared with their adversaries.

London. Although England's capital was occupied continuously from pre-Roman times, very little evidence of Dark Age occupation is visible today. Only one church is worth a visit by anyone in search of Dark Age remains, and that is All Hallows by the Tower in Great Tower Street, EC3, which was found to be of Saxon origin when German bomb damage exposed a Saxon arch in the south wall. The original church was of eighth century date. There is, however, plenty to interest the Dark Age student in London's Museums, the foremost of which is, of course, the British Museum. In addition to the finds from the Taplow barrow, this houses the famous Sutton Hoo collection, a collection of Kentish goldwork inlaid with garnets, late Saxon metalwork and sculptures. Celtic metalwork and carvings are also well represented. Dark Age finds made in and around London are housed in the London Museum, London Wall, EC2, which has a good collection of Saxon and Viking artefacts, while there are some beautiful examples of Anglo-Saxon art in the Victoria and Albert Museum, South Kensington.

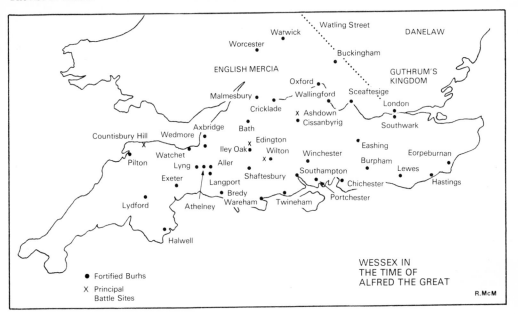

WESSEX IN
THE TIME OF
ALFRED THE GREAT

R.McM

● Fortified Burhs

X Principal
Battle Sites

Sensing the danger that the Danes were close to turning the Isle of Thanet into a secure base for future operations, an English force led Ealdorman Elchere of Kent and Ealdorman Huda of Surrey attacked them there in 853. The battle resulted in an English victory, but there was an appalling loss of life on both sides and the two English commanders were killed. Driven out of Thanet, the Danes began to winter more and more in Sheppey. There were there in 854, when King Aethelwulf made a year-long pilgrimage to Rome. That he chose to do so appears odd, considering the ever-present and growing threat to his kingdom. It is hard to believe that he was irresponsible; history leads us to believe quite the contrary, What is far more likely is that he was supremely confident in the ability of his military commanders to deal with the threat in his absence. At this stage, the regional militia, under the command of an ealdorman, were adequate to deal with pirate incursions.

Aethelwulf seems to have been no mean judge of military affairs, in fact that is oddly at variance with our other information on his character. He is described as sluggish, heavy and indolent, of a mild disposition and very devout; his vigorous father, Egbert, seems to have been mildly disappointed in him. Yet Aethelwulf led his armies into battle on several occasions, and never once was an accusation of cowardice or poor leadership levelled against him.

That he was devout—perhaps overmuch so—was never in dispute, however, and according to some accounts he had wanted to become a priest when he was young. Certainly, before his departure for Rome he granted every tenth hide of land in his kingdom to the church with a charter decreeing that it '. . . be free from all things, for the release of our souls, that it may be applied to God's service alone, exempt from expeditions, the building of bridges or for forts; in order that they may more diligently pour forth their prayers to God for us without ceasing'.

The 'hide' was a unit of land of uncertain acreage on which the Anglo-Saxons had long based their status as men of property. It must have been quite a substantial holding, for in the laws established by Ine of Wessex in the late seventh century a man holding ten hides was expected to provide for his king an annual food-rent amounting to 10 vats of honey, 300 loaves, 12 measures of Welsh ale, 30 measures of clear ale, 2 full-grown cows or 10 calves, 10 geese, 20 hens, 10 cheeses, a full measure of butter, 5 salmon, 20 pounds of fodder and 100 eels.

Aethelwulf made more donations to the church on his arrival in Rome. According to Bishop Asser, his gifts included: 'A gold

Margram (Glamorgan). The Margram Abbey Museum, which is in an old school house next to the abbey, has a good collection of Dark Age crosses and sculpted stones. The earliest date from the fifth to the seventh centuries, but some of the finest are from the ninth to eleventh centuries. The earliest of the crosses bears the inscription, in translation: 'The stone of Boduocus, here he lies, the son of Catotigirnus, great-grandson of Eternalis Vedomavus'. Margam is reached by following the A48 westwards from Cowbridge through Pyle, north of Porthcawl. The abbey is about a mile to the south-east of Margram village. *(OS Sheet 170, 802863.)*

Sockburn (County Durham). Sockburn Hall is famous in County Durham as the ancestral home of the Conyers family, one of whom, Sir John Conyers, passed into legend for his exploit in slaying the 'Sockburn Worm' which allegedly terrorised the surrounding countryside in the Middle Ages. Of more immediate interest, however, is the Sockburn Chapel, which holds a collection of 25 stones from the Dark Age period, including a Mercian cross shaft elaborately decorated with both Scandinavian and Saxon patterns. To reach Sockburn, take the A167 south from Darlington, and on reaching Croft turn left through Hurworth to the village of Neasham. There, a minor road leads off to the right to Sockburn, which lies in a loop of the river Tees.

Bywell (Northumberland). There are two Saxon churches in this little village, which nestles in a bend of the River Tyne about seven miles east of Hexham. The first is the church of St Andrew, which stands near the entrance to Bywell Hall; it is originally eleventh century, although much of the early work is now obscured by post-Conquest renovations. However, the belfry windows and three circular windows above them in each face are Saxon. The second building, the church of St Peter, is partly of eighth century date, but such early work is confined to the chancel and the north wall of the nave. The west parts of the chancel are late Saxon, and in the north wall there is a blocked doorway with Escomb-style jambs. *(OS Sheet 87, 049614/5.)*

crown of four pounds in weight, two dishes of the purest gold, a sword richly set in gold, two gold images, silver-gilt Saxon urns, stoles bordered with gold and purple stripes, white silken garments for celebrating the mass, decorated with figures, and other costly articles of clothing . . . He also bestowed rich alms in gold and silver on the bishops, the clergy and on the dwellers of Rome of every rank . . . The Saxon schools, which had already been twice destroyed by fire since their establishment, he rebuilt at his own cost and further enriched them by the most liberal endowments.'

On his journey to Rome Aethelwulf was accompanied by his youngest son, Alfred, who had already been there two years earlier—in order, some accounts state, to be anointed future king by the Pope after the fashion that had now become time-honoured. The overland journey ran through the territory of Charles the Bald, king of the Franks, with whom Aethelwulf was on very friendly terms; Charles showed all honour and courtesy to the English party, supplying an escort of Frankish men-at-arms. Friendly relations were consolidated even further when, after spending several months at Charles' court on the return journey, Aethelwulf married the Frankish king's daughter, Judith. He was in his fifties; she was only 13.

Little is known about Aethelwulf's first wife, Osburga, whom he married in 830 after being made underking of Kent. She is said to have been the daughter of Oslac, Aethelwulf's steward or armour-bearer, who was supposedly able to trace his lineage back to Earl Hengest or one of his relatives. Osburga bore Aethelwulf several children: Alfred, Aethelbald, Aethelbert, Aethelred and at least one daughter, Aethelswitha. The marriage ceremony between Aethelwulf and Judith was celebrated at Charles' palace of Verberie, on the River Oise, and was performed by Hincmar, Archbishop of Reims. Unknowingly, by placing a crown on the young queen's head, he broke a taboo that had been in force among the West Saxons since 802, when King Boerhtic was said to have been poisoned by his queen, Eadburh, daughter of the great Offa. She escaped to the continent, where Charlemagne made her abbess of a large convent, but repeated sexual misconduct brought her career to an abrupt end and she finished her days a pauper. The West Saxons' hatred for her had been so great that the council of Wessex had sworn that never again would a crown be placed on the head of a woman who married one of their kings—yet now it had happened, and the repercussions were to be widespread.

In Aethelwulf's absence, Wessex had been governed by a council of ministers led by Bishop Swithun of Winchester (later St Swithun) and Bishop Ealstan of Sherborne, together with the king's eldest surviving son, Aethelbald. The latter was tough and energetic, very much a warrior and a 'man's man', unlike his mild-mannered father, and many of the West Saxons apparently regretted that Aethelwulf was now back to take over the reins of power once more. Some of those in authority held that the fact that he had returned with a crowned queen held some sort of sinister purpose, and the divisions were so strong that for a while there was a great possibility of civil war. The danger was averted by Aethelwulf himself, who abdicated and retired to Kent, leaving Aethelbald to rule Wessex. He was well received in Kent, where the people had no objections to the young queen sitting by his side, and there he died in 858. Even after his death, his care for the common folk shone through; he left a will ordering his successors to provide, from every tenth hide of the kingdom for as long as the land should be cultivated, food, drink and lodging for one poor man. It was a far greater epitaph than had been written of many a more powerful and respected king who had gone before.

His son, Aethelbald, survived him by only 2½ years, dying in 860. He was widely mourned and seems to have been a popular king; no major threat to the realm developed during his brief reign. Yet historical records have sometimes been less than complementary about him; Bishop Asser called him 'headstrong and arbitrary', while William of Malmesbury, writing much later, labelled him 'base and perfidious'. It should be noted that these comments were made by monks, in whose eyes Aethelbald had committed a terrible crime: he married Judith, his father's widow, who was still only about 16.

Aethelbert ruled for only five years before

Alton Barnes (Wiltshire). Lying close to the Wansdyke, the Church of St Mary the Virgin in Alton Barnes has a nave that is of Anglo-Saxon date. Lying amid beautiful countryside in the Vale of Pewsey, Alton Barnes may be reached by taking the minor road that branches off the A361 eastwards a mile or so north of Devizes. *(OS Sheet 173, 116620.)*

Ramsbury (Wiltshire). In the church of the Holy Cross at Ramsbury there are the fragments of possibly two crosses dating from the ninth century, both showing Danish influence. Decoration includes vinescroll and a dragon biting its tail. To find Ramsbury, take the A419 Swindon–Hungerford road, turning south-west on to a minor road at Knighton, four miles north-west of Hungerford. *(OS Sheet 174, 274715.)*

Winchester (Hampshire). Although it was once the capital of England and the royal seat of the kings of Wessex, nothing today remains visible of the city's important Anglo-Saxon past. However, the museum in the Square houses an excellent collection of objects unearthed during excavations in the 1960s and 1970s in Winchester and the surrounding area. It includes a carved ivory plaque of about 1000, sculpted architectural fragments from the old minster, and pottery, brooches and a sword from pagan cemeteries at Winnall and Worthy Park. The Saxon name for Winchester was Uintancaestir (Venta Castra, the Fortress of Venta).

his death in 866 at the age of about 35. Sporadic Danish attacks began again during his reign and intensified in the time of his brother and successor, Aethelred I. While Aethelbert still ruled, part of a Danish force which had been plundering on the Continent crossed the Channel and made a surprise attack on Winchester, the principal city of Wessex; the defenders could do nothing to forestall the onslaught, but the men of Hampshire and Berkshire quickly assembled an army under Ealdorman Osric and Ealdorman Aethelwulf and cut the Danes' line of retreat, trapping them before they could regain their ships and inflicting a bloody defeat on them, retaking much of the spoils the enemy had removed from Winchester and the surrounding area. The survivors, however, managed to regroup and worked their way around the coast to Thanet, where they later received reinforcements from across the Channel, and late in 865 they concluded a treaty with the ealdormen of Kent. Its terms were simple; the Danes would leave Kent alone if the men of Kent would pay for peace. But, as Asser later commented: 'These robbers knew nothing of truth and good faith; they were well aware that they could obtain a much larger sum by pillage than by treaties of peace. Scarcely was the league concluded than they again broke it, and like cunning foxes secretly and by night left their camp and ravaged all the eastern side of Kent.'

What Asser probably failed to appreciate, however, was that two separate groups of Danes were probably involved. Danish raiding forces operated in independent groups, and although there was contact between the various commanders there was no system of overall command or control. The commander of the force that carried out the 'treacherous' attack on Kent may have been aware of a peace treaty reached by his predecessor, but he would regard it as having nothing to do with him.

The Danish incursions into the south were part of a much wider campaign, which we shall examine in detail in the next section. Our concern now is with Wessex, and the stand made by its successive rulers against the invader. During this turbulent phase, however, the fortunes of Wessex and Mercia was intermingled through ties of marriage. Mercia's king, Burghred, had married King Aethelwulf's daughter Aethelswitha, and in 868 Alfred of Wessex married Aelswitha, the daughter of a Mercian chieftain. In that same year a Danish host invaded Mercia from the north, and it was natural that Burghred should ask his royal kin-by-marriage in Wessex for help. Aethelred I was now king of Wessex, and he marched to attack the Danes at Nottingham, only to find that Burghred had been forced into making peace with the enemy

Two views of the seventh century church of St Andrew, Corbridge. The original building was destroyed by the Danes, but the lower part of the western tower and the walls of the nave arcade survive.

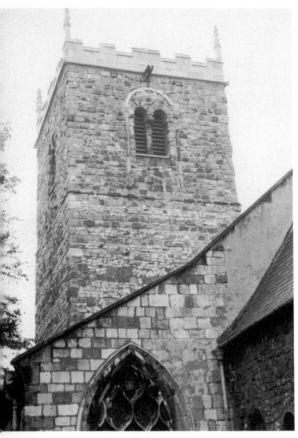

Geddington (Northamptonshire). Lying on the A43 between Corby and Kettering, the interior of the church of St Mary Magdalene shows some very interesting Saxon work, probably dating from the ninth century, including the remains of a round window in the north wall. A pleasing feature of the church's fabric is the way in which the Saxon and Norman architecture blend almost effortlessly with one another. *(OS Sheet 141, 896830.)*

in the meantime. There appears to have been some skirmishing, but no fighting of a serious nature, and the army of Wessex went home. After a while the Danes also returned to their main base at York. For a year both sides concentrated on gathering their strength. Then the Danes renewed their offensive, and by the end of the 869 they had overrun Mercia and East Anglia. The stage was now set for a great drive with the aim of crushing Wessex, now recognised by the Danish leaders as their principal opponent.

They made Reading their base of operations; two forces made rendezvous there, one marching overland and the other sailing up the Thames, plundering on all sides as it came. The site they occupied was a former West Saxon fortress situated on a peninsula at the confluence of the Thames and the Kennet; part of the force stayed there and set about building an earthwork across the peninsula, while the rest spread out to forage and reconnoitre. The reconnaissance force was met by the West Saxons under a local ealdorman Aethelwulf (probably the same leader who had helped to smash the Danes after the earlier sack of Winchester) at a place called

Above left and left *The tower of the Church of St Mary, Bishophill, York, incorporates typical Saxon windows and herringbone work. Remains of a carved Saxon cross are preserved inside the church, and there is a fine round arch between nave and tower which is constructed in the full thickness of the tower wall. The church is tenth century.*
Opposite page *King's Square, York, was once the site of the royal palace of the Viking king Eric Bloodaxe.*

Englafield, which is most likely Englefield, five miles west of Reading. There was a fierce fight in which many of the Danes were slaughtered, together with one of their earls, and the rest streamed back to Reading in disorder. This fight was in the nature of a holding action, designed to buy time until the main Wessex army under King Aethelred, with Alfred as his second-in-command, arrived on the scene, which it did four days later.

The Wessex men's intention was to besiege the Danes in Reading and starve them into submission, but the Danes, realising their purpose, waited until Aethelred's forces were busy setting up their camp and then stormed out in a lightning attack. There was a fierce battle, with the advantage swaying one way and then the other, until at last the Danes triumphed and put the English to flight. Aethelred and Alfred escaped across the Thames by a secret crossing near Windsor. The Danes can not have been strong enough to pursue the English army to destruction, because after another four days Aethelred and Alfred succeeded in rallying their scattered forces and once again prepared to do battle.

On January 8 871, the Danish army left Reading and marched along the Great Ridgeway that runs into Wessex across the Berkshire Downs. At a spot south of Uffington, however, where the ancient road passes by an Iron Age hill fort at Whitehorse Hill—so called because of the great White Horse carved into the chalk centuries earlier—the Danes found their path blocked by the army of Wessex. The *Chronicle* calls the place Aescendun, Ashdown—but that name was applied not to a single spot, but to the vale of the White Horse. The actual battle site may have been a little to the west of the Uffington White Horse, at an old Saxon meeting place called 'Nachededorne' or the naked thorn; Bishop Asser, who was later shown over the battleground by Alfred, says that the fiercest fighting took place around a lone thorn tree.

The Danes held the high ground and, taking cover in thick scrub, showered arrows on the Saxon army below. The Danish force was split in two, one echelon being commanded by two kings, Bagseg and Halfdan, and the other by a group of earls. Aethelred, being of senior rank, faced the Danish kings, while Alfred confronted the contingent led by the earls. The story goes that Aethelred, being very devout, lingered so long in his tent praying for victory

Buried forever beneath modern construction, this is the Coppergate archaeological site where York's Viking tanneries flourished. The photograph was taken in October 1982, not long after archaeological work had ended. Note the depth of the site below the present street level.

Liverpool. Lancashire is not notable for its Dark Age remains, but the City Museum, in Liverpool's William Brown Street, has an excellent collection of early Saxon work, including a beautiful ornament of gold and garnet known as the Kingston Brooch, a gold medallion which once belonged to Bishop Liuhard, a follower of St Augustine, and a lot of grave goods from pagan Saxon cemeteries in Kent.

Heysham (Lancashire). The church of St Peter in Heysham has a ninth century west doorway and south-west window, as well as a cross shaft fragment and a hogback tombstone with bears at either end in the churchyard. On a promontory overlooking Morecambe Bay there are also the ruins of a ninth century chapel, known as St Patrick's Chapel, with some graves cut into the rock to the west of the building; these may predate the chapel itself by a considerable margin. *(OS Sheet 97, 408617—'Chapel'.)*

Croft (North Yorkshire). There is a very fine cross shaft in the church of St Peter in this village, which lies on the river Tees three miles south of Darlington on the A167 road to Northallerton. The shaft is of ninth century date and is beautifully decorated with vinescroll.

Melsonby (North Yorkshire). The church of St James in Melsonby, north of the A66 two miles from Scotch Corner, contains two ninth century grave slab fragments, one depicting a curious camel-like animal with a human head. There is also a cross fragment, with interlace work, on the west of the south aisle. Approaching Melsonby along the A66, a few hundred yards before turning on to the minor road, there is a fragment of the Scots Dike on the left; this was a Dark Age earthwork which formed one of the boundaries between British and Anglo-Saxon territory, and may date from the time of Urien of Rheged.

that Alfred grew impatient and led his men in a wild charge up the hill, engaging the enemy in fierce hand-to-hand combat. The fight lasted all through the day, with Aethelred's forces joining in at some point, and it may be that the sudden appearance of these fresh troops tipped the scales in the Saxon's favour. At any rate, the Danes began to break off the action at nightfall. Leaving King Bagseg and five earls dead behind them and the whole face of the Down strewn with corpses. The victorious Saxons harried the fleeing enemy throughout the night, giving no quarter, until the survivors found refuge in the safety of their Reading stronghold. Despite this reverse, the Danes were ready to fight again only a fortnight later. They encountered a Wessex force at Basing, and the outcome seems to have been inconclusive; the *Chronicle* merely reports that the Danes 'carried off no spoils'.

The months that followed were marked by constant skirmishing between the two sides, as the Danes strove to penetrate deeper into Wessex. The forces involved may not have been large, and for the most part fighting probably occurred when local Wessex militia came into contact with foraging parties. Unfortunately, apart from some patchy references in the *Chronicle*, there is no real record of the war; in many ways, the campaigns of Aethelred and Alfred are as enigmatic as those of Ambrosius Aurelianus and Arthur, four centuries earlier, waged against the Saxon kings' ancestors.

About two months after the fight at Basing, however, the *Chronicle* records a bitter struggle at a place called Meredune. Once again, the Danes fought in two echelons against Aethelred and Alfred, who '. . . put them to flight, enjoying the victory for some time during the day; and there was much slaughter on either hand; but the Danes became masters of the field'. The site of this battle may have been Marden, near Devizes, or Martin, in Hampshire. In either event, the Danes had pushed a long way into Wessex territory. Some historians believe that the Hampshire location is the more likely of the two, for King Aethelred is believed to have died soon afterwards at or near Wimborne, about five miles away, and according to one account he died in agony from wounds he had suffered. The crown of Wessex now passed to Alfred. The year was 871, and the desperate struggle for English survival was only just beginning.

The church of St John Baptist at Kirk Hammerton, on the Harrogate-York road, is probably the most complete Anglo-Saxon church in Yorkshire. The nave and chancel are seventh or eighth century, and the tower is tenth century.

Part Three:
'From the fury of the Northmen, O Lord, deliver us'

Chapter 9

The coming of the Northmen

For the English, the latter half of the eighth century was a time of peace. There were no wars between the Saxon kingdoms, and fighting seems to have been confined to skirmishes between Mercia and the Welsh. In Europe, too, under the rule of Charlemagne, there was a glimmering of hope that some kind of *Pax Romana* might be re-established, and the former frontiers of the empire made inviolate once more. It was a false dawn. In 787 AD, gathering storm-clouds were already on the horizon, as the *Anglo-Saxon Chronicle* recorded: 'In this year King Beorhtric took Edburga the daughter of Offa to wife. And in his days came first three ships of the Northmen from the land of robbers. The reeve then rose thereto, and would drive them to the king's town; for he knew not what they were; and there he was slain. These were the first ships of the Danish men that sought the land of the English nation.'

The phrase 'he knew not what they were' is significant, for it reveals that the Vikings and their ways were utterly strange to the English. When the tempest eventually crashed about them, therefore, the shock and the horror were all the greater. The prayer of the monks of western Europe—'from the fury of the Northmen, O Lord, deliver us'—was uttered in mortal fear. It must indeed have seemed that the warlike, merciless men from the cold north were no mere mortals, but instruments of darkness. But who in fact were the Vikings, as the Scandinavian raiders are generally described—and why did they suddenly burst out of their homelands in a series of invasions

that brought fire and bloodshed to Europe as far south as the Mediterranean between the ninth and eleventh centuries? These are questions which are only now beginning to be satisfactorily answered, and the picture which is slowly emerging is completely at variance with the traditional one of axe-wielding, bloodthirsty warriors bent only on rape and plunder.

The first of the Scandinavian peoples to make their presence felt in the outside world were the Swedes. In the early eighth century, nearly a hundred years before Britain was seriously affected by Viking attacks, they crossed the Baltic and moved south and east, following the great rivers of what is now western Russia and establishing trading posts at such places as Novgorod and Kiev. From Kiev, the broad Dnieper took their vessels on to the Black Sea, which lay between two of the

Gosforth (Cumbria). The finest cross of Scandinavian design in the north-west, this example stands in the churchyard of St Mary, seven miles south-east of Egremont on the A595. The cross is tall and slender, 15 ft high with a round shaft which gradually becomes square higher up. Christ crucified is depicted on its east face, above two soldiers, one of whom holds a javelin; there is a man on horseback on the north face, a mounted figure and two fighting men on the west, and several odd beasts on the south face. The nearby church contains hogback tombstones and a cross fragment showing a snapping dragon. *(OS Sheet 89, 073036.)*

richest states of the known world: Byzantium and Baghdad. To Byzantium they took gold and precious stones, looted from European monasteries and royal halls, and possibly furs as well; to the Arab caliph's kingdom, in all probability, they took mainly slaves and girls, captured on their hit-and-run raids. The fair-haired girls of the north-west must have brought a high price in the harems of the east. It is quite possible that the Swedes created a supply-and-demand situation in Scandinavia, and that booty brought home by their neighbours, the Norwegians and the Danes, found its way to the east through Swedish trading outlets. Many treasures from the Dark Age period have been found in the royal burial mounds of the kings of the Ynglinga, the Swedish dynasty, at Uppsala; but by the middle of the eighth century the vigorous period of Swedish expansion was over, and the initiative gradually passed to Norway and Denmark.

Melbury Osmond (Dorset). In the north chancel of the church of St Osmund here there is part of a cross shaft bearing a carving of a somewhat curious animal surrounded by interlacing. One interpretation is that it represents the Biblical ram, caught in a thicket. Melbury Osmond is seven miles south of Yeovil. In the neighbouring village of Melbury Bubb, the font in the church of St Mary was once part of a round cross shaft of late Anglo-Saxon date. It is decorated with interlace and with animals, including an expertly-carved stag. (OS Sheet 194, 574079.)

Codford St Peter (Wiltshire). In this village, on the A36 Salisbury road five miles south-east of Warminster, there is a cross shaft bearing a curious carving which depicts a man, gazing upwards, holding what seems to be a mallet in his left hand and a tree branch in his right. The cross is probably of ninth century date.

Brompton (North Yorkshire). The churchyard at Brompton, just north of Northallerton beside the A684, is notable for its Scandinavian 'hogback' gravestones dating from the tenth century. There are also three crosses of similar date. (OS Sheet 99, 374964.)

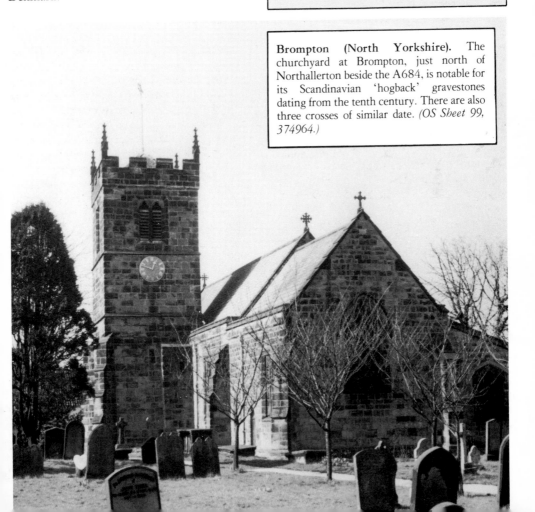

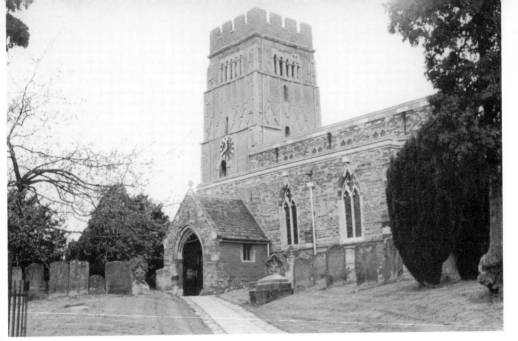

The church of All Saints at Earl's Barton, Northamptonshire, features a door leading to the first floor. This could be entered by means of a ladder, and the building used as a refuge at the time of the Danish invasions.

It has been suggested that climate was a contributory factor in encouraging the Norwegians to seek more temperate settlement areas to the south, but modern meteorological research has proved fairly conclusively that during most of the 'Viking Age' the whole of north-west Europe was warm and dry. There is, however, some evidence of very cold conditions in Scandinavia for about 80 years after 860, the time of the heaviest Viking onslaughts on the British Isles.

A much more valid argument might be that the Viking migrations resulted from pressure of population. At some point in the eighth century, there was a small but steady flow of colonists from western Norway to the islands to the north and north-west of Scotland. The movement may have coincided with the advent of the Viking 'long ship', the graceful culmination of a long period of trial and error by Scandinavian shipbuilders who sought to tame the stormy northern seas. The development of new shipbuilding techniques may have gone hand-in-hand with improved navigational methods; the use of a rudimentary compass, described as a 'sun-stone' in later

sagas, during this period must not be ruled out. To answer the question as to why the emigrations occurred at all, however—and westward over the uncharted sea, into the bargain, with all the superstitious dread of what might lie beyond the horizon—requires a 'Sherlock Holmes' technique of eliminating all the impossibilities in order to be left with what must be the right answer.

The climate, for reasons discussed above, could not have been the root cause; and if the climate was favourable, there would be no reason for crops to fail. Neither—as was the case with the earlier Anglo-Saxon migrations—were the Norwegians being pushed out of their own lands by external forces. The problem must therefore have been an internal one, and only over-population provides a satisfactory answer. The Norwegians were polygamous, each man having as many wives as he could afford and as many slave-concubines as he could acquire. A man took huge pride in fathering as many sons as possible—girl-children were not highly prized—and this must have created enormous problems when the time came for the sons to claim their inheritance. It passed to the strongest; and for the weaker brothers, voluntary exile must have seemed the only sensible course of action. Either that, or they might attempt to re-emphasise their status and bravery by returning home from a pirate

The church of All Saints at Brixworth, near North-ampton, is an impressive building originally dating from the seventh century. A monastery was originally founded here, in 675, but this was later destroyed by the Danes.

expedition laden with booty and slaves.

The emphasis on siring male children, and on turning all of them into warriors, gave the Scandinavians an enormous manpower advantage on their Viking expeditions. They could afford to take losses which would have crippled many of their adversaries, for they had the benefit of a steady flow of replacements as their young men reached maturity. Never, in any account of the campaigns they fought, do the Vikings appear to have been starved of reinforcements. Yet they were prudent

fighters. In the early days at least, they would avoid combat whenever possible. They exploited the element of surprise to the full, storming ashore to sieze their plunder in lightning raids and then making their escape before the defence forces had time to muster. If they thought they might have to fight, they made certain that their line of retreat was secure; once they were safely on their ships, none could follow them. Only very rarely are there recorded instances of a Viking force being cut off before it could return to its vessels.

Their weaponry was much the same as that used by their foes—swords, spears and arrows—but they also used a battleaxe which was far from being the unwieldy weapon it has often been made out to be. A skilled man using an axe could almost certainly have got the better of a swordsman, unless the latter managed to get under the axeman's guard. Armour consisted of chainmail coats, and helmets which were usually of leather; the shields they carried were round, and it is thought that the Norwegians carried white shields and the Danes black ones. A further advantage enjoyed by the Vikings was that they were excellent horsemen and therefore highly mobile on land as well as at sea, which must have posed additional problems for the defenders who had to meet their attacks.

The problem of overpopulation, especially with regard to young males seeking to make their fortunes, was one that seems to have been common to the Norwegians and Danes alike, although in the case of the Danes there were other contributory factors. At the end of the eighth century Denmark was a single united kingdom, and its king, Godfred, also had some claim to lands in north Germany. Since the forces of the Frankish ruler Charlemagne were operating in this area in an effort to secure the frontiers of what was later to become the Holy Roman Empire, it was inevitable that Godfred should view them as a threat to the security of his own realm. He therefore had a huge earthwork—rather like Offa's Dyke, and known as the Danevirke—built across the neck of the Danish peninsula, and put his men on a war footing. Indeed, it is quite probable that hostilities would have broken out between Charlemagne and Godfred if the latter had not been murdered in 810.

A lengthy civil war between the Danish earls who fought each other for possession of the throne effectively removed any threat the Danes might have presented to Charlemagne, who left them alone for the time being and remained an interested onlooker, for this was the first time that the Roman world in the west and the Scandinavians had come into close contact. Then, in 825, an earl named Horik triumphed over his rivals and established a united Denmark once more; his 30-year reign was characterised by a growth of trade and a general increase in contact between Denmark and the rest of Europe. Danish diplomats were accredited to the court of Louis the Pious, who succeeded his father Charlemagne in 814, and the way was opened for Christian missionaries

to preach the gospel in the north.

Closer relations between Denmark and the empire, however, had an unexpected result. For the first time, the rich pickings of Europe became apparent to the considerable number of landless Danes who had reached maturity in the civil wars and who were now eager to grasp what they could. Despite all Horik's efforts to hold them in check, their piratical exploits were a constant embarrassment to him; the market for loot and slaves was too lucrative for any central figure to put a stop to the sporadic raiding, just as authorities are unable to stamp out one of the great evils of our own time, drug trafficking. When Horik and most of his family were assassinated in 854, the Danish kingdom once again dissolved in civil war, and now there was no steadying influence to keep the freebooters under control. Within a decade, Danish piracy had become the major threat to European stability.

The British Isles had already felt the first lashings of the storm. In 787, as we have seen, there was a hit-and-run raid on the Kentish coast; in 793 and 794 Viking raiders from

Lindisfarne (Northumberland). Probably better known by its more modern name of Holy Island, Lindisfarne, off the Northumbrian coast, was the place beloved of St Cuthbert, who spent his last years living as a hermit on the Farne Islands. Before that, however, it is on record as the island of 'Metcaud', where Urien of Rheged besieged the Bernicians 'for three days and three nights'. Although none of the visible remains of buildings on Lindisfarne date from the Dark Age period, the site is well worth visiting for the scenery; and in the small museum there are some early pillow-stones— small, flat stones inscribed with a cross and a name—taken from the Anglo-Saxon burial ground. Lindisfarne was one of the first places in Britain to suffer the ravages of the Vikings; standing on its rocky, windswept shore, it is easy to imagine the long ships sweeping down on the island, and the terror of the defenceless monks. To reach Lindisfarne, take the A1 Alnwick-Berwick road and turn right through Beal, making sure to check on the state of the tide before venturing across the causeway that links the island with the mainland over the tidal flats.

Norway sacked Lindisfarne and Jarrow; and, also in the 790s, there were Danish attacks on Wales, but the British seem to have been better equipped than the Anglo-Saxons to meet the threat and drove off the raiders with heavy losses.

Early raids on Wessex in the 830s were also beaten off, whereupon the Danes turned their attentions elsewhere for a time, making the coast of France their principal target. In this enterprise they were aided by the death of Louis the Pious and the division of Charlemagne's empire into three parts, ruled by Louis's three sons Charles, Ludwig and Lothar. Charles, who ruled what is now

France, was the king who had most to fear from the Viking threat, and the fact that his brother Ludwig bore enmity towards him did not help. In fact, on one occasion, when Charles and Lothar joined forces to drive a force of Danes from the mouth of the Seine, Ludwig—ruler of Germany—attacked France from the rear. Meanwhile, another force of Vikings arrived, and being enterprising businessmen offered to fight their own countrymen on the side of the Franks if the latter would pay them 5,000 pounds of silver.

Meanwhile, the Norwegians had established firm settlements in the Orkneys, Shetlands and the Outer Hebrides, driving out the thinly-scattered Pictish population, and had turned their attention to Ireland. For four centuries, since the collapse of Rome, Christian Ireland had remained one of western Europe's principal centres of culture and learning, and although its chieftains had frequently fought one another their wars had by-passed the religious centres. Secure from the threat of external attack, the Irish chiefs had not deemed it necessary to build strong fortifications around their towns, and there was no centralised defensive system under which neighbouring states could call upon each other for help.

When the Viking onslaught came, it was traumatic. The first attacks came in 795, when a raiding force sailed south after plundering Iona and sacked the monastery on Lambay Island, off the east coast near Dublin. For the next 30 years, no religious community near the Irish coast was safe; the monks were butchered and the Norsemen made off with priceless booty, accumulated over the centuries. In the words of one Irish chronicler: 'If a hundred heads of hardened iron could grow on one neck, and if each head possessed a hundred sharp tongues of tempered metal, and if each tongue cried out incessantly with a hundred ineradicable loud voices, they would never be able to enumerate the griefs which the people of Ireland—men and women, laymen and priests, young and old—have suffered at the hands of these warlike ruthless barbarians.'

By the 830s, Norse raiding on Ireland had given way to permanent settlement. The Viking leader who stands out in this respect is

---

Halton (Lancashire). In the village of Halton, north of the junction between the M6 and the A683 Lancashire-Kirkby Lonsdale road, there is an eleventh century cross combining Christian carvings of the crucifixion and resurrection with pagan Scandinavian effigies, one of which is said to depict Grim, the horse of the Viking leader Sigurd. *(OS Sheet 97, 499647.)*

Kirkleavington (Cleveland). In the church of St Martin here there is a Scandinavian cross depicting figures from Norse mythology, including a man with a skirt and helmet and two birds, and another man with two animal heads in profile. The village—also spelt without the 'a'—is on the A19 a mile and a half south of Yarm.

Middleton (Yorkshire). There is a small collection of finely-worked cross shafts in the church of St Andrew here, carved by English sculptors for Scandinavian masters. The best shows a Viking warrior with his weapons and shield, with a dragon on the reverse. The church lies on the A170, two miles north-west of Pickering.

Brigstock (Northamptonshire). The church of St Andrew in Brigstock, five miles south-east of Corby, is a fascinating mixture of Saxon and Norman architecture. The lower part of the west tower and the nave walls dates from the early ninth century, the upper part of the tower and the round stair turret being added later, before the conquest. The chancel, chapel and spire are all post-conquest. *(OS Sheet 141, 946853.)*

a shadowy and heroic figure named Thorgils (Turgeis, in Celtic) who captured Armagh and whose forces subsequently spread out to set up coastal strongholds at Anagassan on the coast of Louth, Waterford, Wexford, and—most important of all—Dublin. Further settlements sprang up at Limerick on the Shannon and at other points on the west coast. Thorgils was a pagan of the old school, and spared no effort to stamp out Christianity in the lands he had captured. In the end, he was taken prisoner by a group of Irish who, appalled by his excesses, drowned him in a loch in 845.

Six years later, in 851, the desperate Irish called in Danish mercenaries to help them fight off the Norwegians, and for a time the latter suffered a series of reverses; then reinforcements arrived and the Danes were routed, leaving the Norwegians free to consolidate their hold on the fortified coastal towns. From these strongholds, during the century that followed, they launched repeated attacks westwards across the Irish Sea; the Viking encirclement of Britain was complete. Ireland, too, provided a base for Viking onslaughts against the west coast of France. In 844, for example, a large Viking force which may have been of mixed Danish and Norwegian composition sailed down the coast of western France and northern Spain to Galicia, where they tried to attack Corunna but were beaten off. Afterwards they sailed through the straits of Gibraltar and sacked the Arab towns of Cadiz and Seville. There was a further Viking expedition to the Mediterranean in 859, consisting this time of 62 ships which assembled in the Loire estuary and then moved south, their crews plundering the Spanish coastline before moving into the Mediterranean and sacking Algeciras. They then crossed to North Africa, acquiring more plunder—including some negro slaves—before swinging north once more to the Camargue, where they appear to have spent several months. In 860 they sailed southwards along the west coast of Italy, sacking Pisa and Luna. According to some accounts, they then sailed as far east as Alexandria before returning home in 862 at the end of a three-year expedition in the course of which they lost 40 of their original fleet.

This odyssey clearly demonstrates the magnitude of some expeditions the Vikings were able to undertake; it cannot have been an easy matter for even a force of 62 vessels, reducing all the time through battle and attrition, to operate for three years in hostile waters. That they did so, and that the survivors returned home in triumph laden with booty, clearly demonstrates the Vikings' skill in warfare, and indicates the severity of the problem the Anglo-Saxon kings had to face when fleets of 30 or more Viking ships swooped on their coasts in the fateful years between the 830s and 860s.

It was in 865 that the storm burst over Britain in all its fury, with East Anglia and Northumbria the areas that suffered most. The story goes that the massive invasion that took place in 865 was the paying off of an old score. Twenty years earlier, the Viking chieftain Ragnar Lothbrok (Leather Breeches) had been captured and executed by Aelle, a chieftain of Northumbria. The manner of his death was unpleasant, for Aelle had thrown him into a pit full of adders. How Ragnar's sons reacted when they heard the news is told by Sir Winston Churchill in his *History of the English-speaking Peoples*, drawing on the poetic Norse saga:

'Bjorn ''Ironside'' gripped his spear shaft so hard that the print of his fingers remained stamped upon it. Hvitserk was playing chess, but he clenched his fingers upon a pawn so tightly that the blood started from under his nails. Sigurd ''Snake-eye'' was trimming his nails with a knife, and kept on paring until he cut into the bone. Ivar ''the Boneless'' demanded the precise details of his father's execution and his face ''became red, blue and pale by turns, and his skin was swollen with anger''.'

It was Ivar the Boneless who, in the years that followed, was the driving force behind the Viking attacks on northern England, constantly probing the Northumbrian defences and biding his time for an all-out assault. Then in 865, a great fleet of Viking ships descended on East Anglia, carrying an invading army which spent most of a year there—living at peace with the East Angles, according to the *Chronicle*—and marshalled its strength for a drive northwards. In particular, the Danes took pains to equip themselves with large

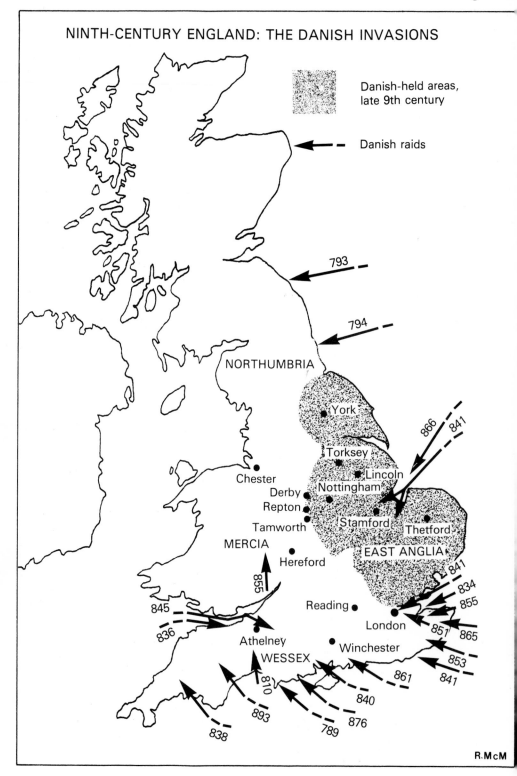

NINTH-CENTURY ENGLAND: THE DANISH INVASIONS

Danish-held areas,
late 9th century

Danish raids

793

794

NORTHUMBRIA

York

Torksey

Chester

Lincoln

Derby

Nottingham

Repton

Tamworth

Stamford

Thetford

MERCIA

Hereford

EAST ANGLIA

866   841

Reading

845

London

834

855

836

Athelney

Winchester

851   865

WESSEX

853

810

861   841

840

893

876

838

789

R.McM

numbers of horses, for Ivar, who was no mean military strategist, realised that it was a cavalry campaign that would bring him victory. The Danish plans were undoubtedly aided by Northumbrian disunity. Instead of strengthening their defences to meet the threat which they must surely have known was coming, the Northumbrian leaders chose this very time to become embroiled in a civil war, with Aelle—who had killed Ragnar Lothbrok—fighting to depose King Osbert, who had reigned for 18 years. The war was still in progress when, in 866, the great Danish mounted army began its push north; it appears to have operated at first along the Yorkshire coast, for it was at this time that Whitby was attacked and the great monastery sacked.

It may have been that the Danish plan was to secure coastal harbours in order to bring in reinforcements. In any event, the army suddenly turned south-west across the Yorkshire Wolds and occupied York on 1 November 866. Thoroughly alarmed by this turn of events, Osbert and Aelle temporarily patched up their quarrel and assembled an army to re-take the ancient city, but the onset of winter brought a halt to military operations and it was not until March 867 that the Northumbrian force was in a position to launch its counter-attack. The size of the Northumbrian army was considerable and it managed to break through the Viking defences of York at several points, but when Osbert was killed and Aelle captured the Northumbrians lost their cohesion and fell apart, leaving the Danes masters of the city.

It was now that the awful vengeance reserved for Aelle was put into effect. In a rite known as the 'Blood Eagle', the luckless Northumbrian was spreadeagled on the ground and, while he still lived, his ribs and lungs were hacked from his body and spread out on either side of him, like an eagle's wings.

Later, the Danes installed a puppet king named Egbert at York and, with their domination of Northumbria now assured, they made plans to expand their territorial gains in England. Moving south, they occupied Nottingham, which was within the boundaries of Mercia. As we saw in Chapter 9,

the Mercians made peace with the invaders, even though the army of Wessex marched north to Mercia's assistance. The year 869 was crucial in the history of the Midlands and East Anglia. As the Danish army moved south to Thetford, where it set up winter quarters, more Danish forces landed in East Anglia and plundered the monastery of Bardney. The invaders were opposed by local militia led by an ealdorman, Algar, who defeated them somewhere near Kesteven. Then more Danish reinforcements arrived and the Angles, severely outnumbered, found themselves fighting for their lives. There was a terrible struggle that lasted all day—the date was September 22—with the Anglians standing firm behind their shield-wall and beating off every Danish onslaught. Then, towards sunset, the Danes pretended to retreat; the Angles broke ranks to pursue them, thinking that they had the victory. Instead, the Danes suddenly reformed and turned on them, cutting them to pieces. Algar and a few survivors made a desperate last stand on a hill before being overwhelmed. Two hundred years later, a carbon copy battle was to be fought at Senlac, between the forces of Harold Godwinsson and William of Normandy. With no further opposition to contend with, the Danes swept on to destroy the abbey at Croyland and monasteries at Peterborough, Huntingdon and Ely. At Peterborough, in the words of the *Chronicle*, they went on an orgy of 'burning and breaking and slaying abbot and monks and all that they there found. They made such havoc there that a monastery, which was before full rich, was now reduced to nothing'.

The Danes at Thetford, meanwhile, had also emerged triumphant from a battle against a militia force led by Ealdorman Ulfketel, who

---

Portchester (Hampshire). The old Roman fortress of Portus Adurni, commanding Portsmouth harbour to the south of the A27, endured throughout the Saxon era as a fortress refuge; a community flourished within its walls from the time of the earliest Saxon settlement, and an Anglo-Saxon gateway can still be seen. *(OS Sheet 196, 625045.)*

was killed. The East Anglians rallied and joined battle again, led this time by their king, Edmund, but they were routed and Edmund was taken prisoner. Some accounts state that he was put to death by volleys of arrows, others that he was sacrificed to Odin by the 'Blood Eagle' rite. Whatever the truth, he was later revered as a saint and martyr, giving his name to the town of Bury St Edmunds. The date of Edmund's death was November 20 869. He was East Anglia's last native Christian king. The brief flowering of Roman-style culture in the east of the Island, nurtured by kings such as Redwald, who were then still pagan, had been torn out at the roots.

With Northumbria, East Anglia and Mercia now under the Danish heel, the time was ripe for the last great trial of strength with the only English kingdom that still posed a real threat to overall Viking supremacy. It was to become a bitter contest between two men, each of whom in his own fashion wore the mantle of greatness and between whom, even in desperate conflict, there grew a bond of respect that was almost kinship. One was Guthrum, the Dane; the other Alfred of Wessex.

Chapter 10

The high tide—and the turn

Alfred had been king of Wessex for only a month when his army once again engaged a Danish force that penetrated deep into Wessex. The battle took place at Wilton, in Wiltshire, and once again the Danes employed the tactics they had used in East Anglia; they pretended to retreat, then turned in good order and fell on the English troops who streamed after them. Wilton was an Anglo-Saxon defeat; in fact, Ashdown was the only English victory of 871. As the *Chronicle* records:

'This year were nine general battles fought with the Army in the kingdom south of the Thames; besides those skirmishes, in which Alfred the King's brother, and every single eolderman, and the thanes of the king, oft rode against them; which were accounted nothing. This year also were slain nine earls and one king.'

Alfred must have realised, by the year's end, that only one course of action was open to him if he was to save his tottering realm from complete extinction. He made peace with the enemy, paying over what must have been a vast sum of money. For the time being the Danes withdrew, leaving Alfred free to re-organise his defences. Why the Danes chose to accept a bribe and pull out, rather than go on to conquer the whole of Wessex—and the odds must have been heavily in their favour at this time—is something of a mystery. They may have chosen their course of action for tactical reasons, for elsewhere in the Island Danish forces were heavily committed, and—assuming that some sort of overall command structure existed, which by this time was quite probable—

the Danish force which had attacked Wessex may have been required to provide reinforcements in the north.

There was certainly unrest in Northumbria in 872, when a rebellion flared up against the puppet king, Egbert. Danish reinforcements were sent to put down the uprising but appear to have been unsuccessful, for Egbert was replaced by a Northumbrian king name Ricsige, who ruled for three years before dying of natural causes. The Danish army wintered at Torksey, in Lincolnshire, then when the campaigning season opened in the spring of 873 they moved into Mercia to complete their occupation of Penda's old kingdom. The Mercian king, Burghred, fled to the Continent and ended his days in Rome; in his place the Danes installed another puppet ruler, Ceolwulf.

In 875 the great Danish army divided. One part, led by a man named Halfdan, moved north into Northumbria. In the following year, the *Chronicle* records that Halfdan 'shared out the land of the Northumbrians, and they began to plough and support themselves'. The same thing happened in Mercia. In the north and the midlands, the terrible years of conquest were at an end; the Vikings, quite literally, were beating their swords into ploughshares.

In the south, meanwhile, the peace purchased by Alfred had lasted five years. The time had been put to good advantage. Not only had Alfred been able to strengthen and re-organise his forces; he now also had the beginnings of a fleet. In 875, the *Chronicle* says that 'in this summer King Alfred went

The church of St Michael at Edenham, Lincolnshire, contains two notable Dark Age sculptures—a two-foot diameter decorated roundel and part of a ninth-century cross shaft.

Singleton (Sussex). A reconstruction of a single-storey Anglo-Saxon hut, built of flint rubble with thatch and sunken floor, may be seen at the Weald and Downland open air museum. It is based on an original excavation carried out at Hangleton, near Brighton. There is also a plan of a timber hall excavated at Chalton in Hampshire.

out to sea with an armed fleet and fought with seven ship-rovers, one of whom he took, and dispersed the others'. At long last, the English were in a position to challenge the Vikings on their natural element. The half of the Danish army which had not gone to Northumberland had based itself at Cambridge. It was under the leadership of Guthrum, who appears to have succeeded Ivar the Boneless as the principal Danish commander; Ivar himself had died in Dublin in 872. Guthrum's subordinate commanders were Oscytel and Anund.

In the spring of 876, as soon as the weather was favourable, Guthrum made his move. A Danish force rode through Wessex, slipping past Alfred's army, and occupied the Saxon fortress of Wareham, in Dorset. Why Guthrum chose to to do this is not clear, unless it was a diversionary tactic or else an attempt to secure a strongpoint on the south coast of Wessex for ease of reinforcement by sea. Whatever the Danes' intentions, the plan went badly wrong; the army of Wessex quickly recovered from its initial surprise and surrounded the place. It was now the turn of the besieged Danes to request an armistice, Their leaders swore a terrible oath on the most sacred of their pagan relics that they would leave Wessex for good if Alfred would lift the siege. Alfred agreed, and the two sides reached what nowadays would be called a ceasefire agreement. No sooner had this been concluded, however, than a large part of the Danish force, using all available horses, slipped through the Saxon lines and rode through the night to Exeter, where they entrenched themselves behind the walls of the old Roman town. Alfred's army rode after them in hot pursuit and besieged them yet again, forcing them to parley and, eventually, to surrender. This time, Alfred was taking no chances. He disarmed the enemy and took many hostages, and his army escorted the Danes out of Wessex and into Mercia. They arrived in August 877, at the height of the harvest, whose bounty they promptly siezed for themselves. They centred on Gloucester and built accommodation there in readiness for the winter.

In the meantime, that part of the Danish force left behind in Wareham had attempted to escape by sea. According to the *Chronicle*, the Danes were taken off by a sizeable fleet; it may have brought part of the invasion force in the first place, or else have been hastily assembled elsewhere to mount a rescue operation. In any case, it ended in disaster. The fleet sailed westwards, but off Swanage the ships encountered dense fog and smashed themselves to destruction on a reef which can still be seen on the south side of the bay. The *Chronicle* says that 120 ships foundered; if this was so, the loss of life must have been appalling.

Winter came, and a desperate winter it must have been for the peasantry in Wessex and Mercia, their harvests seized by the warring armies. Alfred disbanded his forces, doubtless believing that there would be no more fighting until the spring, and prepared to celebrate Christmas at Chippenham. In 2,000 years of history, it has ever been the fault of Christian commanders to lull themselves into the belief that enemies are loath to attack during the Christmas period, at Easter or on Sunday mornings. History, as a consequence, has had its share of Pearl Harbors.

Alfred's 'Pearl Harbor' came just after Twelfth Night in 878, when he suddenly found himself surrounded by Guthrum's Danes at Chippenham. Guthrum had done what no Dark Age commander in his right mind would do; scorning all the conventions of warfare, he had ridden through the mid-winter snows to achieve complete tactical surprise. Alfred and his immediate family only just managed to escape before the Danes overran the town and set up their winter quarters there. Doubtless, they found plentiful provisions, to which they added by plundering the countryside all around. The people of Wessex in the area who were not slaughtered were reduced to serfdom; many must have starved to death. When the thaw came, the Viking forces pushed down to the south coast, spreading death and destruction on such a scale that many of the inhabitants fled and sought refuge on the Isle of Wight. In some areas, Wessex ealdormen seem to have come to terms with the invaders in order to spare themselves and their people from the worst of the Danish excesses. Some Wessex ealdormen, however, fought back with whatever forces they could muster. Leaving their homes, they operated as guerrillas with their warbands, using hit-and-run tactics against the Danes

whenever the opportunity arose. Alfred, meanwhile, had sought refuge in the woods and marshes of Somerset. For six weeks he led a nomadic existence, slowly increasing the size of the forces available to him.

What happened next we can piece together from the *Chronicle* and the account of Bishop Asser, Alfred's biographer. At Easter 878, Alfred and his men constructed a small fortress at Athelney, on the northern fringe of West Sedgemoor. No trace of it survives today, for a church and monastery were later built on the site, now marked by a lonely monument. It was small and poor, but it served as a rallying-point and an operational base from which his growing force could strike at the enemy and forage for provisions. From here, too, Alfred sent forth his messengers into Wiltshire and Hampshire, exhorting the men of Wessex to rally to his standard at Egbert's Stone, at a spot somewhere on the junction of the boundaries of Wiltshire, Hampshire and Dorset near Penselwood. The date was Whit Sunday, May 11 878. Says the *Chronicle*: 'In the seventh week after Easter he rode to Ecgbryhtes-stane by the eastern side of Selwood; and there came to meet him all the people of Somersetshire and Wiltshire and that part of Hampshire which is on this side of the sea, and they rejoiced to see him.'

It is tempting to visualise the scene. The king and his entourage, waiting by the stone under a blue summer sky; to the east the vastness of Salisbury Plain, to the west the rolling forest; and the warriors of Wessex,

---

Somerton (Somerset). The boundary bank of a large Anglo-Saxon estate can still be made out along a lane which follows the north and north-west sides of Bradley Hill, 1½ miles north-west of Somerton. Its date is uncertain, but may be tenth century.

Athelney (Somerset). Here, on rising ground above the Somerset marshes, Alfred of Wessex sought refuge from the Danish invaders. A monastery was later built on the site, although nothing of this remains today. There is, however, a rough stone monument overlooking the lonely marshland on the east side of the Taunton-Glastonbury road. *(OS Sheet 193, 344292.)*

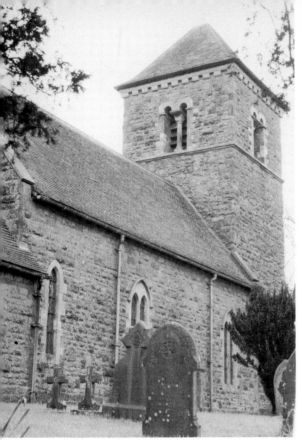

converging on the spot from all sides to cheer and lift their swords in salute to Alfred while one after another the ealdormen came forward to pay homage to him. And so the army of Wessex was assembled; and the following day, the host marched to Iley Oak (Acglea) near Warminster, taking refuge for the night behind some old earthworks surrounded by woodland. During the night, scouts would be keeping a watch on the Danish army, which was camped about seven miles away, so that when the Wessex army prepared to move forward before dawn Alfred would be armed with complete information on the enemy's dispositions.

Meanwhile, a decisive battle had already been fought at Countisbury, near Lynton in north Devon. A second Viking army had spent the winter in south Wales, and when Guthrum moved into Wessex this second force—comprising 23 ships and 1,200 men—had sailed over to Devonshire. There can be little doubt that this was part of a co-ordinated plan, designed to trap the Wessex forces between a pincer movement. However, the Danes were engaged by militia under Ealdorman Odda, and although the enemy appear to have won a marginal victory they lost 800 men and their leader, Ubba. They were no longer in a position to take an active part in the campaign. Alfred's rear was secure, although that security must have been bought at terrible cost to the valiant Devonshire men.

In the pre-dawn darkness, Alfred's army toiled up the ancient trackway leading up the steep chalk edge on to Salisbury Plain. As dawn broke, the men of Wessex poured over the ridge near Bratton and looked down over the rolling land beyond, to the Saxon royal estate at Ethandane—Edington—where Guthrum's army was encamped. Alfred wasted no time. The high ground and the initiative were in his favour, and he attacked at once. In the words of Bishop Asser:

'. . . He fought against all the Army in a dense, shield-locked array, and, long maintaining a stubborn fight, at length by the Divine will be obtained the victory and overthrew the pagans with the greatest slaughter and,

The church of St Nicholas at Cabourne, a mile to the north-east of Caistor, is late Saxon.

striking down the fugitives, followed them as far as their stronghold [Chippenham]. And all that he found outside the stronghold he seized, whether men, horses or cattle, slaying the men at once. And before the gates of the pagan stronghold he with all his army manfully pitched his camp. And when he had tarried there for 14 days, the pagans, worn out with hunger, fear and cold, at last in despair sought peace on this condition, that the king should receive from them as many hostages as he chose to name, while he himself should give them none, these being such terms of peace as they had never before concluded with anyone . . . .'

The victory of Wessex was complete, and at last two of the ninth century's strongest men, Alfred the Saxon and Guthrum the Dane, stood face to face. But the story does not end there. It seems that the two former enemies now became firm friends. Three weeks after the armistice, Guthrum came to Aller, near Athelney, with 30 of his earls to be baptised into the Christian church; Alfred stood as his godfather and afterwards was host to him for 12 nights, honouring him and his attendants with many gifts. Later in the year, the remnants of the Danish army left Wessex for ever. They stayed in Cirencester for a year, then moved back to East Anglia, where they settled as farmers.

Guthrum and Alfred concluded a peace treaty under which the island was partitioned, just as it had been partitioned between Britain and Saxons in Arthur's time. The northern and eastern parts were subject to Danish law—Danelaw—while English law remained in force throughout the rest. There is no suggestion that Guthrum ever broke the treaty, nor is there subsequent mention of him. Quietly, the great Viking warrior fades from the pages of history.

Guthrum must have had a hard time keeping his younger Viking hotheads in check. At one point, a sizeable force assembled at Fulham, on the Thames, possibly with the intention of raiding into Wessex territory; their plans may have been forestalled by the military strength of Wessex, for the *Chronicle* records that Alfred fought a sea engagement off the coast about this time (879), capturing four Danish warships. The Viking force on the Thames then sailed away across the Channel, and for years subjected the land of the Franks to a series of appalling ravages.

Alfred's fleet was in action again in 885, when the Danes of East Anglia—presumably under new leadership—suddenly broke the peace treaty and attacked Rochester, in Kent. The town held out until reinforcements arrived, led by Alfred, whereupon the Danes withdrew to their ships. Alfred decided to launch a punitive expedition against them and despatched his own fleet to the East Anglian coast; at the mouth of the Stour the English ships engaged 16 Danish vessels and captured them all, killing their crews. On the homeward voyage, however, the English fleet was intercepted by a superior Danish naval force, and this time got the worst of the encounter. Apart from these engagements, the years between 878 and 893 were years of peace for Wessex. During this time, Alfred proved himself to be as able a civilian administrator as he had been a military commander. As Bretwalda, the English-held areas of the island looked to him for leadership, and for the first time in the history of the Anglo-Saxons there came about a kind of unity between the English kingdoms, a unity that would eventually reach full fruition in an Anglo-Danish nation under the rule of Alfred's grandson.

Alfred revolutionised the whole structure of English life, and he achieved it by skilful planning. He was shrewd enough to realise that England's future lay in commerce, the success of which depended on settled urban life; his first concern, therefore, was to lay the foundation of a new system of fortified towns throughout Wessex. It is only recently that archaeology has shown that the spread of such towns—known as burhs—across southern England in the latter years of Alfred's reign was due to deliberate royal planning, rather than a haphazard need for defence. Much information on the new towns is contained in a document called the *Burghal Hidage*, which was compiled not long after Alfred's death. It lists 29 Wessex burhs and also gives details of the taxable plots of land allocated to the inhabitants who, in return, were responsible for manning the town's defences; this, in turn, makes it possible to assess fairly accurately the

extent of the burh's perimeter, and the number of men assigned to its defence.

Alfred's defensive strategy becomes clear when one examines the position of each burh across the kingdom; no part of Wessex is more than 20 miles distant from one of these fortified centres, and the strongest of all are built on the rivers leading inland. The Wessex defenders were now in a position not only to block any inroad into their territory by the shallow-draught warships of the Vikings, but also to muster rapid support in any area in the event of a threat developing overland. Perhaps the best example of a burh of Alfred's time is the Dorset town of Wareham, where the rectilinear grid system of Anglo-Saxon streets survives to this day. So do the defensive ramparts, part of which were turned into anti-tank defences when Britain was threatened by invasion in 1940. Excavations have revealed, too, that the street plan of Winchester dates from Alfred's time; 15,000 tons of flints were laid in the

The tower and west stair turret of the church of St Mary at Broughton, near Scunthorpe, are late Saxon. Comparatively few stair turrets of this kind still exist.

street pattern, and fine Anglo-Saxon royal buildings stood in the cathedral area, which was once the site of the Roman *praetorium*. This was where Alfred had his palace, which may have been modelled and decorated on the style favoured by the Frankish emperors.

Another paramount concern of Alfred's during the peaceful years of his reign was to raise the educational standards of his subjects. One of his complaints, when he came to the throne of Wessex, was that as far as he knew not a priest south of the Thames could translate a Latin letter into English. Admittedly, Alfred himself could not read or write his native Anglo-Saxon until well into his teens, and he was a grown man before he acquired a knowledge of Latin. His intention, however, was to arrest the cultural decline that beset the monasteries of his day; a decline hastened in part by the ravages of the Vikings, but made more profound by the fact that the religious houses were administered in general by untutored men who had obtained their

The late Saxon church of St Peter at Barton-on-Humber has a 70-foot tower and, among other early features, a triangular-headed doorway.

promotion through the king's favour. Part of Alfred's own royal house in Winchester was turned into a school for boys of noble birth, and it may be that some commoners were educated there, too. Under his patronage, an embryo university was started at Glastonbury by a group of Irish monks; one of its more illustrious future pupils was St Dunstan.

On Alfred's insistence, English became the official written language throughout his kingdom—a bold step in an age when the language of literature was Latin. Once the overall plan was formed in his mind, the king had selected passages of various Latin works read out to him so that he might decide which would best further the knowledge of his people in English translation. At least six major works were translated; they were the *Dialogues* of Gregory the Great, dealing with the lives of the early saints, and also his *Pastoral Care*, which was a code of practice for bishops; the *History of the World* by Orosius; Bede's *Ecclesiastical History of the English People*; the *Consolation of Philosophy* by Boethius, which showed that men could be masters of their own destinies; and the *Soliloquies* of St Augustine. Alfred himself had a hand in much of the translation work, adding his own comments and notes whenever he felt it necessary, discussing their contents with the learned men with whom he had surrounded himself. Perhaps his greatest literary achievement of all was the complete revision of the *Anglo-Saxon Chronicle*, which may have been compiled on his instructions by Bishop Asser. He had many copies made, and decreed that these be placed in all the leading monasteries and churches and constantly updated. Some of the original copies survive to this day, as testimony to the thoroughness with which Alfred went about the task of preserving his nation's written heritage.

Sadly, his cultural work was to be rudely interrupted by further outbreaks of hostilities with the Danes. Guthrum, it is recorded, died in 890, and the leaders who followed him— one of whom was named as Haesten—were no friends of Alfred or of Wessex. In 893, according to the *Chronicle*, 250 Danish ships sailed into an inlet on the coast of Kent and the vessels moved upriver for about four miles before their crews made camp at Appledore. Shortly afterwards, 80 more ships entered the

Thames estuary and their crews, commanded by Haesten, made camp somewhere between Gravesend and Sittingbourne, where they were reinforced by further contingents of Danes from East Anglia and Northumbria. For several weeks the Danes appear to have ventured out of their camps in relatively small numbers to plunder the surrounding area. Alfred, meanwhile, had assembled an army and positioned it in the Weald, to the west of and midway between the two enemy armies, so that either could be intercepted if it tried to move into Wessex. In due course one of the Danish forces did make a move westwards, but was trapped and defeated by part of Alfred's army at Farnham. The survivors crossed the Thames and found temporary refuge on an island in the River Colne near Iver, Buckinghamshire, where they were besieged by the English.

While most of Alfred's forces were thus occupied, the other Danish army—presumably the one camped at Appledore—re-embarked in its warships and sailed along the south coast to Devon, where it divided. One part moved

---

Wareham (Dorset). The finest surviving example of any burh created in Alfred's time, Wareham, which is reached by taking the A352 south from Dorchester, still has a Saxon rampart on the east, north and west sides, and the street plan closely follows that of the original burh. The chancel and nave of St Martin's church in Wareham date from the tenth century.

Cricklade (Wiltshire). One of the defensive 'burhs' created by Alfred the Great, Cricklade lies beside the A419 Cirencester-Swindon road. The defensive earthwork can still be made out. *(OS Sheet 173, 103933.)*

Halwell (Devon). Another early Saxon burh, the village of Halwell lies at the junction of the A381 Totnes-Kingsbridge road and the B3207, which runs east towards Dartmouth. Follow the latter road for about a mile to discover the earthwork and ditch which once formed part of the burh's perimeter. Halwell was abandoned after a fairly short time, and a new burh created at Totnes. *(OS Sheet 202, 784532.)*

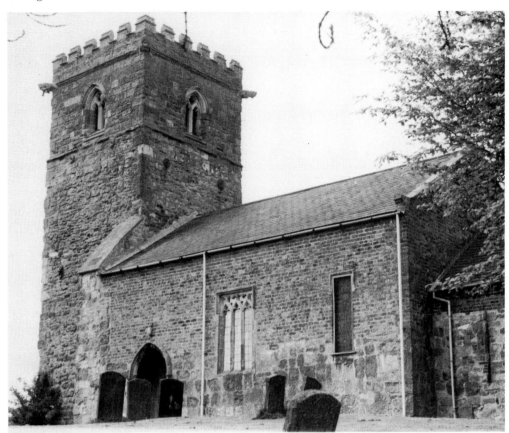

Much Saxon work is evident in the tower of the church of St Peter at Holton-le-Clay, on the A16 south of Grimsby.

inland to attack Exeter, while the other sailed round Land's End to plunder north Devon. Alfred also divided his forces, leading one army to engage the enemy in Devon while his son, Edward, kept an eye on the Danes north of the Thames. However, the Danish raiding force in Devon managed to elude Alfred, and the next intelligence the English had was that the fragmented enemy forces had regrouped at Benfleet, in Essex, in a fortified camp constructed by Haesten. This was stormed by an English army, probably led by Edward, which destroyed the earthworks and, as well as seizing considerable booty, captured all the women and children in the camp, including Haesten's wife and two sons. This suggests that the Danish defences were very depleted; Haesten was away at the time, probably

Left *South of Holton-le-Clay on the A16, the little church at Waithe stands in a picturesque setting.*
Above *The tower of Waithe church is of very late Saxon origin; the rest of the fabric is the result of nineteenth century restoration work.*

leading most of his forces on a plundering expedition.

The English towed as many ships as possible to London and burned the rest. Afterwards, Alfred returned Haesten's family to him unharmed, but this chivalrous gesture does not seem to have had much effect on the Viking, for he immediately reassembled his forces at Shoebury and set about preparing a fresh campaign. This time, there was no slow movement, no digging in behind earthworks: Haesten launched what amounted to a blitzkrieg, his army storming along the line of the Thames, plundering to left and right before swinging across the rich Cotswold country and moving northwards along the Severn into Mercia. There they were intercepted by a joint force of Mercians and Wessex men, under the command of the Mercian Ealdorman Aethelred, and were besieged on an island in

Lydford (Devon). To reach the Wessex burh of Lydford, take the A386 Tavistock-Okehampton road, then turn on to a minor road that branches off westwards midway between the two towns. This was a natural site, fortified during Alfred's reign by a stone-faced rampart. *(OS Sheet 191, 510847.)*

Pilton (Devon). Yet another Wessex burh of Alfred's time, this is actually an Iron Age fort which was conveneintly converted. Known as Burridge Camp, it lies two miles north of Barnstaple a little to the east of the A39. *(OS Sheet 180, 569352.)*

the Severn near Welshpool. After a period of several weeks the Danes, half-starved and desperate, stormed out of the trap and large numbers managed to cut their way through the English forces, making their way across the country to the fortified camp at Shoebury.

Haesten was a determined man. Calling up reinforcements from Northumbria, he struck westwards again, then turned his army north to Chester, making a forced marched along the old Roman road of Watling Street. At Chester the Danes made themselves secure behind the strong fortifications of the Roman fortress town, where once again they were besieged by the English. The latter were not strong enough to make a straightforward assault, or to prevent the Danes sending out frequent raiding parties; instead, they cleared a wide area around the town of all cattle and provisions, so that the enemy were once again faced with the prospect of starvation. Blocked by the English to the east, the Danes made a series of devastating raids into north Wales, seizing plunder and provisions. They then broke out to the north, finding sanctuary in Northumbria and eventually returning to Essex via the friendly territory of Yorkshire and East Anglia. In 894 they set up a new base on Mersea Island, and as harvest-time approached they advanced menacingly towards London. The local militia

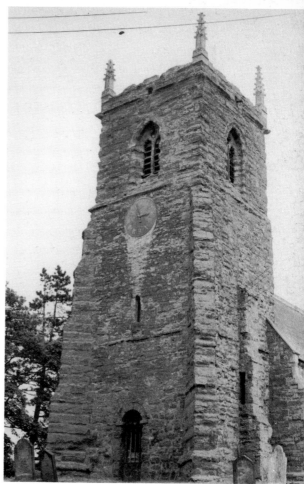

A good deal of Saxon architecture is visible in the church of St John the Baptist at Nettleton near Caistor, although one needs to look closely, as much of it is partly obscured by later work.

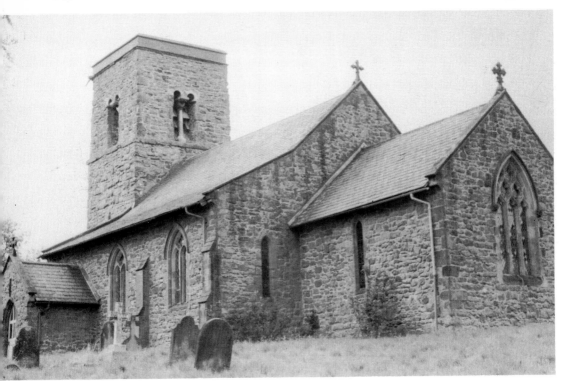

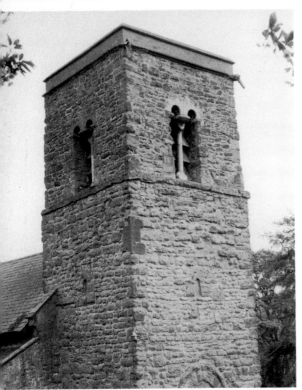

Two miles to the east of Caistor, at Rothwell, the church of St Mary Magdalene is of late Saxon date.

attacked them, and although the English were repulsed the Danish advance seems to have been checked.

The Vikings had moored their ships on the River Lea, which flows into the Thames, and this proved their downfall. While English forces guarded the area around London, enabling the citizens to gather their harvest in relative safety, Alfred's engineers threw a barrier across the Lea and built a fort on either side, trapping the enemy fleet. After sending their women and children into East Anglia, the Danes once again made a long forced march across country, eventually making camp at Bridgnorth in Shropshire. There they spent the winter, watched all the while by the English army.

With the coming of the spring thaw, the English once again prepared to meet a renewed Danish onslaught. It never came. Quietly, and without much fuss, the Danes went home to East Anglia and Northumbria and there the Great Army dispersed for the last time, in the

The tiny Saxon church at Escomb, County Durham, has been in almost continuous use since the eighth century.

summer of 896. The Danes had been out-fought and outmanoeuvred at every turn, and they had at last realised the futility of continued military operations against Wessex. Through-out their latest campaigns, the fact that they had been accompanied by their families indicated that their wish had been to settle on the rich farmlands of the south; but the deter-mined English opposition had denied those lands to them.

During the rest of his reign, Alfred had to contend only with periodic pirate raids, possibly launched from across the Channel, and his warships seem to have been more than a match for the Danish long ships, known as 'esks'. 'Then King Alfred gave orders for building long ships against the esks,' says the *Chronicle*, 'which were full-nigh twice as long as the others. Some had 60 oars, some more; and they were both swifter and steadier and also higher than the others. They were not shaped either after the Friesian or the Danish model,

Wallingford (Berkshire). The Saxon burh at Wallingford, 20 miles north-west of Reading, was built on the west bank of the Thames to command a strategic river crossing. A rectangular bank and ditch enclose an area of about 100 acres and are best defined on the eastern side of the town, whose street plan—similar to that of Wareham—probably follows the original Saxon pattern.

Old Sarum (Wiltshire). Once an Iron Age hill fort, this was refurbished and turned into a burh during Alfred's time, and King Edgar is known to have held court there in 960. During the reign of Aethelred II a royal mint was set up at Old Sarum and this functioned until the time of Henry II. Most of the visible earthworks are Norman, and excavations have revealed very little of the Anglo-Saxon occupation. The burh lies about two miles north of Salisbury on the west of the A345 Amesbury road. (Perhaps significantly, Amesbury recalls the name of Ambrosius Aurelianus; it may be that one of his actions was fought at Old Sarum.) *(OS Sheet 184, 137327.)*

but so as he himself thought that they might be most serviceable.'

Alfred died on October 26 899, aged 50. Throughout most of his life he had suffered from a mysterious illness which struck without warning and left him incapacitated for lengthy periods. Some historians think that he may have been afflicted by some form of hereditary syphilis, but the symptoms described by Bishop Asser—including severe depression that preceded each attack—may point to the possibility that Alfred suffered from migraine. Much of his undoubted strength in the face of great adversity seems to have lain in the closeness of his family ties. He was on good terms with his brothers, with the possible exception of Aethelbald, and what we know of his own household reveals a picture of domestic contentment, with his wife, Elswitha, happily busying herself with bringing up her children

Another early Anglo-Saxon church, that at Bolam in County Durham. Like the church at Escomb, a few miles to the north, it features Roman stone in its construction, probably from the Roman fort at Binchester or Piercebridge.

and looking after the royal home while Alfred was occupied with warfare or the affairs of state. With him, she shared the long, hard months of fear and exile in the marshes around Athelney; that time must have left its mark on her, and was probably the cause of several miscarriages she endured.

In his later years, Alfred undoubtedly received much comfort and support from his eldest son, Edward, although the two appear to have been of much different character. If Edward was Alfred's strong right arm, however, the son who must have basked in his father's love was Aethelward, the youngest, a gentle youth who was gifted in literature. He might have inherited his father's kingdom, for he was regarded as crown prince in Alfred's lifetime; but he died prematurely, and it was the stronger Edward who—perhaps fortuitously, as things were to turn out—came into the Wessex inheritance.

Alfred also had three surviving daughters. The eldest, Aetheflaed, married Aethelred of Mercia; the youngest, Aelfrida, married Count Baldwin of Flanders. He was the son of Judith, who as a teenage girl had married Aethelwulf. The middle daughter, Aethelgeda, never married at all; described as 'delicate', she entered a nunnery and eventually became Abbess of Shaftsbury.

Alfred was dead, but behind him he left an unrivalled legacy of power and greatness which, sadly, was to be squandered by lesser kings who followed him. Wisdom and humility were also part of that legacy, shining through in the preface he himself composed to the *Consolation of Philosophy*:

'What I set out to do was to virtuously and justly administer the authority given me. I desired the exercise of power so that my talents

Llantwit Major. Situated on the south coast of Wales some 15 miles south-west of Cardiff, Llantwit Major featured an important monastery in the Dark Ages, and the kings of Wales were buried here from the ninth to the eleventh centuries. The original monastery was founded on the estate of a landowner turned monk. There are several Dark Age stones in the church, one believed to commemorate Hywel ap Rhys, who ruled the kingdom of Glevissig (Glywysing) late in the ninth century. *(OS Sheet 170, 966687.)*

Cardiff. There is a Dark Age gallery in the National Museum of Wales, incorporating many early Christian stones from all over Wales as well as objects from excavations at the important Dark Age forts of Dinas Emrys and Dinas Powys.

and my power might not be forgotten. But every natural gift and every capacity in us soon grows old and is forgotten if wisdom is not in it. Without wisdom no faculty can be fully brought out, for any thing done unwisely cannot be accounted as skill. In short, I may say that it has always been my wish to live honourably, and after my death to leave to those who come after me my memory in good works.'

Those who came after, however, did not always treat Alfred's memory with the fairness it deserved. There have been attempts, over the centuries, to strip his mantle of greatness from him, and to denigrate his achievement. Let us be under no illusion about that achievement. If Alfred had not stood firm when other kings and kingdoms fell in ruin about him, the English-speaking world of today would not exist.

Chapter 11

The English on the offensive

Alfred's son Edward was the natural choice to succeed his celebrated father. He had already proved himself in battle, and the West Saxons looked to him for leadership. Nevertheless, when he stepped up to the throne at the age of about 30 on his father's death, his accession did not go unchallenged. The man who disputed Edward's right to rule was his cousin Aethelwald, the son of Alfred's elder brother Aethelred, who had died of wounds at Wimborne during the campaign in 871. Immediately on Alfred's death, Aethelwald assembled a force of supporters and seized the royal estates at Wimborne and Christchurch, declaring that he was there to stay. Within hours, however, Edward arrived with his troops and set up camp in the old Iron Age hill fort of Badbury Rings, some distance to the north, whereupon Aethelwald thought better of it and made his escape, leaving his followers to face the consequences.

Aethelwald seems to have been a born troublemaker. He sought refuge with the Danes of Northumbria, who, doubtless with an eye to future settlement prospects in the south, recognised him as a legitimate king. For the next two years he plotted and schemed, and then, in 902, he suddenly turned up in Essex at the head of a sizeable fleet and persuaded the Danes of East Anglia to take up arms in his support. The East Anglians, no doubt considering that they had been at peace for too long, launched a major plundering expedition into Mercia, fording the Thames at Cricklade and spreading devastation across the country-side before returning home. It was a raid in the

classic Viking style, and nothing like the decisive campaign that Aethelwald probably desired. The reaction from Edward, too, was swift and sharp. Quickly gathering his army, the Wessex king pursued the Danish army northwards and 'overran all their land between the foss and the Ouse, quite to the fens northward'. Having made his point, and given the East Anglian Danes a taste of their own medicine, he then ordered his forces to withdraw; the contingent from Kent, however, failed to obey and was cut off by a Danish force led by Aethelwald himself. There was a fierce battle, with heavy casualties on both sides, and Aethelwald was killed.

The demise of Aethelwald was followed by a peace treaty between Edward and the Danes of Northumberland and East Anglia. Hostilities, however, were resumed by Edward in 909, possibly as a punitive measure against continued Danish raiding; the Northumbrians must have been at the root of the trouble,

---

Barnack (Lincolnshire). The church at Barnack, south-east of Stamford on the B1443, is of late Saxon date. The windows and the lower part of the tower are original. *(OS Sheet 142, 079050.)*

Barton-upon-Humber (Lincolnshire). Also late Saxon, the Church of St Peter at Barton-upon-Humber, on the A1077 14 miles east of Scunthorpe, has a 70 ft tower and, among other early features, a triangular-headed doorway. *(OS Sheet 112, 035219.)*

because he led a large army into their territory to burn and destroy for five weeks before the Danes agreed to make peace on English terms. It lasted barely a year before the Danes went on the rampage again; Edward received intelligence that they had assembled a fleet and were sailing down the east coast, apparently with the intention of landing in Kent. Edward hurried with his army to strengthen the Kentish defences and assembled about a hundred ships to intercept the enemy at sea. It was soon apparent, however, that the Danish fleet movement was a clever ruse, designed to draw the greater part of the English forces into the south-east while the main body of the northern Danish army struck deep into Mercia. In one of the biggest plundering expeditions for 30 years they advanced as far as Bristol before turning north again, laden with booty. They had underestimated the speed with which the English army was now able to move. At Tettenhall, in Staffordshire, Edward caught up with them and cut them to pieces, slaughtering several thousand of them. The Danish losses included two kings.

Edward's clear intention was now to secure the frontiers of Wessex and Mercia against further Danish invasion for all time. His plan was to take the offensive deep into Danish territory, eliminating their strongholds one by one until they no longer had any bases from which to launch future raids.

In 911 Aethelred of Mercia, who had consistently supported the kings of Wessex even though his own kingdom had been terribly mauled by the Danes, died. His widow, Edward's sister Aethelflaed, was to prove a formidable ally, collaborating loyally with her brother in his efforts to inflict a series of crushing blows on the enemy. With her full approval, Edward annexed the Mercian towns of London and Oxford, which were turned into strong bases to support the campaigns that were to follow; then she and Edward set about fortifying selected Mercian towns on the lines of the Wessex burhs. The Roman walls of Chester were rebuilt, and Bridgnorth was turned into a key base for operations against the Welsh, should be latter become troublesome and attempt to strike Mercia in the back. Other centres fortified during this period, listed in the *Chronicle*, were Stafford, Tamworth,

Boarhunt (Hampshire). Lying north-west of Portsmouth between the A27 and A333, the chancel arch of Boarhunt church and the walls are tenth century. *(OS Sheet 196, 604083.)*

Bosham (Sussex). The church at Bosham, south of the A27 about three miles west of Chichester, has a structure which is almost entirely eleventh century. On the Bayeux Tapestry, Harold Godwinsson is shown sailing from Bosham. *(OS Sheet 197, 804039.)*

Breamore (Hampshire). The Church of St Mary at Breamore, on the A36 Salisbury–Christchurch road, has a fascinating south transept arch with a Saxon inscription that reads 'Here is the Word revealed unto you'. A badly battered rood in the south porch dates from about 1040. *(OS Sheet 195, 153189.)*

Britford (Hampshire). The nave of St Peter's church at Britford, on the outskirts of Salisbury to the east of the A338, is ninth century. The south doorway is one of the best to be found anywhere; one of the arches at the east end is finely decorated, while the other features Roman tiles. *(OS Sheet 184, 163284.)*

Warwick, Eddisbury, Warburton, Chirbury and Runcorn. Some of these towns were well inside Danish-held territory and had clearly been picked because they commanded vital river crossings.

The *Chronicle* records several battles in 912-3, and the joint forces of Wessex and Mercia seem to have been successful in reducing a number of Danish strongpoints. In 914, however, possibly as a result of a request for help, a Danish fleet sailed from Britanny and made landfall in the Severn, where the crews disembarked and began to plunder in Wales, presumably in the area immediately to the west of Offa's Dyke. Aethelflaed, realising that the Danes might strike into Mercian territory at any moment, got in the first blow and sent her army to engage the enemy in a pitched battle, which resulted in a complete Mercian victory. The Danish survivors, having handed over hostages, were escorted to

the Severn and sent packing in their ships. They subsequently tried to land in Somerset, only to be trapped by English forces and beaten once again. The remnant gave up and sailed away to Ireland.

While Aethelflaed's army guarded the western flank, and provided support where necessary, Edward once again turned his full attention to the Danish colonies in the east. By 916 he had constructed a line of 27 fortresses stretching from Essex to the Mersey; the Danes hurled themselves against the strongholds but were repulsed time and again. There was a good deal of fighting around Towcester, commanding a strategic position on Watling Street, and Derby, which Aethelflaed's troops took by storm; Bedford was also captured by the English and the local Danish earl, Thurketil, submitted to Edward. However, a Danish army from East Anglia made an attempt to retake the town, advancing as far as Tempsford, some six miles to the north, and building fortifications there. After beating off several assaults Edward counter-attacked, storming into the Tempsford strong-hold and destroying most of the enemy

The church of St Andrew at East Lexham, Norfolk, has a tenth century round tower, nave and chancel.

garrison, including the last Danish king of East Anglia.

In the summer of 917 Colchester, too, fell to the English army. Edward chose not to fortify the town, preferring to rely on strongholds he had built a few miles further south, at Witham and Maldon. The latter was particularly important, for it commanded the estuary of the river Blackwater into which marauding Danish fleets had periodically sailed. A Danish naval force, in fact, arrived to assist in a siege of Maldon later that summer, but once again the English emerged triumphant and the enemy forces were scattered. Edward completed his campaign of 917 with a resounding victory over the Danes of Northampton. It was achieved at very little cost. Edward led his forces from London along Watling Street to the river Ouse, where they encamped while a detachment moved ahead to strengthen the defences of Towcester. At that point the Northamptonshire Danes seem to have given up, and their leader, Earl Thurferth, acknowledged Edward as his overlord. Afterwards, Edward moved on to occupy Huntingdon, and now the Danes of East Anglia at last realised the futility of further resistance. In the words of the *Chronicle*: '. . . And all the Army in East Anglia swore union with him; that they would all that he would, and would protect all that he protected, either by sea or land. And the Army that belonged to Cambridge chose him separately for their lord and protector.'

In the spring of 918 it was Aethelflaed's turn. Her Mercian troops occupied the Danish stronghold of Leicester, apparently without resistance, and soon afterwards the Danes of York also made peace overtures to her. On June 12 918, however, the formidable Mercian queen died at Tamworth, and so a formal peace treaty was never concluded. The Mercians accepted Edward as their king, although for several months Aethelflaed's daughter Edfwina held the Mercian throne as regent. Then, for some unexplained reason, she was deprived of her authority and taken to Wessex, where she lapsed into obscurity.

In 919 Edward divided his time between strengthening his own position in Mercia and making further gains in Danish territory. He occupied Nottingham, and after its fortifications were strengthened the *Chronicle* tells us that they were manned by a mixed force of English and Danes. Later, in 923, he built a bridge across the Trent and built a second fort on the southern bank of the river. In the meantime, he had constructed more fortifications at Manchester and Bakewell, in Derbyshire.

According to the *Chronicle*, 920 was the year that found Edward at the peak of his power. Several rulers submitted to them in that year, including Raegnald a Viking leader from Dublin who had established a kingdom at York, Ealdred of Bamburgh, ealdorman of the Northumbrians, the king of Strathclyde, three kings of north Wales and others. The list may have been somewhat fanciful, for Edward must have had his hands full in preserving the

Eliseg's Pillar (Clwyd). This ninth century cross shaft was apparently erected by the grandson of Eliseg of Powys, an old adversary of Offa of Mercia. The pillar was vandalised during the Civil War and its inscription is now illegible, but it is claimed to trace Eliseg's descent from Vortigern. The pillar stands by the side of the A542, 1½ miles north of Llangollen.

Dover (Kent). The late Saxon church that stands above the castle in Dover is surrounded by a defensive earthwork that may have been fortified just before the Norman invasion. An interesting feature is the door that leads from the western gallery of the nave to the Roman lighthouse. *(OS Sheet 179, 326418.)*

Bedford. The scene of much fighting in the times following the Danish invasions, Bedford was a Saxon stronghold in the tenth century, but was captured by the Danes in 1010. One of its churches, the church of St Peter, shows traces of its original Saxon structure in the tower and the chancel, which was the original nave. There is an excellent sculpture portraying two fighting dragons above the chancel arch.

Clapham (Bedfordshire). The church of St Thomas Becket in Clapham, although extensively rebuilt in the nineteenth century, has a Saxon tower displaying four round-headed windows. Clapham is two miles north of Bedford on the A6. *(OS Sheet 153, 034526.)*

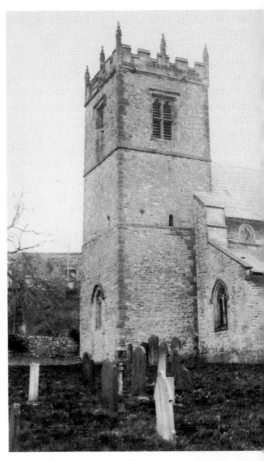

integrity of Wessex and Mercia, and in reality the rulers who were said to have acknowledged him as their lord and protector may have regarded him merely as a potential ally; but he was unquestionably the most powerful ruler in Britain. Unfortunately his personal triumph was destined to be short-lived, for he died at Farndon-on-Dee on July 17 924.

His family life seems to have been unusual for a Wessex king, for he had at least two official wives, which must have brought him into conflict with the Church; a matter that probably did not trouble him unduly, for he is not on record as being excessively devout. In fact, the Church in Wessex appears to have been sadly neglected during his reign. It was only a strong reprimand from the Pope, threatening to excommunicate Edward and all his subjects, that made him pay more attention to religious matters in his later years. He had at least 12 children. One of his sons,

Above left *The church of St James at Nunburn-holme, East Yorkshire, contains a fine tenth century cross that shows both Northumbrian and Danish influence, with Christian figures carved above scenes from Scandinavian mythology.*

Above right *The lower part of the tower of the church of St Helen at Skipwith, North Yorkshire, is Saxon.*

Hough on the Hill (Lincolnshire). The church of All Saints at Hough on the Hill, seven miles north of Grantham, has many visible Saxon remains. These include a tenth century west tower, stair turret with original steps, and nave walls. The south side of the turret has four interesting windows, two circular, one diamond-shaped and one pentagonal. The stone bench in the tower is original, and the square-headed door leading into the stair turret is built in Escomb style. *(OS Sheet 130, 923465.)*

Aethelward, died shortly after Edward himself, but two more, Edred and Edmund, were both destined to rule at a later date. Some of his daughters made good marriages into the royal houses of Europe; others became nuns.

Yet it was an illegitimate son, fathered in Edward's youth, who was to succeed him to the throne of Wessex. According to Bishop Asser, Edward had fallen in love with a shepherd's daughter named Egwina; she bore him a son and a daughter, although there is no record that he ever married her. The son, Athelstan, was brought up in the royal household and was a firm favourite with Edward's father Alfred, who gave him 'a mantle of purple, a girdle set with precious stones, and a Saxon sword in a gold scabbard'. Later—possibly after Edward married—Athelstan was sent to Mercia to be brought up with Aethelred and Aethelflaed. He was therefore well known in Mercia and popular, and when Edward died the Mercians readily accepted the young man as king. The West Saxons, however, appear to have been a little more reticent and some of them may have supported other claimants, among whom was Athelstan's half-brother Edwin, who conveniently disappeared from the scene when he was drowned at sea in 933.

Athelstan was crowned king at Kingston-on-Thames on September 4 925; the delay between his father's death and this date may in itself indicate that some disputes had to be settled before he could step up to the throne. It was not long before he proved himself worthy of the precedents set by his illustrious father and grandfather. Shortly after his coronation, a Viking ruler of York named Sihtric—a cousin of Raegnald and a leading member of the Clan Ivar, the Viking dynasty from Dublin which had seized York earlier—approached Athelstan and proposed an alliance with him. The two rulers concluded a treaty at Tamworth, and to seal the bargain Athelstan gave one of his sisters in marriage to the Viking. Unfortunately, Sihtric died only months later and his inheritance was claimed by Anlaf, a son by a former marriage in Dublin, who arrived in Northumbria with an army provided by his uncle Guthfrith, who was then the Norse king of Dublin. Anlaf's forces were quickly engaged by Athelstan's English army, which stormed York and tore down the Danish fortifications.

Mayburgh (Cumbria). This prehistoric 'henge', which lies south of Penrith on the north side of the A592, may have been the site of King Athelstan's famous court at Eamont Bridge, where the northern kings swore allegiance to him. The henge is a circle 360 ft in diameter, with a single stone at its centre, and is surrounded by a high turf-covered stone bank with an entrance on the eastern side. *(OS Sheet 90, 523284.)*

The church of All Saints at Kirby Hill, near Boroughbridge, incorporates Dark Age stones in its structure. They are built into the nave, which is ninth century and may come either from an earlier church built on this site or from one founded by St Wilfrid in Ripon.

THE ANGLO-SAXON
EMPIRE CREATED
BY ATHELSTAN

PICTS

WESTERN ISLES

Dunnottar

SCOTS

Perth   (Fleet to Caithness)

STRATHCLYDE   St. Andrews
BRITISH

Dumbarton   Edinburgh

LOTHIAN

Bamburgh

ULSTER   CUMBRIANS

Chester-Le-Street

Eamont Bridge

Armagh   MAN   NORTHUMBRIA

Ripon   York

Dublin

Chester   Lincoln

GWYNEDD   Derby   Nottingham

POWYS   Leicester

Tamworth   Thetford

Wexford   MERCIA   Stamford

Waterford   Brecknock Hereford   EAST ANGLIA

DYFED   GWENT Gloucester Buckingham

Malmesbury   London

WESSEX   Winchester Kingston

Exeter

WEST-WELSH   R.McM

◄------ Route of Athelstan's
         Expeditionary Force
         934 AD

The Norse army was put to flight and the remnants, along with Anlaf, sought refuge in Scotland.

Following up his advantage, and sensing a golden opportunity to bring the whole of the island under his complete control, Athelstan marched north and attacked Bamburgh, driving out Ealdorman Ealdred, although the latter was reinstated once he had sworn complete allegiance to Athelstan. Following this, Athelstan sent out messengers summoning all the northern kings to meet him; among them were Constantine, king of the Scots, Owain of Cumbria, and unnamed representatives of the Strathclyde British. The meeting took place on July 12 927 at Eamont Bridge, near Penrith, and one outcome was that Constantine undertook to surrender the Viking refugees from the York battle, including Anlaf and Guthfrith, who had entered his territory. Guthfrith, however, escaped somehow and managed to raise another army, with which he attempted to recapture York. The citizens of York themselves fought him off until the main English army arrived to beat him soundly for a second time. After spending some time on the run, Guthfrith gave himself up. Athelstan decided to be merciful and sent the Viking back to Ireland.

With the north secure, Athelstan decided to fix a permanent frontier with Wales, and to this end he summoned the Welsh princes to meet him at Hereford. There had been some Welsh resistance to the idea of English domination, led principally by Idwal Foel of Gwynedd, but nevertheless the five kings who ruled Wales between them came to Hereford and agreed to pay Athelstan a yearly tribute that included 20 pounds of gold, 300 pounds of silver and 25,000 oxen—a vast fortune in those days.

There was trouble, too, in Cornwall, where the British of that area seem to have instigated an uprising that may have spread as far as Exeter. It was speedily crushed by Athelstan, who strongly fortified Exeter and fixed the boundary between Wessex and Cornwall on the River Tamar. At Easter 928, the king held a great court at Exeter; it was attended by all his underkings, bishops, earls, judges, chiefs and dignitaries, 'rejoicing with great festivities'. It was exactly 50 years since King

> **Earl's Barton (Northamptonshire).** The Church of All Saints at Earl's Barton, four miles south-west of Wellingborough on the B573, served as a strong place of refuge as well as a place of worship during the Anglo-Danish wars. The main door could be sealed and the tower entered by a ladder leading to a door on the first floor. The church has some typical Anglo-Saxon features, including long vertical stones alternating with horizontal ones and a belfry opening with a central shaft supporting a single stone slab. *(OS Sheet 152, 852638.)*

Alfred, his kingdom reduced to a few square miles of marshland, had built his tiny stronghold at Athelney; now Athelstan, his grandson, was ruler of all Britain.

Nevertheless, unrest was always just under the surface. In 934, Constantine, the king of the Scots, suddenly broke his peace treaty with Athelstan. Why he did so is not on record—it may have been a simple matter of refusing to pay tribute in a bad year—but Athelstan's reaction was rapid and decisive. On May 28—Whit Sunday—he assembled a great army at Winchester; it included contingents from Wales and some from the Danes of East Anglia, and as it moved north it was joined by more forces. It paused for a time at Nottingham on June 7 and then marched relentlessly northward again. As it passed through Northumbria, the king halted at the principal shrines to pray for the support of the saints; at Chester-le-Street he prostrated himself before the tomb of St Cuthbert and then, uncovering the saint's remains, he had them wrapped in rich silks from the orient, fragments of which can still be seen in Durham Cathedral. It must have been the biggest army ever to march to war in Britain, and as it progressed it was accompanied by a powerful war fleet which sailed along the East Coast. Crossing the border into Scotland, the army ravaged the country as far north as Kincardine and penetrated to the old Pictish rock fortress or Dunnottar south of Aberdeen, while the fleet sailed on to strike at the Norse settlements in Caithness. The Scots did not offer battle, and in due course their leaders, realising that they were hopelessly outnumbered, surrendered.

Standing solid and square in the centre of Ripon, the Cathedral of St Peter and St Wilfrid is the latest in a line of religious houses that have stood on this site since 660. Only the crypt survives of the original building; it is one of the earliest Christian structures in England, and today serves as a treasury where silver from all over the diocese is on display.

Once again, Athelstan elected to show mercy, restoring both Constantine and his ally, Owain of Cumbria, to their kingdoms as his underlings.

Dictatorship, however, breeds rebellion, and there is no doubt that Athelstan *was* a dictator. In the mid-930s a widespread revolutionary movement grew against him, instigated by Constantine, king of the Scots; it involved both the Celtic peoples of Britain and the Scandinavian settlers. It was as though the clock had been turned back five centuries, to the day when the Romano-British and their mercenary allies had striven to hurl the Saxons back into the sea and so uphold the heritage of Rome in the island; but ironically, it was the West Saxons who now held the Roman inheritance of Britain in their hands.

From Ireland, with a great fleet, came Anlaf, expelled from York during the early days of Athelstan's reign. Joining forces with those of the Scots and the Britons of Strathclyde, he marched through Northumbria and made York his campaign headquarters. Shrewdly— and, it must be said, this was the target of much criticism at the time—Athelstan let the enemy come on. Like Montogmery a thousand years later, he did not intend to make a move until his own forces were strong enough to be sure of victory. The enemy army advanced 'deep into England', possibly as far as the Don valley in south Yorkshire, and there at last— at a fort called Brunanburgh, which has never been identified but which is said to have been at a place also known as Holy Hill, where there had been a pagan temple—they came face to face with the English army. It was the autumn of 937. Athelstan struck first, mounting a fast dawn assault. He had divided his army in two; the West Saxons were thrown against their old enemies, the Celts, while the Mercians took on the Scandinavians. The battle was a savage one, with both sides fighting desperately, but in the end the superior training and discipline of Athelstan's troops won the day and the enemy broke and streamed from the field. The West Saxon cavalry pursued them until nightfall, cutting down the fleeing warriors 'cruelly, with blades whetted on grindstones', according to the *Irish Annals.*

The English victory was complete, but the cost had been heavy; it included two of Athel-

---

Great Paxton (Huntingdonshire). The Church of the Holy Trinity at Great Paxton, on the B1043 Godmanchester-St Neots road, is eleventh century and features a very wide chancel arch and an aisled nave, which is unusual for this period. *(OS Sheet 153, 210641.)*

Greensted (Essex). The Church of St Andrew is the oldest surviving example of a timber Saxon church, with nave walls made from split oak trunks standing on end. The building dates from 850. In this heavily-wooded area, 12½ miles west of Chelmsford off the A113, timber was easier to obtain than stone. The body of Edmund the Martyr lay here for a while in 1031 on its way to Bury St Edmunds. *(OS Sheet 167, 539030.)*

---

stan's cousins, two earls and two bishops, as well as 'a multitude' of ordinary soldiers. The enemy had lost five kings, including the Norse ruler of the Western Isles and Owain of Cumbria, as well as two sons of Sihtric and five of Anlaf Guthfrithson's earls. The son of Constantine was also numbered among the dead. Anlaf himself escaped, arriving back in Dublin early in 938 with 'very few' survivors. The victory won by Athelstan was celebrated for generations, and ranks among the greatest achievements of English arms. It made Athelstan secure for the rest of his reign, and increased his status enormously throughout Europe. Even Harold Fairhair, king of Norway, sent his son to be brought up at Athelstan's court. Four of his half-sisters married into European royal families, and in 939 he despatched a fleet to Flanders at the request of Louis d'Outremer, king of the Franks, to help repel a German invasion. It was the first recorded instance of an English expeditionary force intervening in the affairs of the Continent.

Athelstan was by no means modest about his position of supremacy. He called himself 'King of all Britain' and sometimes 'Basileus (the Byzantine word for emperor) of the English and of all the nations round about'. Cenwald, bishop of Worcester, called him 'King of the Anglo-Saxons, Emperor of the Northumbrians, ruler of the pagans and

Above *The parish church at Stanwick, North Yorkshire, partly dates from the eleventh century, but it is possible that an earlier Saxon church stood on the present site. It stands at the centre of Stanwick fort, stones from which were used in its construction.*

Below *Fragment of an Anglo-Saxon cross shaft in Stanwick churchyard.*

guardian of the Britons'. He died at Gloucester on October 27 939, aged 44, after reigning for 14 years. The impact he had made was such that, 200 years later, William of Malmesbury was still able to write: 'The firm opinion is still current among the English that no one more just or learned administered the state'.

When Athelstan fought at Brunanburgh, Edmund, his half-brother and the legitimate son of Edward, had fought by his side with distinction. Then, the boy had been only 16 years old; now, two years later, tried in battle and popular with the West Saxons, he was accepted without hesitation as Athelstan's successor. There was to be no respite for him; no time in which to consolidate his position as Bretwalda. Within weeks of Athelstan's death, Anlaf Guthfrithson once more landed in Northumbria at the head of an army and occupied York, from which base his forces began to plunder southwards. Local militia defeated them at Northampton, but then they turned west and spread devastation into Mercia, destroying the old Mercian royal seat of Tamworth. Edmund, meanwhile, had managed to assemble an army and confronted the Vikings at Leicester as they were homeward-bound with their booty; a major battle seemed inevitable, and since Edmund was in command of little more than a scratch force the outcome would probably have been an overwhelming English defeat. Somehow, however, the Archbishops of Canterbury and York managed to come between the opposing armies and arrange a peace treaty, which in effect ceded to Anlaf almost the whole of the former Danelaw—Leicester, Derby, Nottingham and Lincoln.

Two years passed; then, in 942, Edmund—sure now of his position and at the head of an army which was more than a match for the Vikings—launched a campaign that won back all the surrendered territory. In this he probably had the full support of the Danish settlers; after 15 years of peace, it is hardly likely that they would have taken kindly to being overrun by Norse invaders. After being expelled from East Anglia and the Midlands the Norsemen moved north, plundering in Northumbria. Then Anlaf died, to be replaced for a short time by Anlaf Sihtricson, whose rule lasted only a matter of months before he was ousted by a brother of Anlaf Guthfrithson, Raegnald.

Both Anlaf and Raegnald sought an alliance with Edmund, and became Christians in order to achieve it. Each, however, hotly contested the other's claim to the Viking kingdom of York, and Edmund, fearing that their dispute would involve the country in a far-reaching civil war, launched an attack on them in 944 and drove them both out. His army then moved north to devastate Strathclyde, whose king, Dunmail, had supported Anlaf, and in 946 Edmund turned over the whole of the Strathclyde area to Malcolm I, the new king of the Scots, with whom he had formed an alliance. At the age of only 24, Edmund had succeeded in re-establishing Athelstan's authority over the island. His promising reign, however, was cut brutally short in May 946, when, during the feast of St Augustine at Pucklechurch in Gloucestershire, he was stabbed to death by a criminal expelled from his kingdom a few years earlier. He left two sons, Edwy and Edgar; but since both were under age the throne passed to his brother Edred. He received the submission of all the underkings who had been ruled by Edmund, including the Northumbrians, at Pontefract in 947; the Northumbrian delegation was led by Archbishop Wulfstan of York, who was to prove a devious and unreliable ally.

The problems of the north were intensified with the death of Harold Fairhair, the Viking leader who had succeeded for the first time in uniting all the kingdoms of Norway. Harold was followed by one of his sons, Eric, whose prowess in battle had earned him the nickname 'Bloodaxe', but a family feud broke out in which Eric killed two of his brothers. A group of powerful Norwegian earls managed to depose Eric; they replaced him with his half-brother, Haakon, who had been educated at Athelstan's court and who, aged only 15, was now brought back from England. Eric, faced with overwhelming opposition to his violent ways, gathered his supporters and set sail across the North Sea. After plundering in Scotland, he eventually arrived in Northumbria, where he was welcomed and invited to be king at York; the Northumbrians presumably saw in Eric a man strong enough to restore their kingdom to full independence.

Following the precedent of the earlier West Saxon kings, Edred reacted quickly to this new threat. Gathering an army, he marched north and ravaged Northumbria; then, satisfied that he had taught the northerners a lesson, he

Ovingham (Northumberland). The church of St Mary at Ovingham, which lies just across the Tyne a mile north-west of Prudhoe off the A695, has a tower that is late Saxon from ground level to the belfry, and also several original windows (OS Sheet 88, 085637).

Warden (Northumberland). The present church of St Michael at Warden, three miles north-west of Hexham, was built in the eleventh century and rebuilt in the eighteenth, but there may have been a religious house here much earlier than the eleventh century —perhaps as early as the seventh. The present church has late Saxon windows in the tower (OS Sheet 87, 915665.)

Aspartia (Cumbria). More tenth century stones—and some perhaps of earlier date— may be seen in the church of St Kentigern, on the A596 about ten miles north-east of Maryport. There is also an excellent hogback coffin-lid, richly decorated with interlace and animal sculptures (OS Sheet 85, 147419.)

Penrith (Cumbria). There are two crosses outside the parish church in the town centre, both dating from very late in the tenth century, with four Scandinavian hogback coffin sides nearby. The piece of ground on which the crosses stand is known as the Giant's Grave. One of the crosses is decorated with the figure of a woman, a serpent and a Lamb of God, the other with a small human head. Both have interlace work. Another stone in the same churchyard, standing north-west of the tower and known as the Giant's Thumb, is a wheel-headed Anglian cross.

Dearham (Cumbria). The church of St Mungo at Dearham, off the A596 two miles east of Maryport, contains a good collection of Dark Age stones, including a tenth century wheel-headed cross and another depicting a mounted horseman, a bird and a man. A third cross, in addition to carved figures, carries a runic inscription *(OS Sheet 89, 073364.)*

Ilkley (West Yorkshire). The Manor House Museum in Castle Yard has a small collection of cross fragments, one of them dredged from the River Wharfe; this fragment has a fox and grapes in scroll work. The museum is close to the church of All Saints, where there are three Anglo-Saxon crosses of mid-ninth century date in the churchyard. The tallest bears symbols of the four evangelists and curious twisting beasts. Elsewhere in West Yorkshire, cross fragments are also to be seen at Collingham (St Oswald's Church), on the A58 ten miles north-east of Leeds; Dewsbury (church of All Saints), to the south of Leeds; the church of St Peter in Leeds Kirkgate, where there is a fine free-standing cross, 11 ft high and dating to the tenth century; Addingham (church of St Peter), on the A65 three miles west of Ilkley; Crofton (church of All Saints), on the miles east of Wakefield on the B6378; Otley (church of All Saints), ten miles north-west of Leeds at the junction of the A659 and A660; West Marton (church of St Peter), six miles west of Skipton; Thornhill (church of St Michael), about a mile south of Dewsbury on the B6117; and Walton Cross, off the M62 four miles north-west of Hartshead, where there is a large and finely decorated cross base standing next to a minor road.

withdrew. Behind him he left wholesale slaughter and towns in ruins; his troops burned St Wilfrid's minster at Ripon, which appears to have been a mistake and which aroused the north to outraged fury.

As Edred's army marched south once more, it ran into an ambush. At Castleford, on the River Aire, part of the Northumbrian army waited until the main body of the English force had passed, then fell upon the rearguard and destroyed it. Eric himself, according to one account, led this action. On hearing the news, Edred was all for turning round and striking deep into Northumbria again, turning the land into a desert. He was quite capable to doing so, and the Northumbrians knew it; in panic, they expelled Eric and once again submitted to the English king, forestalling great bloodshed in the nick of time.

The new Viking king of York was our old friend Anlaf Sihtricson, who returned from Dublin presumably with Edred's approval. His rule lasted for four years, from 948 to 952; and then, unexpectedly, Eric Bloodaxe returned. No one knows what Eric had been up to in this four years of exile; fragmentary clues suggest that he plundered and traded in Spain and the Mediterranean. At any rate, he was once again welcomed by the Northumbrians—led it seems by Archbishop Wulfstan—and the unfortunate Anlaf was thrown out yet again. Eric's second reign in York lasted only two years, but in that time he established himself in a position of power which no Northumbrian ruler had known for generations, and left a lasting impact on the north. He styled himself 'Eric Rex' and minted his own coinage, ruling in some splendour from the Viking hall whose position in modern York is still commemorated in the name of King's Square. Edred, in the meantime, made no overt move against him, although he took the precaution of imprisoning Wulfstan when the latter made the mistake of visiting the Wessex court; he doubtless blamed the archbishop for many of the north's intrigues. The place of his confinement was 'Iudanbyrig', which has been variously identified with places as far apart as Bradwell-on-Sea and Jedburgh, although the latter seems unlikely.

Forces were at work, however, which were to result in Eric's downfall, which may well

Middleton (North Yorkshire). The church of St Andrew at Middleton, on the A170 a mile west of Pickering, has a late Saxon tower and, in part, nave walls, although an earlier building may have stood on the site. There are some tenth century Anglo-Danish crosses in the church, one showing an armed warrior and another a hunter and his dog. More Anglo-Danish sculptures are to be seen in the church of St Hilda at Ellerburn, which lies two miles east of Pickering a little to the north of Thornton Dale.

Nunburnholme (East Yorkshire). On a minor road to the south of the B1246 and about three miles east of Pocklington, the church of St James at Nunburnholme contains a cross, dating from the mid-tenth century, that shows both Northumbrian and Danish influence, with a Virgin and Child and other Christian figures carved above scenes from Scandinavian mythology, including the hero Sigurd devouring a dragon's heart. Other Dark Age sculptures in East Yorkshire may be seen at Folkton (church of St John Evangelist), just off the A1039 five miles west of Filey; North Frodingham (church of St Elgin), on the B1249 five miles east of Great Driffield; Aldbrough (church of St Bartholomew), on the B1242 seven miles south of Hornsea, where there is a Saxon sundial with an inscription dedicated to a man named Ulf, who had the original church built; and Stillingfleet, on the B1222 eight miles south of York, where the south door of the church of St Helen has unique Viking ironwork depicting a long ship.

Wharram le Street (East Yorkshire). The church of St Mary here, on the B1248 six miles south-east of Malton, is of late Saxon origin, and original work is still to be seen in the nave and chancel as well as in the belfry windows.

Kirby Hill (North Yorkshire). The church of All Saints at Kirby Hill, just off the B6265 two miles north of Boroughbridge, incorporates several Dark Age stones in its structure. These are built into the nave, which is ninth century, and may come either from an earlier church built on this site or from one founded by St Wilfrid in Ripon (OS Sheet 99, 394686).

Stonegrave (North Yorkshire). There are several interesting sculptures in the church of the Holy Trinity at Stonegrave, which lies on the B1257 ten miles north-west of Malton. One of them, which stands on a mediaeval grave slab, is a tenth century Anglo-Danish cross. There are other tenth century cross shaft fragments, and some pieces of hogback gravestones. More sculpture work may be seen in the church of All Saints in Hovingham, two miles south of Stonegrave on the same road, which also has a late Saxon tower.

York: the Viking Kingdom. Little is known of the history of York—the Roman Eboracum—during the 200 years which followed the end of the Roman occupation. In the seventh century, however, the Saxons began to settle within the fortress walls, giving the city their own name of Eoforwic; it was there, in 627, that Paulinus baptised King Edwin of Northumbria into Christianity, and the tiny wooden church built on the site was the first York Minster. In the eighth century, a school was founded in York and pupils came from all over Europe to be taught there by Alcuin. It is claimed that the school stood on the present site of St Peter's School, Clifton. In 866 York was captured by a Viking army. Ten years later, part of this army returned as settlers, and made the city their capital, changing its name once again to Jorvik. A succession of independent kings ruled here until 954, when the last of the line, Eric Bloodaxe, was expelled by the English king Edred. Excavations in York have shown a constructive side to Viking life that is completely at variance with the Norsemen's traditional image. The existing coinage was taken over and extended in use, quality and quantity, while trade flourished with Dublin, Scandinavia, the Continent and beyond. The most important excavations took place at Coppergate, which means the 'street of the woodturners' and lies at the very heart of Viking York; the site is now hidden under modern construction, but the archaeologists uncovered an astonishing quantity of material, including the remains of wooden houses. Many of the artefacts are housed in the Yorkshire Museum, which stands in the city's Museum Gardens.

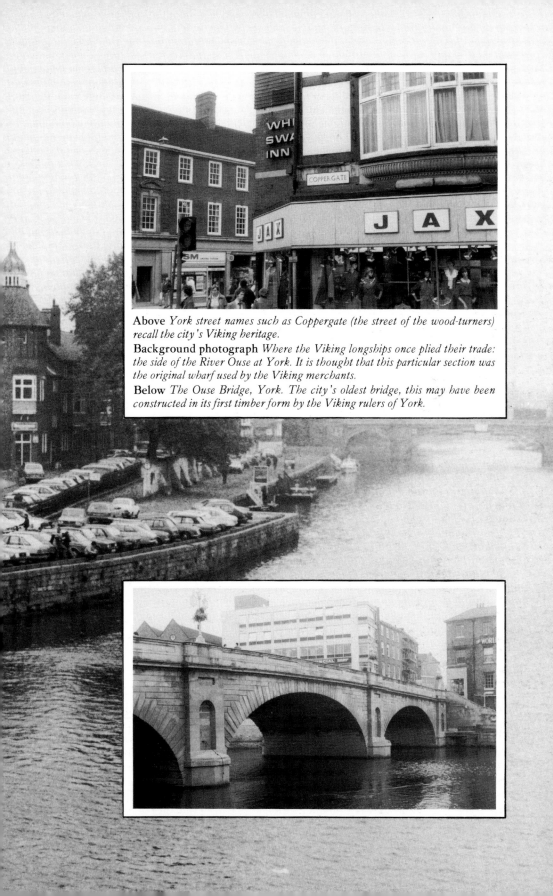

Above *York street names such as Coppergate (the street of the wood-turners) recall the city's Viking heritage.*

Background photograph *Where the Viking longships once plied their trade: the side of the River Ouse at York. It is thought that this particular section was the original wharf used by the Viking merchants.*

Below *The Ouse Bridge, York. The city's oldest bridge, this may have been constructed in its first timber form by the Viking rulers of York.*

Kirkdale (North Yorkshire). The church at Kirkdale, north of the A170 between Helmsley and Kirbymoorside, has a Scandinavian sundial above the south porch. It is framed by an inscription which reads, 'Orm, son of Gamal, bought St Gregory's Church when it was all broken and fallen down and he had it made new from the foundations for Christ and St Gregory in the days of King Edward and the Earl Tosti [Tostig]'. The dial therefore is dated between 1055 and 1065. *(OS Sheet 100, 677857.)*

have been engineered by Edred's agents. Little is known of the circumstances, but it is said that Eric was 'betrayed'. It seems likely that he was the victim of some kind of coup and that his 'betrayer' was Earl Oswulf, of the northern English at Bamburgh. At any rate, we know that Eric and his followers made their last stand at Stainmore, on the Roman road between Brough and Bowes. Eric himself was killed by Earl Maccus 'the son of Anlaf', who was probably the Anlaf Sihtricson chased by Eric out of York. Later tradition says that English forces were involved in the battle, yet the *Chronicle* makes no mention of it, stating simply that 'the Northumbrians expelled Eric, and Edred succeeded'. Today, the stump of a stone cross stands on the lonely moor at Stainmore. Its name is Rey Cross, which is derived from the Norse word *hreyrr*, meaning boundary. No-one can say who erected it, or why; but it may be a lasting memorial to Eric Bloodaxe, the last Viking king of York.

Edred outlived Eric by three years. He died in 955, in his mid-thirties, having reigned for nine and a half years. In that time he had succeeded in recovering all his father's territory; his most important achievement, however, was to prevent the fusion of Dublin and York into a single Viking state. Edred was the last of the warrior kings of Wessex. This does not mean that those who followed him, Edwy and Edgar, were weak or lacked courage, but simply that Edred and his predecessors had fought so successfully that there was no longer any fighting to be done, at least not of a serious nature. Edred left no children when he died, so the succession naturally passed to his nephews, Edwy and Edgar, the sons of Edmund. Edwy

was the elder of the two, but even then he was barely 15 when he assumed the mantle of kingship; he was an extremely good-looking youth and very popular with the girls, and the story goes that on one occasion, when he should have been in session with his ministers, he had to be dragged away from a noble lady's bedroom by Bishop Dunstan, whom he detested but who, as a close friend of the late Edred, had risen to a position of considerable power in the kingdom. Edwy later married the lady in question, Elgifu, but the quarrel with Dunstan continued unabated and the bishop was driven into exile. This certainly did not endear Edwy to the Church, and his irresponsible behaviour in other areas seems to have stripped him of much support he would otherwise have enjoyed. He stripped his grandmother, Edward's widow, of all her possessions and and handed out grants of land left, right and centre to his favourites; he issued no fewer than 60 land charters in the first year of his reign.

In the end, the councils of Northumbria and Mercia rejected him outright in favour of his brother Edgar, and although Edwy continued to rule in Wessex for a while longer, it was Edgar who held the reins of power in England north of the Thames. When Edwy died in October 1 959, after a four-year reign that had done nothing but damage to the image of the royal house of Wessex, the general feeling was one of relief. His brother Edgar is on record as being a small man—less than five feet tall—yet he seems to have had no trouble in persuading his underkings of his fitness to rule. This may have been due at least in part to the efforts of Dunstan, who was immediately recalled from the monastery at Ghent, where he had spent his exile, and enthroned as bishop of Worcester. Later, in 959, he was moved to London, and in the following year Edgar made him Archbishop of Canterbury.

Edgar, in fact, had been educated by a great friend of Dunstan's, Aethelwold, who was abbot of Abingdon. Under Dunstan's influence he was made bishop of Winchester in 963; another friend, Oswald, had already become bishop of Worcester when Dunstan moved to London in 961. With Edgar's full support, these three powerful churchmen were to dominate the English church—not to mention

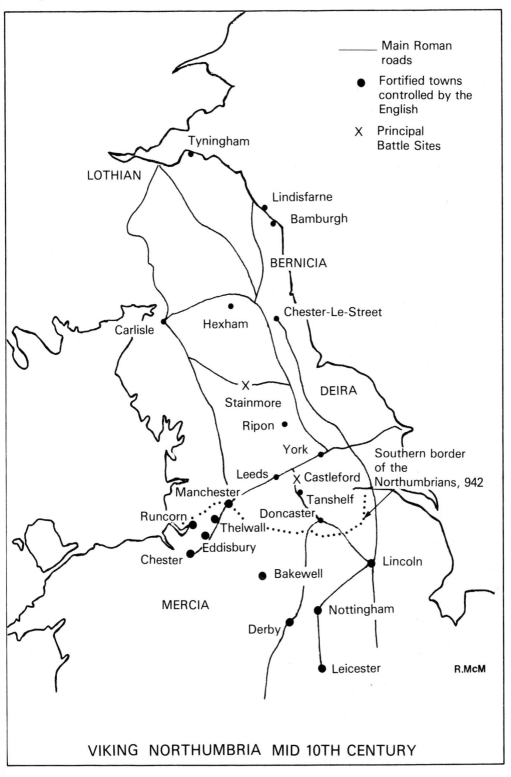

VIKING NORTHUMBRIA MID 10TH CENTURY

English politics—during the 15 years of the young king's reign.

Immediately after his coronation, Edgar summoned his underkings to a meeting at Chester, where a demonstration of English naval power seems to have been made in the estuary of the River Dee. Some of the kings in attendance are named as Kenneth of Alba, Donald of Strathclyde, Maccus of the Western Isles (the same Maccus, presumably, who had slain Eric Bloodaxe) and Iago of Gwynedd. According to one account, the kings rowed the royal barge while Edgar reviewed his fleet, which sounds more like a good-natured after-dinner exercise than a conscious attempt by Edgar to assert his power.

Edgar's reign would appear to have been peaceful; apart from an Irish raid on the coast of Cumbria, and some disturbance in Thanet that was dealt with speedily by English troops in 969, the *Chronicle* makes no mention of any serious military challenge. The years of peace allowed the king to make sweeping changes in England's administrative structure; it was he who organised the kingdom into 'shires', each subdivided into 'hundreds', a system which was to last for a thousand years. He also gave considerable autonomy to the Danish-settled districts: 'It is my will,' he declared, 'that secular rights shall be in force among the Danes according to as good laws as they can best decide on. Among the English, however, that is to be in force which I and my councillors have added to the decrees of my ancestors.'

Edgar died suddenly on July 8 975, aged 32. Little is known about his private life; what information we have comes from the pens of ecclesiastics, who have glossed over what might be called the seamier side. However, he appears to have been involved with three women, only one of whom became his legal wife. The first was Wulfryth; she bore him a daughter, Edith, who became a nun. Then there was Aethelflaed, nicknamed the 'White

North Elmham (Norfolk). At North Elmham, which lies about six miles north of East Dereham on the B1110, can be seen the foundations of a small Saxon cathedral, just beyond the parish church. It was destroyed by the Danes in 870, and they probably built the earthwork which surrounds the site. The cathedral was rebuilt in the tenth century. *(OS Sheet 132, 988216.)*

Bygrave (Hertfordshire). First recorded in a Saxon charter of 973, the village of Bygrave stands a little to the west of the Icknield way, 1½ miles from Baldock. It was a completely self-contained Saxon settlement, and its name means 'the place by the ditch'. The present-day cluster of houses lies almost exactly within the original settlement plan.

Duck', who was the mother of a boy named Edward; and lastly Aethelfryth, widow of Aethelwold of East Anglia, who shared Edgar's throne and who was the first consort since Judith to be styled 'queen' in Wessex. She bore Edgar two sons, Edmund and Ethelred, but the first died in childhood, and so the right of succession was between Edward and Ethelred. Being the oldest—although still only barely 16—Edward was the son who was chosen. He was a violent, ill-tempered youth who quickly made himself thoroughly disliked by both the nobility and the common people. He reigned for three and a half years until, during a visit to Queen Aethelfryth at Corfe in Dorset, he was stabbed to death by one of her men on March 18 978, presumably at her instigation. He was buried at Wareham, apparently with no honours whatsoever, and no one was punished for his murder. Within a month, his step-brother Ethelred had been crowned at Kingston-on-Thames amid great rejoicing. The jubilation, however, was to be short-lived. Once again, the Viking storms were about to burst over Britain.

Chapter 12

The years of darkness

The transition from Edward to Ethelred, especially in view of the dislike that had attended the former king, ought to have been simple. It was not. Edward's body was hardly cold when England was swept by a wave of superstitious awe, engendered by portents such as a 'cloud as red as blood . . . with the appearance of fire, which usually appeared about midnight; it took the form of rays of light of various colours, vanishing at the first sign of dawn'. In those times, even the Aurora Borealis could arouse abject terror. Then the rumour began to spread that strange lights had been seen dancing over the tomb of the murdered Edward, and that the horse of Ethelred's mother had shied in fright and refused to approach the burial place. It all added up to a general feeling that Ethelred's reign was doomed from the beginning, that God's vengeance was hanging over his head. We may laugh at such opinions now, but in the tenth century they were strong enough to topple kingdoms.

The 'vengeance' began to make itself apparent in 981, when seven Viking ships suddenly descended on Southampton. Their crews sacked the town, killing or capturing most of the inhabitants. More Norse raiders struck at points on the coasts of Devon and Cornwall, and Portland was ravaged. The sudden renewal of Viking attacks was due to the consolidation of Norway and Denmark into one kingdom under the iron rule of King Harald Gormsson. He was a Christian, and issued edicts that all his subjects be converted to the faith; those who demurred were ruthlessly weeded out and sent into exile, and it was natural that they should follow the age-old Viking trade of plundering.

After the early attacks there was a six-year respite; then, in 987, the raiders struck at Watchet. It was only a small attack, but in the following year a sizeable Viking force landed in Devon. It was opposed by local militia, and in the ensuing battle the Saxons were heavily defeated and their commander killed.

Ethelred was now 19 years old. He had been barely 12 at the time of his accession, and the kingdom had been virtually ruled by his mother, her brother Ordulf, and Archbishop Dunstan, none of whom were capable of commanding a united English army as the earlier Saxon kings had done. Only Dunstan might have been in a position to advise the young and weak king on the best course of action to take, but the archbishop died in 988, and there was no shrewd adviser to take his place. In 991, a massive Viking raid hit the

---

Sompting (Sussex). The Church of St Mary Blessed Virgin at Sompting, on the eastern fringe of Worthing, dates in part from the early eleventh century. The tower roof is original, as are the tower arch and the interior. *(OS Sheet 198, 161056.)* Visitors may like to make the short journey eastward to **Battle** where, of course, the Normans overcame King Harold's army and ushered in a new era in our history. *(OS Sheet 198, 747160.)*

east coast of Britain. Ninety-three long ships, under the command and Olaf Tryggvason, who was later to become king of Norway, swept down on the area between Sandwich and Ipswich. The latter town went up in flames, and then the Viking fleet anchored in the Blackwater river and the raiders advanced on Maldon. There they were met by a force of Essex militia commanded by Ealdorman Brythnoth. The Danes, it appears, were assembled on Northey Island, which ˙ is separated from the mainland by tidal mudflats and reached by a causeway, covered by the sea at high tide; the English forces took up station on the shore opposite. When the tide ebbed the Vikings launched an attack along the causeway, but were beaten back with considerable loss; then, for some inexplicable reason, the English commander allowed the whole enemy force across before joining battle with it. A savage fight followed, with the Danes—who may have had superior numbers—gradually gaining the upper hand until they surrounded Brythnoth and his personal bodyguard. The Englishmen fought to the bitter end, their shield-wall gradually shrinking as they were cut down, until at last Brythnoth himself fell. At that, the English forces broke and scattered, leaving the Vikings in possession of the field.

The battle was later dramatised in an English epic poem, the 'Battle of Maldon', which made much of the heroic last stand made by Brythnoth and his men. It tells us that the battle took place because Brythnoth flatly refused to pay to the raiders the tribute they demanded, telling them that 'point and blade shall bring us together first, grim battle-play, before we pay tribute'. The pointed message of

the poem is that if other English leaders, notably the king himself, had met the raiders with cold steel instead of gifts, they would have given up and gone elsewhere, just as they had done in the time of Alfred and Edward the Elder.

History, which nicknamed Ethelred the 'Unready'—in other words, lacking in counsel—has placed the blame for the tragic events of the next few years squarely on his shoulders. This may not have been wholly fair. He did take diplomatic steps to reduce the Viking menace; for example, he reached an agreement with Duke Richard I of Normandy that neither would give safe harbour to the other's enemies. This was a very important step, for hitherto the Vikings had always been able to depend on the assistance of their Norse kindred in France. The real cause of the disasters of Ethelred's rule, as his nickname suggests, was most probably the unreliability of his advisers and his military commanders. In 992, when Ethelred ordered all his warships to assemble at London and tried to organise his forces to combat Viking raiders who were plundering around the Thames estuary, the *Chronicle* records that: 'Ealdorman Elfric sent and gave warning to the enemy; and on the night before the day of battle he slipped away from the army, to his great disgrace. The enemy then escaped, except the crew of one ship, who were slain . . .'.

Incredibly, the treacherous Elfric appears to have remained in a position of authority. In 1003 we come across him again in the *Chronicle*, at the head of a great army raised in Wiltshire and Hampshire to do battle with the Danes. Instead of leading his men into action, however, he pretended to be sick; leaderless, the English forces retreated, leaving the enemy free to plunder at will. If this was the calibre of the men upon whom Ethelred was forced to depend, there is little wonder that tragedy followed tragedy, or that the king came to believe that his only course of action was to buy peace. In 994 he made the first of his notorious 'Danegeld' payments to Sweyn, the Viking leader; the sum agreed was 16,000 pounds. The payment brought only a temporary respite; the Vikings were soon back for more, and like any gangsters running a lucrative protection racket they constantly

---

Wickham (Berkshire). The church at Wickham, on the B4000 road that runs north-west from Newbury, had a strong defensive tower with an entrance on the first floor, like the one at Earl's Barton. It is of tenth century date. *(OS Sheet 174, 394715.)*

Worth (Sussex). The church of St Nicholas at Worth, on the eastern outskirts of Crawley, has a chancel arch 22 ft high, which is said to be the largest of its kind. *(OS Sheet 187, 302362.)*

increased their demands. Their tactics were simple. They would descend on some point on the coast, pillage the district to make it absolutely clear what they would do if their demands were not met, and then name their sum. In 1001, after plundering in Devon and Hampshire, it was 24,000 pounds, and this was only the beginning. In great lumps, the wealth so carefully accumulated by Ethelred's predecessors was being squandered.

In 1002, Ethelred—doubtless panic-stricken and overwhelmed by pressures from all sides—gave an order that was to have fearsome consequences on future Danish operations against the island. On November 23, St Brice's Day, he ordered the massacre of every Dane living in England, whether man, woman or child. There is no reason to suppose that his subjects took the frenzied order literally—to do so would have been impossible, anyway, because about a third of the island's population was Danish or of Danish descent—but local massacres may have taken place. It is said that Gunhild, sister of the Viking Sweyn, was among the victims, together with her husband and children. The whole story may well be an exaggeration; it may be that the Danes who were massacred were hostages, and that they were killed because Sweyn's men had broken an agreed truce. The act in itself, however, aroused the Vikings to new heights of violence. During the next four years, in the raiding season, they devastated large areas of England, from East Anglia to Wiltshire, 'harrowing and burning and slaying as they went', defeating the English militia at every turn and departing only when they were paid off. By 1006, the annual Danegeld had risen to 30,000 pounds. Adding to the general misery, in 1005 England was in the grip of the worst famine in living memory, the product perhaps of harvests destroyed or neglected in the previous year's fighting.

By 1007, central government in England was well on the way to collapsing. In east Kent, local leaders made a separate peace with the Danes, paying them 3,000 pounds to be left alone, and the same thing doubtless happened in other areas too. Nevertheless, Ethelred continued to make attempts at keeping the invaders out of Britain. In 1008 he ordered a new fleet to be built, with every man

Penzance (Cornwall). A tenth century cross, with a wheel head and ornamented panel, stands outside Penlees Museum in Morrab Road, Penzance. Known simply as the Penzance Cross, its base bears the inscription REGIS RICATI CRUX (The Cross of King Ricatus).

Sancreed (Cornwall). Of the five crosses to be seen in the churchyard of the little village of Sancreed, at least two date from the Dark Age period. One stands by the path and is 9 ft tall; it carries an inscription which may be of fifth or sixth century date, but which now is almost illegible. The other cross, standing near the south porch, dates from the tenth century and bears a crucifixion together with some fine ornamental work. Sancreed lies three miles west of Penzance. *(OS Sheet 203, 420293.)*

Cardinham (Cornwall). There is a very fine Dark Age cross here, with a tapered shaft and circular head; it stands outside the south porch of the church and displays ornamental work of carved interlace, running spirals and ring-chain. It is, in fact, the only cross with ring-chain work in southern England, and probably dates from the tenth century. Cardinham is three miles north-east of Bodmin. *(OS Sheet 200, 124687.)*

Winterbourne Steepleton (Dorset). The church of St Michael and All Angels here has a nave which is of Anglo-Saxon origin. The church was built sometime between 950 and 1100, and the external south wall boasts a carved angel in a rather awkward upside-down posture. *(OS Sheet 194, 629898.)*

Corhampton (Hampshire). The Saxon church here has a nave and chancel dating from the eleventh century, and the jambs of the chancel arch are of similar style to those of the famous church at Escomb in Co Durham. The chancel was extensively rebuilt and extended following a collapse in 1855. Corhampton village lies 11 miles south-east of Winchester, from where it can be reached by following minor roads or, alternatively, by taking the A32 Alton-Fareham road. *(OS Sheet 185, 612202.)*

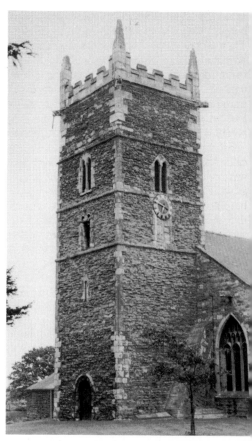

The church of St John the Baptist in Alkborough, close to the Humber, was first built very shortly before the conquest, and there are traces of original Saxon work in the lower stages of the tower.

who owned 310 hides of land commanded to provide the funds for one ship, while those who owned as little as eight hides had to provide a helmet and breastplate. The ships were ready by the following year, and the *Chronicle* tells us what happened next.

'In this year [1009] the ships . . . were ready, and there were more of them, according to what the books tell us, than there had ever been before in England in the days of any king. They were all brought together off Sandwich, to be stationed there to protect this realm against every invading host. But no more than on previous occasions were we to enjoy the good fortune or the honour of naval operations which would be advantageous to this land. About this same time or a little before, it happened that Beorhtric, the brother of the ealdorman Eadric, made an accusation to the king against Wulfnoth, a nobleman of Sussex, and he then fled the country and succeeded in winning over as many as 20 ships, and went

harrying everywhere along the south coast, and did all manner of evil. Then information was brought to the fleet that they [the rebel ships] could easily be surrounded if the opportunity were seized. Then the aforesaid Beorhtric procured 80 ships, and thought to win great fame for himself by taking Wulfnoth dead or alive. But when his ships were on their way, he was met by a storm worse than anyone could remember: the ships were all battered and knocked to pieces and cast ashore. Then that Wulfnoth came straightway and burned the ships. When news of the fate of these ships reached the rest of the fleet under the command of the king, then it was as if everything was in confusion, for the king, the ealdormen and the chief councillors went home, abandoning the ships thus irresponsibly. Then those who remained with the ships brought them back to London, thus inconsiderately allowing the effort of the whole nation to come to naught, so that the threat to the Danes, upon which the whole of England had set its hopes, turned out to be no more potent than this.'

Ethelred was certainly not of the same calibre as his forebears. Yet some Englishmen were prepared to stand and fight in the face of all odds; one such was Ulfketil, who struck hard at the invaders in East Anglia whenever the opportunity arose. The tragedy was that such men were in no position to weld together the scattered English defenders into a cohesive fighting force; there was no Arthur or Alfred to emerge and take the leadership.

Meanwhile, Ethelred and his councillors were chasing their own tails and trying to make up their minds what to do. The *Chronicle* tells us that whatever course of action was decided upon, it was not followed even for a single month, and that the Saxon militia was sent off on one wild goose chase after another. Either the Danes had become expert at eluding the local levies, or the latter had no idea where to look for the enemy. In the end, '. . . there was no leader who was willing to raise levies, but each fled as quickly as he could; nor even in the end would one shire help another'.

In 1011 Ethelred and his councillors sent emissaries to the Danes, begging for peace on almost any terms. By this time, according to the *Chronicle*, the enemy had overrun East Anglia, Essex, Middlesex, Oxfordshire, Cambridgeshire, Hertfordshire, Buckinghamshire, Bedfordshire, half of Huntingdonshire, Kent, Sussex, Surrey, Berkshire, Hampshire and much of Wiltshire. They also took Canterbury, apparently with the help of a treacherous abbot named Aelfmaer, and demanded 48,000 pounds to leave Kent alone, seizing Archbishop Aelfheah as security. He was held at Greenwich until Easter 1012, when the necessary sum was raised and paid over to the Danes in silver. Even then, the Danes were not content; they demanded a separate ransom for the archbishop, and when it was not forthcoming—Aelfheah himself having forbidden

> **Daglingworth (Gloucestershire).** The nave and chancel of the church of the Holy Cross at Daglingworth, three miles northwest of Cirencester, are of late Saxon date. There is a Saxon sundial in the porch (although the building of the porch at a later date effectively obscured it from the sun) and some notable sculptures, including a crucifixion above the east gable, a seated Christ and a figure that probably represents St Peter inside the church itself. *(OS Sheet 163, 994050.)*

anyone to try and raise it—they pelted him to death with bones of cattle, one of them delivering the coup de grace with the blunt end of an axe-head.

By the middle of the following year, the English 'empire' created by Athelstan had fallen apart. In August, a large Viking fleet commanded by Sweyn appeared off the East Coast, sailing inland via the Humber and the Trent to Gainsborough, where the Danes set up a base camp. Within a few months, Sweyn's forces, striking south, had secured control of almost the whole of the country; Oxford and Winchester surrendered to him, although the citizens of London continued to put up a spirited resistance, only submitting to him after most of England had acknowledged him as king.

Ethelred, who had taken refuge in London while the Danes hammered at its gates, now fled to the Isle of Wight, where he spent a miserable Christmas before crossing to Normandy with his wife and sons. The last obstacle to complete Danish domination of the island had been removed—or so it seemed. Then, in February 1014, Sweyn died at Gainsborough, and the Danish army chose his son Canute (Knut Sweynsson) as their king. Instead of making some immediate move to consolidate the position won by his father, however, Canute did nothing, and the English councillors saw a golden opportunity to break the Danish stranglehold. They recalled Ethelred from exile, saying that he was dearer to them than any other lord, if only he would govern his kingdom more justly than he had done in the past. Ethelred grasped the olive branch with both hands, promising that he would be a gracious lord and forgive all the wrongs that had been done or said against him, if all his subjects once more gave him their full allegiance. He came home during Lent, to be 'received with joy'.

On learning of Ethelred's return Canute decided to act at last, and began raising levies in the north, particularly in the Lindsey district. It was Ethelred, however, who struck the first blow, sending his troops into Lindsey to ravage the countryside by way of punishment for his subjects who had supported the Danes. Canute got away by sea, taking with him some hostages who had originally been held by his father; he landed them at Sandwich, minus their hands and noses, before sailing away to Denmark to confer with his elder brother Harold, who was now king there.

Ethelred, meanwhile, negotiated with the Danish army that was encamped at Greenwich and forestalled any military action they might take by paying over 21,000 pounds in Danegeld. It seemed that he had not learned by his earlier mistakes. Even so, the Danes might

---

Oxford. The Ashmolean Museum in Beaumont Street has a fine collection of objects from Anglo-Saxon cemeteries, including gold, jewellery and weapons. Among the latter is the Abingdon Sword, which was found in a tributary of the Thames; it is iron, with a silver decoration on the hilt. The most famous exhibit is the so-called Alfred Jewel, which is probably a kind of book-mark and was discovered near Athelney in 1693. It is made of gold and bears the inscription 'Alfred had me made' in Anglo-Saxon. Apart from the museum, the west tower of the church of St Michael in Cornmarket Street is of Saxon origin and has some fine Saxon windows.

Diddlebury (Shropshire). About four miles further north of Ludlow, on the B4368 close to Wenlock Edge, the church of St Peter in Diddlebury has a Saxon north nave wall. The original church was built very shortly before the Norman conquest. An interesting point is that the structure incorporates a good deal of herringbone work, one thought to be exclusively Norman but, in this case, definitely Saxon. *(OS Sheet 138, 508854.)*

---

have moved against him if the south-east had not been hit by appalling floods in the autumn, drowning many people on both sides and depriving many more of their winter shelter and stores.

So 1015 dawned in misery; it was to be a decisive year for England, and it began with a domestic squabble between Ethelred and his eldest son, Edmund. In February or thereabouts, a Mercian ealdorman named Eadric murdered two East Anglian thanes, whose property was then taken over by Ethelred. Edmund, however, determined to seize the estates for himself; breaking away from his father, he assembled a small army and marched on Lindsey, where he was accepted as king by the five boroughs of Derby, Leicester, Lincoln, Nottingham and Stamford and the people round about. He also married the widow of one of the murdered thanes, which was probably why he decided on his course of action in the first place.

Meanwhile, Canute returned from Denmark with a fleet and landed in Wessex. While his men plundered in Dorset, Somerset and Wiltshire, Edmund, in a dubious alliance with Ealdorman Eadric, raised forces to meet the threat, but they failed to agree on a concerted war plan and the two armies separated. It was just as well, for Eadric secretly planned to throw in his lot with Canute.

Edmund's efforts to raise an army during the winter of 1015 were frustrated time after time by the unwillingness of local levies to serve under him. They wanted Ethelred to lead them, but Ethelred was a sick man. The 'campaigns' of those winter months, and of the early spring of 1016, were nothing more than large-scale pillaging expeditions by bands of lawless men, with the forces of Canute and Eadric 'plundering and burning and slaying all they met' in Mercia while Edmund's men, joined by the levies of his brother-in-law Uhtred of Northumbria, harried the west midlands.

Suddenly, Canute's army abandoned their pillaging and swung northwards along the Fosse Way towards York. Uhtred, in turn, broke off his evil work in the midlands and moved to oppose him, whereupon Edmund managed to impose some order on his English forces and marched to London, where he

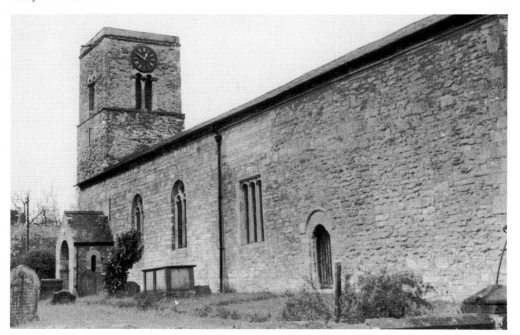

joined his ailing father. He was only just in time, for Ethelred '. . . ended his days on St George's Day [April 23] after a life of much hardship and many difficulties. Then after his death all the councillors who were in London, and the citizens, chose Edmund as king, and he defended his kingdom valiantly during his lifetime.'

The Londoners may have given Edmund their allegiance, but the leaders of the rest of the country did not. Instead, they offered it to Canute, if he would rule wisely and justly. Canute, who was then at Southampton with his warships, agreed, and sailed his fleet round into the Thames to attack London. Edmund, meanwhile, marched on Wessex, where he raised more loyalist forces, and either in May or June he fought two battles, one at Pensel-

The church of St Michael at Glentworth, north of Lincoln, has an eleventh century tower. The original west doorway has been blocked up, but its outline is still visible.

Wootton Wawen (Warwickshire). The church of St Peter in Wootton Wawen, six miles north-west of Stratford-on-Avon, has an eleventh century tower constructed in the years immediately before the Norman conquest. Its four arches show that the original church was cruciform, and display Escomb-style architecture. *(OS Sheet 151, 153633.)*

Stanton Lacy (Shropshire). The village of Stanton Lacy lies three miles north of Ludlow. The north and west walls of the nave of the village church, and also those of the north transept, are of tenth or eleventh century date. Two Saxon doors also remain; one, though blocked up, is particularly fine and has a cross in relief above it. *(OS Sheet 138, 496788.)*

Shelford (Nottinghamshire). At the church of St Peter in Shelford, eight miles north-east of Nottingham, there is a splendid example of Saxon sculpture dating from the middle of the eleventh century. Standing just under 3 ft high, it displays a bearded seraph on one side and the Virgin and Child on the other. The edges are decorated with interlace and scroll work. *(OS Sheet 129, 662424.)*

Leicester. At one time the important Roman city of Ratae Coritanorum, Leicester today boasts the church of St Nicholas, which stands in the town centre and has a nave dating from the tenth or eleventh century. Excavation has shown that an area in the vicinity of the nearby Jewry Wall was occupied in the fifth century.

Stapleford (Nottinghamshire). In St Helen's churchyard here there is a fine cross, 10 ft high, which was substantially restored in the nineteenth century. The original dates from the eleventh century and the shaft is decorated with interlace. Stapleford is just off the M1 eight miles east of Derby.

Bracebridge (Lincolnshire). The church of All Saints in the village of Bracebridge, two miles south of Lincoln, has an eleventh century tower and several other late Saxon features, including chancel arches and nave. *(OS Sheet 121, 968679.)*

Branston (Lincolnshire). Another church of All Saints, four miles south-east of Lincoln, the building at Branston also has a late Saxon tower, but the west wall of the nave is of somewhat earlier date. *(OS Sheet 121, 021673.)*

wood in Somerset and the other at Sherston in Wiltshire. The enemy in both cases were probably Wessex forces who had sided with Canute, rather than an army commanded by Canute himself. Those battles, although not decisive by any means, resulted in victories for Edmund and must have given his followers new heart. With a substantial army behind him, he marched on London to lift the Danish siege, cleverly keeping north of the Thames and then advancing on the city for an entirely unexpected direction through the woods to the north, at Clayhill Farm in Tottenham. Taking the Danes by surprise, the English army stormed their earthworks and drove them out. As the Danes streamed back in disorder to their ships Edmund made a triumphal entry into London. Two days later his troops marched upriver to Brentford, crossing by the ford there, and engaged the Danish forces on the south bank. Once again the English won a victory, but their losses were so severe that Edmund was forced to pull back to Wessex to raise more men.

As soon as Edmund had departed Canute tried to take London again, but was repulsed. His fleet then sailed to the mouth of the River Orwell, in Essex, and from here he despatched raiding parties into Mercia to forage for supplies. With these safely on board his ships, Canute sailed into the Medway and prepared to renew his offensive operations. Before he was ready, however, Edmund was upon him with a fresh army, and in a fierce battle at Otford, near Sevenoaks, the Danes were soundly thrashed. According to the *Chronicle*, the enemy panicked at the first English charge and they streamed back towards Sheppey, Edmund's cavalry cutting them down as they fled.

It was now that Edmund made his greatest mistake. In the wake of the Otford battle, the treacherous Eadric of Mercia approached the king and offered his allegiance, which Edmund accepted. The consequences were to prove disastrous. In the autumn of 1016, however, the English were riding high on a wave of triumph, and Edmund seemed set fair to deal a final, crushing blow to Danish aspirations. He assembled yet another army, or rather three armies in one; as well as the West Saxons, there were forces from East Anglia under

Ulfketil, who had fought so valiantly in previous years, and troops from Mercia under Eadric. On October 18, the English army confronted Canute's forces at Assandun, the hill of ash trees, which is Ashingdon in Essex, where the ground rises slightly a few miles north of Southend between the estuaries of the Thames and the Crouch. Edmund attacked first, and no sooner had he done so than the treacherous Eadric pulled back his Mercian levies, leaving Edmund's flank wide open. There was nothing the English could do to redress the situation. They fought with desperate valour, but in the end they were overwhelmed and all but annihilated. The brave Ulfketil died, as did the ealdormen of Hampshire and Lindsey and many other nobles. Edmund himself barely managed to get away; with a handful of survivors he escaped to Gloucestershire, where, still refusing to acknowledge defeat, he promptly set about raising more levies.

At this point Eadric of Mercia appears on the scene again, this time in the curious role of intermediary. According to the *Chronicle*, he approached Canute, who was pursuing Edmund, and advised him to make peace with the English king. As a result, the two leaders met at Deerhurst, on the Severn, and swore eternal friendship, exchanging gifts as a preliminary to the real business, which was the division of the island between them. The bargain was heavily weighted in Canute's favour; he got everything except Wessex, which Edmund retained. Within a month of this one-sided agreement being concluded, Edmund died at Ross-on-Wye in somewhat mysterious circumstances. According to one account, he was fatally wounded by an assassin at Minsterworth, on the west bank of the Severn. This seems very likely, and if it happened it was probably with Canute's connivance. A live Wessex king would have been a constant threat to him.

It might have given Edmund's spirit some small comfort to know that the man responsible for many of his misfortunes, Eadric of Mercia, was living on borrowed time. Canute gave him Mercia to rule, but clearly did not trust a man who had already betrayed one king. Using a quarrel as a pretext, he had Eadric strangled and his body thrown into the Thames.

Marton (Lincolnshire). The church of St Margaret, three miles west of Stow, has a tower that was built just before the conquest. There is an original window in the west face of the tower, and in the west wall of the aisle there are some fragments of an interlaced Anglo-Saxon cross shaft. *(OS Sheet 121, 840817.)*

Corringham (Lincolnshire). The church of St Lawrence here has an eleventh century Saxon tower and nave walls, and the outline of a Saxon doorway can just be distinguished in the west face of the tower. Corringham is three miles east of Gainsborough. *(OS Sheet 112, 872916.)*

Springthorpe (Lincolnshire). The church of St Lawrence and St George here has an eleventh century Saxon tower, with an original window set high in the west face. The windows in the belfry appear to be Saxon, but are not. *OS Sheet 112, 875898.)*

Canute was accepted as king by the English ealdormen in 1017. In the following year he extracted the last and the biggest Danegeld of all from the English shires; it amounted to 72,000 pounds, and a further 10,500 pounds had to be raised by the unfortunate citizens of London, with whom Canute had a score to settle. Part of the Danish army then sailed away from Britain, Canute retaining 40 ships and their crews to assure his personal defence. On his accession, Canute underwent an extraordinary metamorphosis. He was no longer the cruel semi-barbarian who had mutilated his English hostages only four years earlier, but a devout Christian king who went to amazing lengths to reconcile the English and Danish peoples of Britain. One immediate step he took in this direction was to bring Emma, the widow of Ethelred, out of exile in Normandy and marry her. He was a born showman, as the apocryphal story of efforts to turn back the tide illustrates. When he went on a pilgrimage to Rome in 1027, visiting churches and abbeys en route, he 'advanced humbly and prayed with complete concentration and wonderful reverence for the intercession of the saints, his eyes fixed on the ground and overflowing with a veritable river of tears. And when the time

Left *The church of All Saints at Branston, near Lincoln, has a late Saxon tower and a nave of somewhat earlier date.*
Above *Branston church—window and lower tower detail.*

Below and right *The church of All Saints at Heapham, Lincolnshire, has a late Saxon tower with original belfry windows. The tower arch and the south door to the nave are also Saxon.*

Broughton (Lincolnshire). The tower and the west stair turret of the church of St Mary at Broughton, four miles east of Scunthorpe, are late Saxon. The stair turret, like that at Hough on the Hill in Lincolnshire, makes the church worth a visit, for comparatively few are still in existence. *(OS Sheet 112, 960086.)*

Caistor (Lincolnshire). The former Roman town of Caistor, near the river Ancholme, was occupied in Anglo-Saxon times, and the late Saxon church of St Peter and St Paul was built within the boundaries of the Roman settlement. Traces of the original Saxon work may still be seen in the lower stages of the west tower. In the neighbourhood of Caistor there are three more churches where Saxon architecture may be seen. The first is the church of St John the Baptist in Nettleton, 1½ miles south of Caistor; the second is the church of St Nicholas at Cabourne, a mile to the north-east of Caistor; and the third is the church of St Mary Magdalene at Rothwell, two miles to the east of the Roman town. All are late Saxon. *(Caistor—OS Sheet 113, 116013.)*

Scartho (Lincolnshire). The church of St Giles at Scartho, on the southern outskirts of Grimsby on the A16, shows Saxon masonry in the tower and the nave walls. Late Saxon work is also in evidence in the tower of the church of St Peter at Holton-le-Clay, two miles further south on the same road, and continuing southwards for another four miles or so the village church at Waithe has a very late Saxon axial tower, although the rest of the fabric is the result of nineteenth century restoration work.

Edenham (Lincolnshire). The church of St Michael at Edenham, on the B676 two miles north-west of Bourne, is worth a visit for its two notable sculptures. One is a roundel, 2 ft in diameter and decorated with scrolls at the western end of the south aisle; the other is part of a ninth century cross shaft displaying a carving of St John and another unidentified figure. *(OS Sheet 130, 062219.)*

Heapham (Lincolnshire). This village, standing only a mile from Springthorpe and about four miles south-east of Gainsborough, to the south of the A631, has the church of All Saints, with yet another late Saxon tower. In this case, the belfry windows are Saxon in origin, as are the tower arch and the south door to the nave. *(OS Sheet 112, 878886.)*

Glentworth (Lincolnshire). The church of St Michael in Glentworth, on the B1398 ten miles north of Lincoln, has an eleventh century tower. Although the original west doorway has been blocked up, its outline can still be made out, and inside the church the tower arch is Anglo-Saxon. *(OS Sheet 112, 946881.)*

Alkborough (Lincolnshire). The church of St John the Baptist in Alkborough, close to the Humber, was first built very shortly before the conquest, and the lower stages of the west tower still show evidence of the original Saxon work. To reach the village, take the B1430 north from Scunthorpe and turn on to a minor road at Burton upon Strather. *(OS Sheet 112, 882219.)*

came for heaping the altars with royal offerings, how often did he first press kisses with tears on the pavement . . ..'

He may have been sincere, but one is tempted to doubt whether such was the case. There is, however, no reason to doubt that he ruled wisely. After visiting Denmark briefly in 1019, he spent the early years of the 1020s in England, and among his actions at this time was one that consolidated his position greatly with the English; he reaffirmed that the nation should observe the laws laid down by King Edgar and made his own additions.

In 1023 he returned to Denmark, leaving one of his most trusted advisers, Thorkell the Tall, to act as regent in England during his absence. Making Denmark secure was of paramount importance, for there were warlike rumblings from Norway and Sweden, whose kings had formed an alliance; in 1026 he led an Anglo-Danish naval expedition against the Swedes and fought an engagement which, although inconclusive, forestalled a possible invasion of Denmark. Later, after returning from his pilgrimage to Rome, he laid on a massive show of strength in Northumbria, which had been troubled by a raiding army led by Malcolm II, king of the Scots, and Owen of

Strathclyde. Malcolm, realising that he was not strong enough to try conclusions with Canute, acknowledged him as overlord.

Canute was probably the best-guarded sovereign in English history up to that time. He formed a personal bodyguard of highly-trained and disciplined soldiers called house-carls, all of whom held officer rank and who were paid by an annual levy known as heregeld, or army tax. In other areas, however, military expenditure was gradually reduced; the size of the fleet, for example, was reduced by two-thirds during his reign, an indication of the peace that prevailed.

Canute died at Shaftsbury on November 12 1035, aged about 46. He had ruled England for 18 years; years which, for the first time in centuries, had seen a peaceful and united island freed from foreign attack. But his reign meant more than that. For Canute, Dane though he was, England was home; and it was home, too, for thousands of his fellow-countrymen. At last, the Anglo-Danish kingdom was a reality.

Chapter 13

The end of the beginning

When Canute died, his son by Emma, Harthacnut, was in Denmark, keeping a vigilant eye on the Norwegians who, under a new king named Magnus, were once again becoming troublesome. In his absence, the English earls and thegns elected Harold Harefoot, son of Aelfgifu of Northampton, who was Canute's first wife. The choice created an immediate rift in Wessex, where Queen Emma strove hard to have her son Harthacnut installed on the throne. Then an unexpected complication arose in the person of Alfred, the younger of Emma's two sons by

The church of the Holy Trinity at Great Paxton, Huntingdonshire, is eleventh century and features a very wide chancel arch and an aisled nave, unusual for this period.

Ethelred, who suddenly arrived in England from Normandy. His stated purpose was to be with his mother in Winchester; what is more likely, however, is that he saw some kind of opportunity to seize power with his mother's help. At any rate, he came over with 600 fighting men, which seems rather a large number for a personal escort. He never reached Winchester. He was intercepted at Guildford by Earl Godwin of Wessex, a supporter of Harthacnut's claim, who slaughtered most of the 600 men and took Alfred prisoner. The young man was handed over to Harold Harefoot, who had him so cruelly and savagely blinded that he died of his injuries soon afterwards, while being tended by the monks of Ely.

In 1037, following the acceptance of Harold Harefoot as king everywhere in England, Emma was forced into exile. She went to her kinsfolk at Bruges, where she was later joined by Harthacnut, and it was there, on March 17 1040, that messengers informed mother and son that Harold Harefoot had died of an illness. Harthacnut came to England in June to claim his throne, and was welcomed as Canute's legitimate successor. During his brief two-year reign, however, he succeeded in making himself thoroughly unpopular, mainly because he demanded 32,000 pounds to pay the crews of the fleet he had brought with him. He also outraged churchmen by having the corpse of Harold Harefoot dug up, beheaded, and thrown into the fens. No one, except perhaps Emma, was really sorry when he died in the middle of a drinking bout on June 8 1042.

There does not seem to have been any

Norwich (Norfolk). Any visitor to Norwich should take in the Castle Museum, which contains many Saxon objects from sites all over East Anglia. The city also has several religious houses showing traces of Saxon architecture. These are the Cathedral (west wall of cloister); the church of St John de Sepulcre (transept walls); St John Timberhill (east wall of chancel); St Martin at Palace (east wall of chancel); St Mary at Coslany (Saxon round tower); and St Julian's off King Street, the best example of all, which has a Saxon round tower and nave walls. In addition, some churches in the immediate area of Norwich are worth visiting because of their Saxon connections. The round tower of the church of St Peter in Forncett St Peter, nine miles south-west of the city, has a round tower that is of late Saxon date, as are parts of the west wall of the nave; the church of St Mary at Howe, six miles south-east of Norwich, also has a late Saxon round tower and nave; at Framlingham Earl, five miles south-east, the Saxon round tower, nave and chancel are all intact, as they are in the church of St Mary at Colney, four miles west of the city; and another Saxon round tower may be seen at the church of St Lawrence at Beeston, ten miles north-east.

Stoughton (Sussex). Most of the structure of the church of St Mary at Stoughton, north of Chichester, dates from the years immediately before the Norman conquest. Earl Godwin had a wealthy manor at Stoughton, and it may have been on his initiative that the church was built. Saxon features that can still be seen are the outlines of the north and south doors and the large Saxon windows in the transepts. To reach Stoughton, take the B2178 out of Chichester as far as the junction with the B2146; turn right along this road for two miles, then right again on to a minor road leading to Stoughton village. *(OS Sheet 197, 801115.)*

Carew (Dyfed). There is a very important cross here, beside Carew Castle on the south side of the A4075 road from Pembroke Dock. Standing over 13 ft high, it is covered with fret and interlace patterns and bears an inscription which reads in translation 'The cross of Margiteut, son of Etguin'. Margiteut is Meredudd ap Edwin, who was killed in 1033. *(OS Sheet 158, 047037.)*

Above *The church of St Margaret at Marton, Lincolnshire, has a tower which was built just before the conquest. There is an original window in the west face of the tower.*
Below *Marton church—lower tower detail.*

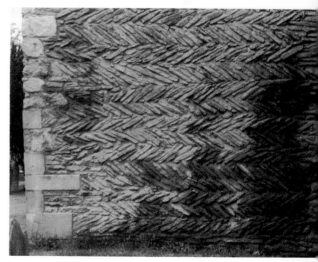

dispute over his successor. Edward, the elder son of Ethelred and Emma, came from Normandy and was unanimously accepted by all the peoples of England. His mother, however, played no part in his rise to power, for there was no love lost between the two. Edward, in fact, confiscated all Emma's estates, although he allowed her to live in comparative luxury at Winchester.

Once again, a king of the royal line of Wessex sat on the throne of England; yet in outlook, speech and manner, Edward was thoroughly Norman and had little affinity with the English after his 25 years abroad. He ruled from a position of isolation, partly because he distrusted the powerful Saxon families who surrounded him, but mainly because he never felt quite at home in England. Of his piety there was no doubt—his nickname of 'Confessor' was not bestowed lightly—but he made the mistake of importing clergy from France and Normandy, much to the fury of the English bishops, particularly when he made a Norman Archbishop of Canterbury. Also, he openly favoured the Norman nobility, and encouraged his friend Duke William of Normandy to think that he was Edward's chosen successor. This may have been part of a scheme to discredit Earl Godwin of Essex, whom he disliked intensely. Godwin, with some support, appears to have openly challenged Edward at one stage, for he was compelled to seek refuge abroad; but he returned in 1052 and his homecoming marked the temporary end of Norman influence, for Edward's English subjects refused to fight against the Wessex nobleman and the Witenagemot, the Great Council of England, voted for the restoration of his lands and the expulsion of all foreigners from Edward's realm. It was a slap in the eye for William of Normandy, who had assembled a fleet in readiness to come to

---

Roughton (Norfolk). The church of St Mary at Roughton, four miles south of Cromer, has a round tower and nave west wall dating from the late Saxon period. One noteworthy feature is the west door from the tower, which opens into the church at a height of 16 ft above ground level. The tower has an interesting mixture of circular and slit windows. A few miles to the west of Roughton, the church of St Mary at Bessingham has a very late Saxon round tower. *(OS Sheet 133, 220366.)*

Cambridge. The Cambridge Museum is well worth a visit, as it contains a good collection of objects from Dark Age cemeteries which have been excavated in the area. The church of St Bene't (an abbreviation of Benedict) near the Guildhall has a tower and nave dating from the mid-tenth century, and although the building was substantially restored in the nineteenth century much original Saxon work is still to be seen.

Great Tey (Essex). The church of St Barnabas in this village, eight miles west of Colchester, shows tenth century Saxon workmanship in the lower stages of the tower. *(OS Sheet 168, 892258.)*

Colchester (Essex). Colchester was the site of the first major legionary fortress, and later (in 49 AD) of the first Roman town in Britain. Subsequent Anglo-Saxon settlers in the area consequently found a wealth of building materials ready to hand, and this fact shows in the church of Holy Trinity, a tenth century building just south of the High Street. Part of the tower and west wall of the nave are original; the tower arch is build of Roman brick.

Strethall (Essex). Three miles north-west of Saffron Walden, the village of Strethall boasts the fine little church of St Mary the Virgin, which has an eleventh century nave and chancel arch, the latter with Escomb-style jambs. Three miles further north, excavation work has been carried out around the church of St Botolph at Hadstock, where there are a few remains of the original tenth century church structure. *(OS Sheet 154, 485398.)*

Guestwick (Norfolk). The church of St Peter in this village, nine miles east of Fakenham, has a late Saxon lower tower, and Saxon masonry is also visible in parts of the chancel. Visitors should look for the blocked arch in the west face, where there is a carving of a muzzled animal, possibly a bear, on the jamb. *OS Sheet 133, 061270.)*

Edward's aid, sensing a golden opportunity of consolidated his own position still further.

The need to call on a Norman fleet arose from the fact that Edward's navy, by 1050, had shrunk to only five ships. This was by deliberate policy, for—apart from one or two sporadic pirate raids, usually by warbands from Ireland—the shores of England were secure. Norway and Denmark were concerned with their own internal affairs, and only once did Norwegian ships attack in strength. The raid, very badly recorded in the *Chronicle*, took place in 1058 and was led by the Norwegian king's son, Magnus Haroldsson.

Earl Godwin died in 1053, and his son Harold Godwinsson succeeded to the earldom of Wessex. He also inherited much of his father's considerable influence, which was extended when his brother, Tostig, became earl of Northumbria. Tostig, however, proved a cruel overlord, and in 1065 his subjects rose

Two views of one of the City of Lincoln's fine Saxon churches—St Peter-at-Gowts, in the High Street.

Beachamwell (Norfolk). The church of St Mary at Beachamwell, five miles south-west of Swaffham, is a thatched building standing in attractive surroundings, has a late Saxon tower, chancel and nave. The tower is round and displays four belfry windows. *(OS Sheet 143, 751054.)*

Newton by Castleacre (Norfolk). Much of the Saxon architecture in the village church here, four miles north of Swaffham, has been obscured by later mediaeval work, but traces of the original Saxon structure are to be seen in the nave, chancel and axial tower. *(OS Sheet 132, 830156.)*

Great Dunham (Norfolk). The church of St Andrew at Great Dunham, five miles north-east of Swaffham, is one of Norfolk's finest Anglo-Saxon structures. The nave and axial tower both date from the late Saxon period, and the arcading inside—the rows of arches on columns—is very fine and unusual in design. The arches themselves are of Roman brick. *(OS Sheet 132, 874147.)*

East Lexham (Norfolk). Two miles north of Great Dunham, the church of St Andrew at East Lexham has a tenth century round tower, nave and chancel. *(OS Sheet 132, 860172.)*

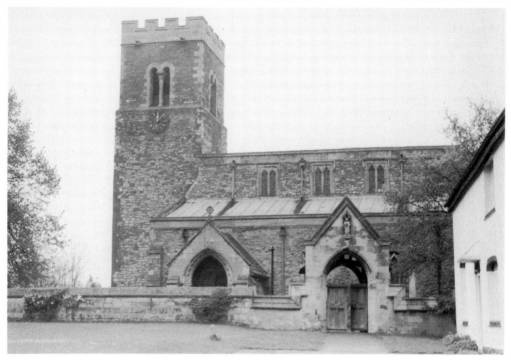

Above *The church of St Lawrence at Corringham, Lincolnshire, has an eleventh century tower and nave walls.*
Left *The outline of a Saxon doorway can just be made out in the west face of Corringham church tower, below the belfry window.*

against him and drove him out, replacing him with Earl Morcar. Tostig, quite irrationally, blamed Harold for not having come to his aid, although his downfall had been the direct result of his own excesses, and spent the next few months in Flanders, brooding on revenge. His intrigues were to play no small part in shaping the destiny of England.

Edward the Confessor died on January 5 1066. He left no children; indeed, it was widely rumoured that his marriage to Earl Godwin's daughter was never consummated. The direct heir to the throne was Edgar, the son of Edward's dead brother Alfred, but he was only a child; the Witenagemot therefore had no hesitation in choosing Harold Godwinsson. He was a Wessex man through and through, and he had moreover proved himself in battle, having fought and defeated a Welsh army ten years earlier.

Haddiscoe Thorpe (Norfolk). The church of St Matthias here, nine miles south-west of Great Yarmouth, is another thatched building. The tower under the belfry is Saxon, as are three of the windows in it. The west wall of the nave is probably tenth century, a good deal earlier than the tower itself. *(OS Sheet 134, 436981.)*

So Harold was king; but it was not his destiny to wear the crown for long, or in peace. From the moment of his accession he was haunted by fears of a Norman invasion, and from the amount of military preparation that was going on in Normandy in the spring of 1066 it was clear that William was planning to assert his claim to the English throne by force of arms. Then there was the problem of Tostig, still plotting in Flanders and in contact with Harold Hardrada of Norway, who also considered that he had a legitimate claim to Harold Godwinsson's realm. That April, terrified people flocked to the churches in their thousands all over England as a great comet trailed its lurid tresses across the night sky. Nothing like it had been seen for more than 70 years, when the Vikings had spread blood and fire over the island in the time of Ethelred. To the Anglo-Saxons, the periodic appearance of Halley's Comet spelled doom and disaster. The Normans, on the other hand, saw it as a harbinger of future victory. When the harvest was safely in, and the winds of early autumn blew from the south—then would be the time to strike.

A window of St Ninian's Chapel on the Isle of Whithorn, on the Solway coast in Wigtownshire. See photograph on page 192.

Part Four:
Scotland in the Dark Ages

Chapter 14

The painted warriors

The early history of Dark Age Scotland, peopled by tribes known to the more southerly British Celts as the Gwr y Gogledd, the Men of the North, is shrouded in mystery. In other areas to which their influence extended, often far beyond the physical boundaries of the Empire, the Romans identified with considerable accuracy the various barbarian tribes and their territory; no such record, however, exists of the Iron Age peoples of the land north of the Forth-Clyde isthmus. Only one people, presumably the most threatening and warlike of all, the Picts, rises to prominence in the writing of Roman historians, and *Picti* is a Latin word, meaning the Painted People. Only scant clues exist as to which tribes comprised them, and what they called themselves; the Irish knew them as the Cruithni, or British, and the land they inhabited as Alba. Their homeland appears to have been a large block of territory in central Scotland comprising Fife, Strathmore, Athol and Fortrenn, but their influence must have extended beyond their tribal frontier; they certainly exercised domination over neighbouring tribes.

Nothing is known of the Pictish kings until the fifth century, and then an Irish source names one of them. He was Drust, son of Erp, and his reign appears to have lasted from 414 to his death in 458. According to Irish tradition he fought 'a hundred battles', which means that he was a warrior of considerable renown. It was in his time that the greatest threat materialised from the north against Vortigern's Britain, compelling Vortigern to enlist the aid of Germanic mercenaries and so,

inadvertently, laying the foundation of what was to become the English nation.

The Picts were masters of eastern Scotland, between the Forth and the Moray Firth. They had nothing in common with the other Caledonian tribes who made their homes among the lochs and islands of the west, or who peopled the Orkneys and built the formidable round stone castles known as brochs. No one knows from whence these people came, but they must have come as conquerors, for once their conquest was completed they abandoned their strongholds and moved into more convenient settlements nearby. Even more enigmatic are the people mentioned by the Romans in the fourth century, the Atecotti, whose tribal area is unknown and who may have been responsible for the undecipherable script, resembling ogham, which has been found on a number of memorial stones.

The Picts were not a single tribe, but rather a confederation of tribes whose names, according to fragmentary Latin sources, may have been Caledonii, Vacomagi, Taezali and Venicones. The Caledonians, grouped in what is now Perthshire, seem to have been the most important; their name survives today in Shiehallion, 'the sacred hill of the Caledonians', and Dunkeld, the 'fort of the Caledonians'. These tribes seem gradually to have merged, but late in the fourth century there was still a clear division, according to the historian Ammianus, who says that the Picts comprised the Dicalydones (Caledonians) and the Verturiones, the latter living to the south in the area of the Antonine Wall.

Jedburgh (Roxburghshire). The museum at Jedburgh, on the A68 (the old Roman Dere Street) is part of the abbey on the southern outskirts of the town, and contains several Dark Age stones, including one from a shrine that may have belonged to St Boisil, abbott of Melrose and friend of St Cuthbert. Travelling further north, it is worth branching off the A68 at Newton St Boswells along the A6091 road to Melrose, taking in the majestic Eildon Hills and the site of the Roman fort of Trimontium (Newstead). Nothing remains of the fort now, apart from a simple monument, but it may well have been used as a base during the frontier wars between Bernicia and Urien's Rheged.

Orphir (Orkney). Here, eight miles south-west of Kirkwall (take a minor road south off the A964 at Swanbister) stand the remains of the only surviving mediaeval round church in Scotland, although the ruins consist only of the little chancel and a fragment of the nave wall. The church is of Norse origin and is mentioned in the Icelandic *Orkneyinga Saga* of the thirteenth century; this also tells of an Earl's drinking hall, the foundations of which can still be made out near the church. There was probably once a large Norse settlement at Orphir, but a lot of it doubtless dates from the post-Dark Age period. *(OS Sheet 7, 334044.)*

Broch of Gurness (Orkney). The brochs of northern Scotland and the Isles were stone towers originally erected in the Iron Age. Most were abandoned in the early centuries AD, but many were subsequently reoccupied and refortified in the Dark Ages. One such was Gurness Broch, eleven miles north-west of Kirkwall on a headland near Evie, a mile and a half north of the A966. This was a Pictish stronghold from about the fifth century, and was the scene of substantial rebuilding with the coming of the Vikings, who among other buildings erected a long house. The site museum contains many objects discovered during excavations in the 1930s; more finds from the excavated grave of a Viking woman, including a pair of tortoise brooches, are in Tankerness House Museum, Kirkwall. *(OS Sheet 6, 383268.)*

Ring of Brodgar (Orkney). The fine stone circle that lies on the isthmus between the Lochs of Harray and Stenness, four miles north-east of Stromness, is prehistoric, but is also notable for its Dark Age graffiti. Counting clockwise from the north-west entrance, stone No 3 has an inscription in an unknown script, No 4 has a cross, No 8 an anvil and No 9 an ogham inscription. The latter is almost certainly Pictish, the rest of Norse origin. *(OS Sheet 6, 294133.)*

Brough of Birsay (Orkney). A tidal island connected to the mainland by a causeway, but cut off at high tide, the Brough of Birsay lies 20 miles north-west of Kirkwall and can be reached via the A966. This is the leading religious site on Orkney, and was occupied by both Picts and Norsemen. There is a good museum on the site, displaying finds from several excavations, most of them to do with the Viking period of occupation. No traces of the Pictish occupation remain, other than a cemetery and what may be part of a wall of an early Pictish church, built over by the later Norse structure. Nevertheless, the Pictish occupation must have been extensive, because excavation of a midden in the 1930s turned up many objects associated with a flourishing metalworking industry. A Pictish grave slab, bearing sculptures of an eagle, a creature resembling an elephant, and three armed bearded figures, was also found, and a recon-struction of this can be seen on the site. The remains of the Norse church stand within the Viking cemetery, and when excavating the interior of the church archaeologists found a wooden coffin with a skeleton which might be that of Earl Thorfinn, whose seat this once was. The church was built in the middle of the eleventh century, and shows some Anglo-Saxon influence. More Dark Age remains lie between the church and the cliff; they include the foundations of a tenth century building known as Earl Sigurd's Hall, over which a later structure, Earl Thorfinn's Palace, was built. The remnants of this are in turn obscured by other buildings erected in the twelfth century and later. On the hillside above the church there are two partly-excavated long houses, dating from either the ninth or tenth century. *(OS Sheet 6, 239285.)*

Above *The building known as St Ninian's Chapel on the Isle of Whithorn is mediaeval, but is thought to stand on the site of a much earlier building. St Ninian founded a religious house at Whithorn in the fifth century and set about converting the pagan tribes of Caledonia.*

Below and **bottom** *Chapel Finian, overlooking Luce Bay in Wigtownshire, was probably founded by Irish monks in the tenth century. The ruins are surrounded by a drystone wall. The original building was dedicated to St Findbar.*

Maes Howe (Orkney). There is a splendid collection of runic graffiti inside the neolithic burial mound at Maes Howe, beside the A965 about nine miles west of Kirkwall, and although all of it probably dates from the twelfth century it should certainly not be missed by Dark Age enthusiasts. Two of the lengthier inscriptions record how Norsemen carried away great treasure from the mound, and another tells how one of a Viking party who sheltered in the howe from a storm went crazy. There is also the carved figure of a dragon, some personal names, a drawing of a walrus and some runic scribblings about women. *(OS Sheet 6, 317127.)*

Jarlshof (Shetland). This very important archaeological site lies a few hundred yards south-east of the airport buildings at Sumburgh, off the A970. There was a settlement here from neolithic times, and it is easy to see why Norse settlers chose the same site, for the bay on which Jarlshof stands provides an excellent natural harbour. Sorting our the various remains seems a formidable task at first sight, but a visit to the site museum helps to clarify things and, in fact, visitors pass the remains of the Bronze and Iron Age broch and dark Age wheelhouses from the entrance. Past the museum, by the edge of the sea, there are the remnants of an Iron Age brooch and Dark Age wheelhouses —circular stone huts with piers radiating towards a central hub where the hearth stood. These are late Iron Age in origin, but were reoccupied during the Dark Ages. To the north-west of the wheelhouses, another structure known as the Passge House is of late Dark Age date; this comprises three chambers with a sloping passage leading to them. Excavation has shown that it was used as a byre, but it may have been a human dwelling before that. Fifty yards west of the Passage House are the remains of some stone huts, where excavators found a cross engraved on a slate slab, probably dating from the eighth century. The Vikings came to Jarlshof in the ninth century, and the principal relics of their occupation lie to the north of the seventeenth century Laird's House; the original Viking building was a classic long house, which had additions made to it at regular intervals up to the thirteenth century. This central house was surrounded in the ninth and tenth centuries by other smaller buildings, but it needs a close examination of the official guide book to unravel their plans. *(OS Sheet 4, 398095.)*

Many of the Picts, in the south at any rate, seem to have embraced Christianity in the early years of the fifth century, for St Patrick, writing in the 440s, denounced them for renouncing it. Who the early missionaries were is not known, although, according to Bede, their work was inspired by Ninian of Whithorn, in Galloway. The move away from Christianity appears to have gained impetus in Drust's lengthy reign, and probably resulted from the renewed Pictish offensive against the Christian Roman province south of Hadrian's Wall. However, Christianity was revived in the years after Drust's death by his successor kings, and in particular by Nectan Morbet, who reigned from 462 to 486.

After Nectan the lists of Pictish kings are confused. It may be that Pictland was divided about 530, probably as a result of the southern part being overrun by the Scots of Dalriada. Not until the 550s does Pictish history begin to untangle itself, and then only because in that decade the Picts looked beyond their own territorial boundaries in their search for a new and strong king. The man they chose to rule them was Bridei mac Maelcon, who was without doubt the son of Maelgwn, the powerful king of Gwynedd. The choice seems strange until one realises that the Pictish royal inheritance passed through the female line, rather than the male; it was a system under which no son ever succeeded his father, so preventing the rise of corrupt and tyrannical dynasties. Bridei, son of Maelgwn, had Pictish blood, for his great-grandmother had been a

Dumfries. The 'Fortress of the Frisians', Dumfries may have been a military stronghold for German mercenaries deliberately settled in the lowlands during the fifth century. Today, the Dumfries Museum houses finds from all over south-west Scotland, dating from the fifth to the eleventh centuries; the splendid collection of Dark Age stones in the basement deserves special attention.

Pict. He succeeded in 554 and for a while ruled only in the north, a rival king—presumably a puppet of the Dalriada Scots—controlling the Pictish lands to the south. Then, in retaliation for attacks on Gwynedd by an alliance of North British kings, Bridei's brother Rhun assembled a great army and marched north; in the course of his punitive expedition to the Clyde he passed through the southern territory of the Picts and appears to have occupied it for a time, driving out the rival king and leaving his brother as sole ruler of all Pictland. In 560, he hammered home the strength of his position by inflicting a decisive defeat on the Dalriada Scots, effectively removing any threat from that quarter for more than a decade.

Under Bridei, Christianity at last became deeply rooted among the Picts. Tradition asserts that Bridei was baptised by St Columba 'in the eighth year of his reign', but this cannot be factual, for Bridei, like Maelgwn before him, was already a Christian, and it is likely that many of his hitherto pagan subjects embraced the religion of their all-powerful sovereign simply because he *was* all-powerful, in the way that Christianity later spread wholesale through the Anglo-Saxon kingdoms after the conversion of their rulers. Bede would have us believe that the conversion of the Picts in Bridei's time was the work of St Columba, but there is some evidence that Columba's Irish brand of Christianity was at first rejected by Bridei and his chieftains. Indeed, for a considerable time Columba and his missionaries lived and preached in the north only because Bridei permitted it, and it was Bridei who granted them the island of Iona.

The later years of Bridei's reign were marked by unrest; his authority was once again challenged by rival kings in the southern part of Pictland, and probably also by rebellion in the Orkneys. The *Irish Annals* record that the leader of the Dalriada Scots, Aedan mac Gabran, led an expedition to the Orkneys in 581, and he probably did so as Bridei's ally, for otherwise his forces would have had to fight their way through 200 miles of Pictish territory and crossed seas that were controlled by the Picts. But the wars against the southern Picts continued, and in 584 Bridei was killed fighting them.

After his death Pictish history is once again confused; there was no leader strong enough to replace him completely. During these years, Aedan mac Gabran might have felt himself sufficiently powerful to subdue Pictland, perhaps in alliance with the British of Strathclyde, and he may indeed have annexed parts of it, but any greater ambition was forestalled by a new threat from the south: the rapid expansion of the Northumbrian English under Aethelferth, who had smashed the British of Gododdin at Catterick and whose forces were now pushing relentlessly northwards to the Forth and Clyde. In 603, a mixed force of Dalriada Scots and Strathclyde British met him at Degsastan, somewhere in Northumberland; the English, although outnumbered, utterly destroyed the enemy army, and, in the words of Bede, 'From that day until the present, no king of the Scots in Britain has dared to make war on the English'.

Significantly, no Pictish army featured in the northern alliance against Aethelferth, and it is probably that the Pictish leaders used the confused aftermath of Degsastan to regain some of the territory lost to Dalriada. They certainly still held the lands around the Firth of Forth, for the English knew the high land of Midlothian as 'Pictland' or 'Pehtland'—a name that survives today as 'Pentland'.

During the first half of the seventh century some kind of alliance appears to have existed between the Picts and the Northumbrian English; at least there is no evidence that they fought one another. There again, the Northumbrians did not make serious inroads into Pictish territory; having dealt with Dalriada and the Strathclyde British, they were now preoccupied with the growing power struggle between Aethelferth of Bernicia and Edwin of Deira, and when the latter triumphed in 617 it was with the Picts that several of Aethelferth's exiled sons sought refuge.

The one serious recorded threat which developed against the Picts in the first half of the seventh century came from Dalriada, whose ruler Domnall Brecc, the grandson of Aedan mac Gabran, sought to expand Dalriada's territory by fighting each of its neighbours in turn. He earned the reputation of being a great warrior and succeeded in annexing some Pictish territory, but he failed in his main aim, and in 636 the Picts defeated

Ruthwell (Dumfriesshire). One of the finest monuments to artistic achievement in the Dark Ages to be found anywhere, the Ruthwell Cross stands in a well in the church at Ruthwell, just off the B724 five miles west of Annan. It is of seventh century date and has been partly restored, having been broken and defaced in the seventeenth century on the orders of the hierarchy of the Church of Scotland after standing intact for a thousand years. The ornamental panels of the cross are beautiful, showing vinescroll with birds and animals, scenes that depict St John and his symbolic eagle, John the Baptist with his lamb, Christ in various biblical scenes, and Saints Paul and Anthony. The cross shaft also bears Anglian runic inscriptions and the text of an Old English poem, the 'Dream of the Rood', which has been attributed to Caedmon. It is thought by some that the cross was first erected about the time of the Synod of Whitby in 664. *(OS Sheet 85, 100675.)*

Pictish stones. North-east Scotland is something of a paradise for anyone interested in Pictish sculpture. At *St Vigeans*, a mile north of Arbroath, there is a collection of no fewer than 32 stones housed in a cottage in the village. The stones were all discovered in the vicinity of the church, which is dedicated to St Fechin, an Irish saint who founded a religious community here in the seventh century, and one of the stones bears Irish lettering. At *Aberlemno*, five miles north-east of Forfar on the B9134, two stones carrying Pictish sculptures stand on the south side of the road, and there is a third and even more splendid stone in the churchyard. At *Kirriemuir*, on the A926 five miles north-west of Forfar, .there are four stones in the cemetery, while at *Eassie*, off the A94 midway between Meigle and Glamis, there is a finely-decorated cross slab. In the grounds of the Manse at *Glamis* there is a famous 9 ft high Pictish symbol stone known as the Glamis Manse Stone, while north of Glamis, on the A928, is to be found St Orland's Stone, standing in a field near Cossans farmhouse. At *Meigle*, on the A94 Coupar Angus–Forfar road, there are 25 Pictish stones in the small museum, including one depicting Daniel in the lion's den and some horsemen. There is a 10 ft high cross slab adorned with Pictish symbols in the village square at *Fowlis Wester*, four miles north-east of Crieff off the A85 road to Perth, while further to the north, off the A827 six miles north-east of Aberfeldy, there is a finely-carved Pictish stone just outside the churchyard in *Dunfallandy*. In the grounds of *Aboyne Castle*, Aberdeenshire, there is a cross-slab bearing ogham script, even though it is of Pictish origin, and there is another stone with an ogham inscription, known as the Brandsbutt Stone, up a farm road off the A96 north-west of Inverurie. At *Dyce* church, off the A947 and adjacent to Aberdeen Airport, there are two symbol stones, while an intriguing stone known as the *Maiden Stone* stands by a side-road to the north-west of the A96, about six miles along the Inverurie–Huntly road. Carvings on this stone represent the biblical tale of Jonah and the Whale, and there are Pictish symbols on the other face. Still more intriguing is the *Newton Stone*, which stands in the grounds of Newton House, ten miles north-west of Inverurie on the B992 (off the A96); one of the inscriptions it bears is in ogham, but the other is in a completely unknown script. Finally, on the outskirts of *Forres* in Morayshire, beside the B9011 in Kinloss, there stands the magnificent Sueno's Stone, probably erected in the ninth century and richly carved. It shows a good deal of Northumbrian influence.

Trusty's Hill (Kirkudbright). The small vitrified stone fort at Trusty's Hill, near a minor road off the A75 at Anwoth, dates from the Iron Age, but was substantially strengthened during the Dark Ages. Pictish symbols are to be seen on one of the stone outcrops that form the main entrance, but is is possible that they were carved by raiders rather than occupiers. *(OS Sheet 83, 590560.)*

Abercorn (West Lothian). The church at Abercorn, on the A904 two miles west of Queensferry, stands on the site of an early Christian monastery, traces of which are to be seen in the churchyard. Bede mentioned the monastery as Aebbercurnig, and the chief priest there in the late seventh century was Bishop Trumwine. Stones from the monastery, unearthed during excavation, include a cross shaft and are to be seen in the church. *(OS Sheet 65, 082792.)*

Abernethy (Perthshire). There is an impressive round tower here, standing in a corner of the churchyard. The lower part is probably tenth century, although the upper portion is a little later in date. Close by, near the gate, there is a Pictish symbol stone. Abernethy is six miles south-east of Perth on the A913. *(OS Sheet 58, 190163.)*

Moncrieffe Hill (Perthshire). Moncrieffe Hill, which lies on a minor road off the A90 two miles south of Perth, is an Iron Age fort refurbished with stone defences at some point during the Dark Ages. It is generally accepted that this was the site of a battle known as Monad Croib, fought in 729. *(OS Sheet 58, 136200.)*

Dundurn (Perthshire). The nuclear fort at Dundurn lies 12 miles west of Crieff to the south of the A85, just before that road joins the shores of Loch Earn. It is mentioned in the Annals of Ulster as Duinduirn, and there was a siege there in 683. The fort was undoubtedly a Pictish stronghold of considerable importance, and is of Dark Age origin. *(OS Sheet 52, 706233.)*

Govan (Renfrewshire). Govan lies on the A8 four miles west of Glasgow city centre. Here, the church of St Constantine houses a collection of 24 sculptured stones, dating from the tenth and eleventh centuries and showing mixed Pictish, Scandinavian and Northumbrian influences in their design. The best stone is one known as the Sarcophogus of St Constantine, who was a sixth century saint; it is engraved with animals and a hunting scene. There used to be more stones in the churchyard, but they were vandalised and removed to Kelvingrove Museum in Glasgow. Other stones of interest in the area are the Barochan Cross, a rather damaged tenth century cross on a hill five miles north-west of Paisley (take the A737 out of Paisley and then the B789 through Houston) and the collection of Inchinnan, dating from the tenth and eleventh centuries and including a sarcophogus cover with an engraving depicting Daniel in the lion's den. Inchinnan is off the A8 to the west of Glasgow, and the stones are in the church.

him in his own territory. After that Domnall turned his attentions to Ireland for a time, but the Picts seemed bent on keeping any threat from the Scots firmly at arms length; in 648 they waged a campaign against the Scots of Kintyre, and four years later, in a move that was clearly designed to extend their influence southwards, they chose an English king, one of Aethelferth's grandsons, who might have contended with King Oswy for the throne of Northumbria had he not suddenly disappeared from the scene in 656; it is not known whether he died naturally or was killed. But Oswy, having beaten Mercia in the south, was not slow to realise that it was now time to subdue the Picts, and he marched north to overrun Strathmore, thus bringing a large slice of southern Pictland under English domination.

Northern Pictland, however, remained intact, and after Oswy's death it became the primary target of his son, Egferth, who perished with his army when the Picts trapped them at Nechtansmere (Dunnichen Moss, in Angus) in 685. With this defeat the English overlords were expelled from southern Pictland, but they left behind many colonies which survived apparently unharmed; Strathmore is still spattered with place-names of Anglian origin.

The man who had defeated Egferth was another Bridei, and in the years that followed he appears to have established cordial relations with the Northumbrians under Aldfrith, Egferth's pacific successor. Bridei established his main seat of government in Fortrenn—Stirlingshire—and so it was to remain for several centuries. In many ways the Pictish nation was more powerful now than it had been under the first Bridei, Maelgwn's son; it was once more ruled by a single king, and was more than able to keep the Scots at bay.

Bridei's successors continued to rule from a pinnacle of strength. In 706 he was succeeded by Nechtan mac Derelei, who after some initial skirmishing with the Northumbrians cemented friendly relations with them still further by inviting guidance from the Northumbrian Church on the method of calculating Easter. Nechtan's reign, however, was turbulent; his throne was bitterly contested by at least three rivals, and he was eventually overthrown by one of them,

Dumyat (Stirlingshire). The hillfort at Dumyat, which lies north of the A91 four miles north-east of Stirling, is of Iron Age origin, but its ramparts were extensively rebuilt at a much later date and it was certainly occupied, although probably not continuously, in the Dark Ages. *(OS Sheet 57, 836977.)*

Traprain Law (East Lothian). No explorer of Dark Age Scotland should miss the famous hill fort at Traprain Law, which lies off a series of minor roads to the south of East Linton on the A1 Edinburgh–Dunbar road. Much of the fort has been destroyed by quarrying, but there is still plenty to see. The original fort dates from the Bronze Age, and was much modified and expanded over successive centuries, becoming a very important tribal capital during and after the Roman occupation. Evidence of long-standing contact with Rome has come in the shape of the objects unearthed at Traprain during excavation; these include quantities of Roman coins and a quite remarkable treasure, dating from the fifth century, of silver vessels smashed ready for smelting. They had apparently been looted from Gaul and may have been a gift to the Votadini, whose northern territory was ruled from here. Other archaeological evidence tends to show that the fort was occupied until at least the seventh century, and Pictish ornaments have been found there. About a mile and a half

south-west of Traprain, fragments of an Anglian cross shaft may also be seen in the wall of the church at Morham. *(OS Sheet 67, 580747.)*

Dalmahoy (Midlothian). Ten miles south-west of Edinburgh, off the A70, there is a nuclear fort (a type built on a rocky hill and utilising natural defences) at Dalmahoy, a mile and a half west of Balerno. Finds have indicated that it was occupied during the Dark Age period. *(OS Sheet 65, 135670.)*

Burghead (Morayshire). Standing on a promontory of the Moray Firth, on the B9013 road that forks north from the A96 from Elgin, are two forts—or rather, one fort in two sections. The upper fort was built in the fourth century, and excavation has turned up Roman coins; the lower fort was a Pictish stronghold throughout the Dark Ages until it was overwhelmed by Viking raiders. Twenty-five stones bearing Pictish bull symbols have been found on the site. The wall that divided the two forts on the promontory can still be seen, but uncontrolled digging in the nineteenth century caused irreparable damage to the structure and many of the objects discovered during that period have been lost forever. There is an interesting well inside the lower fort, cut out of the rock at the foot of a crag, which may date from the Dark Age occupation. *(OS Sheet 28, 107692.)*

Oengus mac Fergus, who launched a succession of campaigns against the luckless Dalriada Scots, who were already seriously weakened by internal disputes. By 741, the Scots were completely under Pictish domination, and Oengus now opened an offensive against the British of Strathclyde, assisted from time to time by English forces. It was a tactical mistake. In 756, the combined forces of Oengus and Eadberht of Northumbria were shattered by the British, defending their territory with customary valour. Oengus died in 761, and his death was the signal for Dalriada to win back its independence; this it achieved over the next 15 years or so under an able leader called Aed Finn, although from time to time over the years that followed the Picts seem to have re-established a degree of

domination at intervals over their neighbour.

The history of the Picts from this point to the middle of the ninth century is once again hazy. They left no written records, and no worthwhile information is to be gleaned from the Irish lists of their kings, who after the time of Oengus were often the products of foreign parents, connected tenuously through the line of female descent. It was this tradition which finally brought an end to the Pictish monarchy in 843, when Kenneth mac Alpin rose to power under circumstances which are unknown, except that he was a rightful claimant to the Pictish throne under the female descent laws; but mac Alpin was also king of Dalriada, and his accession meant that the kingdoms of Pict and Scot were finally united.

Like the Pictish kings before him, Kenneth

mac Alpin ruled from Fortrenn; but he ruled as High King, the first man to do so north of the Wall. The old kingdom of Dalriada gradually lost its identity as a separate power, and in course of time became the province known as Argyle. The Picts, too, gradually lost their identity as they ceased to exist as a power in their own right, for the Dalriada Scots progressively colonised the former Pictish lands after mac Alpin took the throne. But it was not only that; the Scots had an evolved system of administration based on written communication, and the Picts did not. It was probably this factor, as much as any other, that doomed them to failure as a major power. Progress had passed them by, and left them stranded on the shores of the early mediaeval world.

Behind them, they left a few scant clues to the language they used in the form of a few scant inscriptions in Pictish ogham, although they probably acquired this form of alphabet on a very late date from their neighbours, the Scots of Dalriada. Their principal legacy, however, lies in their brilliantly creative art forms, from sculptured stones to silverwork, and their symbolism continues to mystify archaeologists to this day.

Restenneth (Angus). Although the priory at Restenneth, a mile and a half east of Forfar on the B9113, is in the main twelfth century, some of the lower walls may date from the eighth. It has been suggested that the original building may have been the work of Northumbrian masons who were brought from Monkwearmouth to build a church in 710 by the Pictish king Nechtan mac Derelei. The spire is fifteenth century. *(OS Sheet 54, 482516.)*

Craig Phadrig (Inverness-shire). The fort at Craig Phadrig stands south-west of Inverness, on a minor road that leads off the A9 to Leachkin. This was originally a fourth century fort, but it was destroyed while the Romans still occupied Britain and not refurbished until some uncertain date in the Dark Ages. It was certainly occupied in and after the sixth century, for excavation has uncovered pottery and other objects of that date. *(OS Sheet 26, 640453.)*

Kirkmadrine (Wigtownshire). There is a group of fifth century stones recessed into the outside wall of the church at Kirkmadrine, which lies to the west of the A716 that runs southwards down the narrow peninsula ending in the Mull of Galloway. One is a gravestone which, according to its Latin inscription, once marked the resting place of three priests named Ides, Viventius and Mavorius. *(OS Sheet 82, 080484.)*

Farr (Sutherland). In the churchyard at Farr, on a minor road running north from the A836 from Melvich to Bettyhill, there is an interesting monument known as the Red Priest's Stone, which is finely decorated in Irish style. The decorations include two birds with intertwined necks. *(OS Sheet 10, 720633.)*

Whithorn (Wigtownshire). Whithorn, on the A746 11 miles south of Wigtown, is the site on which, according to Bede, St Ninian founded a religious house in the fifth century and from there embarked upon the conversion of the pagan tribes of what is now Scotland. The ruins of the priory are of thirteenth century date and therefore have nothing to do with the Dark Ages, although they may stand on the site of the original church. There is a museum beside the road leading to the priory, and this houses a number of Dark Age stones of which the earliest is the Latinus Stone. Dating from the middle of the fifth century, it bears a 12-line inscription dedicating it to one Lord Latinus and his four-year-old daughter. Another stone, the Peter Stone, has a Latin inscription which translates 'The Place of Peter the Apostle' and is probably of seventh century date. Other stones in the museum come from St Ninian's cave at Physgill, south-west of Whithorn; to reach this, take the A747 to Physgill House near Glasserton and then walk along the path leading to the shore. *(OS Sheet 83, 444403 (Priory).)*

Chapel Finian (Wigtownshire). Further to the north-west along the A747, seven miles or so past Port William, Chapel Finian overlooks Luce Bay and was originally dedicated to St Findbar. It probably dates from the tenth century and may have been founded by Irish monks. The ruins of the chapel are surrounded by a drystone wall. *(OS Sheet 82. 279489.)*

Dunadd (Argyll). One of the most important Dark Age sites in the British Isles, the fortress of Dunadd, off the A816 to the west of Kilmichael Glassary, was the capital of the Scots of Dalriada, and was first occupied in the fifth century. The crag on which the fort stands was once surrounded by marshland, and the modern pathway probably follows the line of the old causeway. Parts of the fort's original stone walling are well preserved, and beneath the summit there is an interesting carving of a boar next to an inscription of ogham. There is also a carving of a footprint, which may have had a ceremonial significance—perhaps the kings of Dalriada stood here to be crowned. The ogham inscription is Pictish, and may be a relic of the time in 736 when Dunadd was besieged by the Pictish king Oengus mac Fergus. Excavation of Dunadd has produced many finds, from the first occupation by the Scots to the ninth century Viking settlement. *(OS Sheet 55, 837936.)*

Iona (Argyll). Although there are few Dark Age remains to be seen today on Iona, the island is well worth a visit for its atmospheric value, for this was where St Columba began his ministry to the Scots of Dalriada in 563. The only relic of his original monastery is the vallum, a low bank and ditch running from the pier to the priory, and a few associated earthworks. On nearby Tor Abb there are the remains of a small dwelling known as St Columba's cell, although this probably has nothing to do with the saint. To the south-west of the priory, however, near the mediaeval chapel, lies Reilig Odhrain, a burial ground where the Dark Age kings of the Scots were traditionally interred, and elsewhere on the island there are three splendid High Crosses—St Martin's, St Matthew's and St John's—of which the most complete is St Martin's. This stands beside the cathedral, together with the lower part of the shaft of St Matthew's Cross and a concrete replica of St John's, the fragments of which are in the nearby museum.

Ardwall Isle (Kirkudbright). There was a sixth century chapel on the island of Ardwall, which lies just offshore in Wigtown Bay. To reach it, follow the minor road from Castle Haven to Knockbrex and then take the track down to the shore, crossing over to the island at low tide. The original timber chapel was replaced by a stone one in the eighth century; a mediaeval hall was later built on top of its ruins. *(OS Sheet 83, 573493.)*

Mote of Mark (Kirkudbright). The history of the Mote of Mark, a hill fort which lies near Rockcliffe, off the A710 five miles south of Dalbeattie, in uncertain. Excavation indicates that the first of its series of defences appear to have been built in the fifth century, but runic inscriptions seem to point to occupation by Anglian peoples, probably in the seventh century. Parts of the stone rampart are vitrified, showing that the fort was burnt at some point. *(OS Sheet 84, 844540.)*

Castle Haven (Kirkudbridge). There is another stone-walled fort at Castle Haven, which is reached by taking the B727 westbound from Kirkudbright as far as Borgue, and then minor roads in the direction of Kirkandrews. The fort is almost certainly of Iron Age origin, but excavation has shown that it was reoccupied and strengthened in the Dark Ages. *(OS Sheet 83, 594483.)*

Islay (Argyll). The Island of Islay was once rich in early Christian communities, some of whose relics are still to be seen. Perhaps the best is the Kildalton Cross, standing in a churchyard on a minor road off the A846 at Ardbeg. The cross, richly decorated and showing much Irish influence of the Iona pattern, is of ninth-century date. On the opposite side of the island, a second monument known as the Kilnave Cross stands in an old graveyard on the western side of Loch Gruinart, reached by a minor road off the B8017 north of Aoradh. The cross, of badly-weathered slate, is of ninth century date.

Keillmore (Argyll). At Keillmore, which branches off the A618 running south from Oban, there is a free-standing slate cross adjacent to the mediaeval chapel, probably dating from the eighth century. It is decorated with fine interlace and figure patterns. *(OS Sheet 55, 690805.)*

Kildonan (Argyll). On the Mull of Kintyre next to the B842, six miles north of Campbeltown, Kildonan Dun probably dates originally from the Iron Age, but the fort was certainly refurbished and occupied during the Dark Age period up to about the ninth century. Another small fort at Ugadale Point, about a mile south of Kildonan, also shows traces of Dark Age occupation up to the eighth century. *(OS Sheet 68, 780277.)*

Eileach an Naoimh (Argyll). North of Islay and Jura, at the entrance to the Firth of Lorne, lie the Garvellach Islands, and on one of them, Eileach an Naoimh, stand the remote remains of a monastery that is traditionally associated with St Columba. The ruins have not been accurately dated, but may be as early as the seventh century; they consist of a rectangular chapel, three round cells and a circular enclosure known as Eithne's Grave, marked by slabs bearing engraved crosses. Eithne, according to tradition, was Columba's mother. *(OS Sheet 55, 640097.)*

Thornhill (Dumfriesshire). A mile out of Thornhill on the A702 road that runs south to Moniave, on the south side of the road near the Nith Bridge, there is a ninth century Anglian cross surrounded by iron railings. The cross has a rosette in its head and the panels on the shaft are decorated with interlacing creatures. There is further testimony to the Anglian occupation of the area a little further along the A702, where a side-road leading north passes the hill fort of Tynron Doon; excavation here has produced Anglian objects dating from the seventh and eighth centuries. *(OS Sheet 78, 868954.)*

Kingarth (Island of Bute). You need to take the car ferry from Wemyss Bay in Renfrewshire to reach the Island of Bute, but the trip is well worth it, for there are several Dark Age sites on the island. The most important are the monastic ruins at Kingarth, off the A844 seven miles south of Rothesay; the original monastery, which stood below the ruins of the mediaeval church, may have been founded by St Blane in the sixth century, and probably flourished until the arrival of the Vikings. to the southwest of the monastery lie the remains of two forts; the larger of the two, Dunagoil, dates from the Iron Age, but the other, Little Dunagoil, is more interesting, for within its perimeter stand the foundations of two Viking long houses, dating from very late in the Dark Age period. Following the A844 round the west coast of Bute, and then taking a minor road to Straad, one comes to St Ninian's Isle, where there are the remains of an early chapel. There was probably a timber structure on the site, replaced by a stone one in the ninth century. *(OS Sheet 63, 034612 (Chapel).)*

St Andrew's (Fife). The mediaeval abbey in St Andrew's is built on the site of a Dark Age monastery which once housed the relics of Scotland's patron saint, Andrew, in the eighth century. It was administered right up to the twelfth century by a strict Celtic religious order known as the Culdees. Today, the tower of St Regulus shows some pre-conquest features, including double belfry windows. There is an interesting museum in St Andrew's Cathedral (which superseded the church of St Regulus as the main religious centre in the twelfth century). It contains over 50 early Christian stones, including the Shrine of St Andrew, which probably dates from the eighth century.

Brechin (Angus). The principal point of Dark Age interest in Brechin is the Round Tower, which now forms part of the cathedral in the city centre. The tower is tenth century and shows a good deal of Irish influence, including a door set above ground level and flanked by sculptured figures of two bishops, one carrying a T-shaped Irish crozier. In the cathedral itself, which was built in the thirteenth century, there is a ninth century slab known as the Aldbar Stone, bearing a sculpture of the Virgin and Child.

Edinburgh. The first port of call for any Dark Age student in Edinburgh is the National Museum of Antiquities of Scotland in Queen Street, where there is a remarkable collection of Dark Age objects including the St Ninian's Isle treasure, beautiful Pictish silverwork from Shetland, Viking treasure and finds from excavations all over Scotland and the Islands. Not to be missed is the Monymusk Reliquary, a small shrine which is said once to have held a relic of St Columba. Another place of interest in Edinburgh is Arthur's Seat, which probably has nothing to do with Arthur but which has a small fort on the summit which may be of Dark Age date. It is worth the long climb from the foot of the Royal Mile simply to take in the tremendous view from the top.

Chapter 15

The Dalriada Scots

The influx of Irish settlers into western Caledonia very late in the fifth century and early in the sixth was, in all probability, the result of fierce rivalry between powerful dynasties in Ireland. No one can say when the first settlers came, but according to the *Irish Annals* the movement gained impetus in 503, when Fergus, the ruler of Dal Riada—a small kingdom in Antrim—found himself in danger of being overwhelmed by more powerful neighbours and moved the seat of his dynasty to safety in Kintyre, only a short sea trip from his original home. The immigrants were called Scotti, the name by which Rome knew the inhabitants of Ireland; it was a name which, in due time, would be applied to the whole of the wild and beautiful land north of the Solway.

The movement made the immigrants neighbours of the north British kingdom of Strathclyde, whose ruler in the early sixth century was Dyfnwal. Irish colonisation of Kintyre must have begun in a limited way before the arrival of Fergus, so arrivals on a larger scale would probably not have been seen as a threat by the British; indeed, troubled as they constantly were by the Picts, they probably welcomed the Irish as allies. In any case, it would be many more years before the Dalriada Scots became a military power in their own right.

According to some sources, Fergus originally arrived with only 150 men, including two who were his brothers: Loarn and Angus. Traditionally, Loarn's family occupied northern Argyll and ruled from Dunollie, a fort near Oban, while Angus occupied Islay. But the naming of Loarn and Angus as the brothers of Fergus was probably artificial, designed to give the impression in later years that the rule of the Dalriada Scots was centralised, which it almost certainly was not. In fact, Loarn and Angus fade conveniently from the scene, and it is the grandsons of Fergus who are remembered as the true architects of Dalriada's power, the men who expanded its territory and consolidated their gains in the face of the formidable power of the Picts.

The greatest of these men was Gabran, who ruled from the stronghold of Dunadd and who, in the middle of the sixth century, appears to have annexed large tracts of southern Pictish territory by force of arms. It was probably as a result of these incursions that the Picts chose the strong Bridei mac Maelgwn as their king; under his leadership the forces of Dalriada were defeated in 560 and Gabran killed.

There was still no unity among the colonies of Dalriada, but in 568 Conall, Gabran's successor, tried to establish it by launching an expedition to the Western Isles. The attempt seems to have resulted in civil war in which Conall perished, but the next ruler, Aedan mac Gabran, succeeded where the other had failed and was acknowledged as sovereign over the separate portion of Dalriada. His achievement was almost certainly supported by Columba of Iona, who had settled in Britain in 563 and who, ten years later, already exercised considerable influence among both Picts and Scots. Columba sought to bring an end to old enmities between the Dalriada Scots and the kings of Ireland, and one of the conditions of his support for Aedan is

Natural inlets such as that on the Isle of Whithorn, on the Solway coast in Wigtownshire, would have provided excellent shelter for sea raiders preparing to launch attacks on the British-held southern side of the Firth.

said to be that the latter was made to promise that he would not make war against the powerful Ui Neill dynasty. Columba himself was a prince of the Ui Neill line, and his first cousin, Aed mac Ainmere, was High King of Ireland. It is recorded that, sometime in the 580s, Columba took Aed mac Gabran to a great meeting of the Irish clans, convened by King Aed at Drumceat, near Derry; the result was a pact between Dalriada and the High King.

Columba may also have been responsible for securing peace between Dalriada and the northern Picts of Inverness; he certainly liaised with Riderch, king of the Clyde British, probably working through the offices of Bishop Kentigern, who was then ministering from the British stronghold of Dumbarton (the name, incidentally, means 'fortress of the Britons'). In this case, it was not so much a question of securing peace, but of consolidating the peace which had already lasted for the best part of a century.

It was at this juncture, in 581, that Aedan launched an expedition to the Orkneys, probably in alliance with Bridei, king of the Picts. Three years later, Dalriada was involved in a war against the Picts for the first time in Aedan's reign, but this was in the south; it is recorded that Dalriada won the battle of Manaan, and Manaan is the 'Manau' of the Votadini, or Gododdin, in the region of the Firth of Forth (the modern name Clackmannan is

derived from it). Other recorded battles fought by Dalriada under Aedan include one at 'Leithrig', possibly near Stirling, in 593, and some of his forces are said to have joined the British in their war against the embryo English kingdom of Bernicia, at Bamburgh. There was an indecisive battle against the southern Picts in Strathmore in 599, with both sides apparently suffering heavy losses. Then, in 603, Dalriada joined forces again with the British to confront the army of Aethelferth at Degsastan, and the result was a total disaster. Although Dalriada remained intact, the English pushed on to overwhelm and occupy the Lothians, the 'Manau of the Gododdin', bringing an end to British rule in south-east Caledonia.

Aedan mac Gabran died in 609, and under the leadership of his son Dalriada regained much of its lost military strength. The real problems began with the accession of Aedan's grandson, Domnall Brecc, an over-ambitious and head-strong man whose successive campaigns undid much of the good work of his predecessors. His incursions deep into Pictland caused the Picts to unite against him, and they defeated him in 636; undeterred, he launched an offensive in Ireland in support of a vain attempt to depose the High King and was defeated there, too. This campaign brought about a rift between Dalriada and Columba's successors in Iona, for by fighting in Ireland he had broken the conditions imposed upon his grandfather. But Domnall Brecc was not yet finished. In 640, only a year after his defeat in Ireland, he was campaigning in the vicinity of Edinburgh, where he was again defeated, either by the British or the Northumbrians. He fought the British again in roughly the same area three years later, and this time

These views of the important hill fort of Traprain Law, in East Lothian, show all too clearly how modern quarrying has destroyed most of it. Traprain was the capital of the northern Votadini; among other things, excavation turned up a remarkable treasure hoard of silver vessels dating from the fifth century. The fort was occupied until at least the seventh century.

they killed him. His repeated and wasteful wars brought about the collapse of the Dalriada monarchy and left the territory of the Scots wide open to Pictish attacks. It was 40 years before the monarchy was restored, and then the new king of Dalriada was not a descendant of Aedan, but of the Clan Loarn; his name was Ferchar the Tall, and he ruled until 696. Nevertheless, he was unable to restore Dalriada to its former power, and for the next century and a half its territory was prey to the ravages of the Picts. Not until 843 was the situation restored, with the rise to power of Kenneth mac Alpin, and he was of the Clan Gabran of Kintyre. Under his rule, Dalriada and Pictland ceased to exist as separate entities; the foundations had been laid for the emergence of the nation that would eventually be known as Scotland.

But that was still a long way in the future. In the ninth century, the new Scottic kingdom was faced with a formidable external threat which effectively denied any hope of unity between what had been northern and southern Pictland. Sometime early in that century—the date is

uncertain—Viking raiders had begun to settle in small communities in the Western Isles, and this was closely followed by the first settlements in the Northern Isles, Orkney and Shetland. The *Orkneyinga Saga* tells the traditional tale of how the Vikings arrived in the north:

'Picts (Peti) and Gaelic priests (Papae) were the first inhabitants of these islands. The Picts were scarcely more than pygmies in stature, toiling wonderfully morning and evening at building their towns, but at midday losing all their strength and, out of sheer terror, hiding themselves in underground dwellings. The islands were called not Orkneys but the land of the Picts, wherefore to this day [the saga was written in the thirteenth century] the sea which separates the islands from Scotland is called the Pentland Firth (Petlandicum mare). We know practically nothing about the people who were then the inhabitants. The priests were called papae because of the white robes they wore, for in the Germanic tongue all priests (clerici) are called papae. There is to this day an island which they call Papey . . . In the days of Harold Fairhair, pirates of the kin of the most powerful prince Ragnall, crossing the north sea with a great fleet, destroyed them and deprived them of their accustomed habitation and subjected the islands to their own power. Whence, protected more securely in their winter quarters, they made their forays in summer, exercising tyrannical rule now among the English, now the Scots and now the Irish, to the point where they subjugated to their authority Northumbria in England, Caithness in Scotland, and Dublin and other seaports in Ireland.'

The tale ignores the earlier Norse settlers, whose existence has since been proven by archaeology, and places the first colonisation of Orkney and Shetland in the time of Harold Fairhair, in other words in the last decades of the ninth century. The main message, however, is clear; the Norsemen used the Northern Isles as a base for their plundering expeditions southwards, and Kenneth mac Alpin's kingdom suffered as much at their hands as did the English kingdoms.

The original Norse settlements in the Northern Isles must have been made with sufficient ferocity and determination to enslave the native Christian inhabitants; with the Orkney and Shetland bases secured, there was doubtless a steady flow of Scandinavian immigrants during the middle years of the ninth century, when Viking plundering—as distinct from large-scale invasion—was at its peak. In the ninth and tenth centuries, then, the Northern Isles were important staging posts on the plundering routes to the south, while the Hebrides—which owed more to Scandinavian influence from Iceland and Ireland than to Norway—served a similar function in support of expeditions down Britain's west coast.

In view of the importance of these settlements, it is a great pity that their early history is so obscure. The main documentary evidence comes in the *Orkneyinga Saga*, but this tells little of the political and administrative structure of the settlers. It does, however, tell us that the leading family in Orkney affairs was that of Ragnald; his brother, Sigurd the Great, acted as Harold Fairhair's regent in the Islands and spread Norse influence deep into Caithness, Sutherland, Ross-shire and south of the Moray Firth—in other words, the northern territory of the Picts. It was this which prevented the unification of the Scottish kingdom ruled by Kenneth mac Alpin and his tenth-century successors, for as the Viking threat increased the northern rulers were compelled to organise their own defence independently of Fortrenn. At the same time, they were too preoccupied with fighting the Norsemen to be in any position to challenge the mac Alpin dynasty, which in turn ultimately benefited from the chaos caused by Scandinavian attacks on the northern English to seize Edinburgh in 960 and the Lothians, south of the Forth, in 1018. At about the same time, the British of Strathclyde also came under Scottish rule, for the last of their native kings had died, the dynasty of Riderch dying with him.

Meanwhile, the house of Ragnald had continued to dominate Norse affairs in the north, and in the time of his youngest son, Turf-Einar, who succeeded Sigurd, the Viking position on the mainland was further consolidated by a series of marriage alliances with Pictish princesses. The same thing happened in the Western Isles, where the daughters of notable Vikings were married off to Irish chieftains. The Islands, both north and west, were still predominantly pagan, but Christianity probably never disappeared entirely and, according to the saga, gained a fresh foothold late in the tenth century following the sudden conversion of the Orkney ruler, Olaf Tryggvasson. The saga tells how Olaf, in 995, con-

Below *Excavation at the hill fort of Tynron Doon, near Thornhill in Dumfriesshire, has produced Anglian objects dating from the seventh and eighth centuries.*

Bottom *The crags rising steeply from Edinburgh's 'Royal Mile' are topped by a small hill fort known as Arthur's Seat. It probably has nothing to do with the legendary Arthur, but may be of Dark Age origin.*

fronted Sigurd the Stout, ruler of the Western Isles, and gave him a straightforward choice between conversion and death and destruction. Sigurd accepted conversion, and in the years which followed rapidly extended his influence throughout all the Isles and Caithness; one of his subordinate earls also ruled the Isle of Man.

At the beginning of the eleventh century, a united Scottish kingdom, known then as Albany, was close to becoming a reality under King Malcolm II, who was lord of Inverness, Glasgow and Edinburgh, and who also ruled the lands to the south of the Forth. One of his daughters married Sigurd the Stout, so encouraging the chances of further unification with the Viking earldoms of the north. It was an ambition that was to be thwarted by the aspirations of two men. The first was the Viking Thorfinn, later known as the Mighty, who succeeded his father Sigurd when the latter was killed in 1014 at the Battle of Clontarf, on an expedition to aid the Norse of Dublin. For 20 years, up to the death of Malcolm, his grandfather, Thorfinn, engaged in continual feuding with his half-brothers as each sought to establish supremacy in the Orkneys. Then, in 1034, Malcolm died, and the throne of Albany was taken by his grandson, the young and headstrong Duncan of Cumbria. Duncan at once levied a huge army, established his authority over Inverness and then marched on Caithness, where he was smashed decisively by the Orkney Norse. Duncan made all the mistakes that the over-ambitious Domnall Brecc had made four centuries earlier; he marched south into Northumbria and besieged Durham, where the English inflicted an even greater defeat on him than the Vikings had done. The latter, meanwhile, had been raiding deep into Albany, and their ravages, added to two major military defeats, at last drove Duncan's subjects to rebellion.

Duncan was killed in 1040, his family driven into exile, and the throne of Albany offered to the one man who had shown himself powerful enough to defeat the plundering Norsemen and throw them out of Albany. He was the King of Inverness; his name was Macbeth. History has treated Macbeth in callous fashion. He was neither a usurper nor the murderer of an old man; he probably had no hand in killing Duncan, who was still in his youth when he died, and he was enthroned as a saviour. Macbeth, in fact, ruled Albany well and wisely for 20 years, maintaining peace and keeping the Orkney Norse at arm's length by treaty and, when necessary, by force. But in 1058 Macbeth was overthrown by Duncan's son, Malcolm III, who was nicknamed Canmore (Big Head) with the support of an English army. Malcolm surrounded himself with English advisors, married an English princess, and it was his English historians who portrayed Macbeth as some sort of devil incarnate, a totally false stigma which was later perpetuated throughout the world by William Shakespeare.

During Macbeth's time, Thorfinn still ruled over the Norse possessions in the north; his control over Britain's northern and western seaways was undisputed, he was said to have held no fewer than nine earldoms, including Ross, part of Moray and Galloway, he was the firm master of Shetland, Orkney and the Hebrides, even though his position had been threatened more than once by internal feuding, and after 1034 he controlled the Isle of Man as well. He was a Christian and an experienced traveller; his journeys took him to Rome and Germany, and probably to other places which are not recorded. At the same time, he recognised the authority of the king of Norway who, after 1047, was Harold Hardrada.

Malcolm Canmore, despite Thorfinn's power, succeeded in reasserting the authority of Albany over most of the mainland during his reign, which was to endure until 1093, but Viking overlordship of the Northern Isles was to continue for two more centuries. Thorfinn died in 1064, and so never witnessed the fleet, commanded by Harold Hardrada, which staged through the Orkneys on its way south to the Humber two years later, carrying Viking forces to support Earl Tostig, outlawed brother of Harold Godwinsson, in an attempt to seize the English throne. Hardrada and Tostig both met their deaths at Stamford bridge, together with all but a handful of their men, on a bloody September day in 1066. It was the first of the momentous events of that Year of the Comet; the second, a few weeks later at Senlac, would shape the destiny of Britain for a thousand years to come.

Index

Aballava 53
Abercorn 195
Abernethy 196
Adeon 15
Adrianople 13
Aedan 90, 91
Aegelsthrep 29
Aegidius 28
Aelfgifu 182
Aelfheah 173
Aelle 30, 133
Aesc 29
Aethelbald 99, 117
Aethelbert 60, 83, 106, 115
Aethelburh 66
Aethelferth (-frith) 65, 194
Aethelflaed 149, 151, 153, 155, 168
Aethelfryth 170
Aethelgeda 153
Aethelhere 74, 97
Aethelred 77, 115, 120, 144, 149-151, 153
Aethelstan 110, 155, 157, 159, 160, 173
Aethelswitha 114, 116
Aethelwald 150
Aethelwulf 112, 114, 115
Agatho 94
Agricola 49
Aire, river 162
Alans 16
Alaric 16
Alcuin 108
Aldbrough St John 21, 63
Aldfrith 94, 97, 196
Alemanni 12, 48
Alexandria 131
Alfred (of Wessex) 124, 138, 147
Alfrid 92
Algar 133
Algeciras 131
Alkborough 180
Allectus 11
Aller 143
macAlpin, Kenneth 197, 205
Alton Barnes 115
Ambrosius Aurelianus 26, 27, 31, 36, 38
Amesbury 35
Ammianus 13, 190
Anastasius 79
Andredescaester (Anderida) 30
Andredeslea 30
Angles 133
Angus 202
Anker, river 100
Anlaf 155, 157, 159, 162
Anthemius 39
Antrim 202
Anund 136
Appledore 142
Aquitaine 48

Arcadius 15
Ardwall Isle 199
Argyle 198
Armorica 15, 31
Arthur 39, 43, 45, 48, 49-52, 81, 121
Ashdown (Aescendun) 120, 135
Aspatria 161
Asser 113, 116, 120, 138, 142, 155
Athelney 137, 149, 157
Athol 182
Attecotti 190
Augustine 82, 83, 84
Austerfield 94
Aurelius Caninus 56
Avalon 50, 53
Aylesbury 59

Badbury 45
Badbury Rings 150
Badon 75
Baghdad 125
Bagseg 121
Bakewell 76
Balkans 14, 16
Baldwin 149
Bamburgh 61, 157, 166, 203
Bangor-is-Coed 65, 83
Barbury 60
Bardney 133
Barnack 150
Barton-on-Humber 150
Basingwerk 107
'Bassas' (Arthurian battle) 40, 42
Bath 59
Battle 169
Beachamwell 185
Bede 20, 44, 84, 86, 96, 105
Bedevere 50
Bedford 152-3
Benedict Biscop 96
Benfleet 143
Benson 102
Beornred 99
Bernicia 61, 63
Berthwald 94
Bewcastle 9, 77
Bichamditch 35
Binchester 21
Birdoswald 9, 53
Blackwater, river 153, 170
Boarhunt 151
Boerhtric 172
Bokerley Dyke 37
Bosham 151
Bracebridge 176
Bradford-on-Avon 99
Branston 176
Bradwell-on-Sea 94
Brancaster 11
Breamore 151
Brechin 200
Brecon 58
Breedon-on-the-Hill 95
Bremenium 43
Brent Ditch 37
Brentford 176
Bretteville 31
Bretwalda 82, 99, 102, 109, 160
Bridei 57
Bridgnorth 146
Brigstock 130
Britford 151
Brixworth 95
Broadstairs 24
Brodgar, Ring of 191
Broughton 180
Brunanburgh 159
Brythnoth 170
Burgh-by-Sands 53
Burgh Castle 86
Burghred 135
Bury St Edmunds 134
Bygrave 168
Byzantium 123

Cadafel (of Gwynedd) 72
Cadbury 28
Caerleon 43
Caewlin 59
Caistor 180

Caithness 111, 157
Caldeonia (-ii) 25, 190
Camboglanna 12, 59
Cambridge 153, 184
Camlann 53
Camolodunum 30
Canterbury 81, 83, 93, 175
Canute 174, 176, 177, 182
Caratacus Stone 55
Carausius 10
Cardiff 149
Cardinham 171
Carew 183
Castle Dore 52
Castleford 162
Castle Haven 199
Catterick (Catreath) 21, 63, 64
Catwallaun 66, 68, 69, 86
Celestine 25
Celidon (Arthurian battle) 40
Cenwalh 72, 75
Cenwulf 107
Ceolfrid 96
Ceolwulf 135
Cerdic 40, 66, 75
Chapel Finian 199
Charlemagne 102, 107, 114, 124, 129
Charles the Bald 114, 130
Chester 43, 65, 145, 151, 168
Chester-le-Street 96
Chippenham 137, 139
Christchurch 150
Chun Castle 29
Cirencester 59, 139
Cissa 30
Clapham 153
Clayhill farm 176
Clontarf (Battle of) 206
Clovis 15
Codford St Peter 125
Coelius 21, 26
Coenred 99
Coifi 86
Colchester 59, 153, 184
Colman 47
Cologne 15
Columba 96, 203
Constans 12
Constantine I 10
Constantine III 16
Constantine of Dumnonia 56, 157, 159
Constantius 11
Corbridge 21, 92
Corfe 170
Corhampton 111, 171
Cornovii 65
Cornwall 109, 157, 169
Corringham 177
Countisbury 130
Craig Phadrig 198
Cricklade 142, 150
Croft 121
Crouch estuary 177
Cruithni 190
Cunedda 21, 48
Cuthbert 94
Cuthred 99
Cuthwin 59
Cymea 30
Cynric 60

Dacians 9
Dacre 82
Daglingworth 173
Dalmahoy 199
Dalriada 76, 193, 194, 197
'Danegeld' 170
Danube, river 13, 15
Dearham 162
Dee, river 108, 166
Deerhurst 99, 177
Deganwy 58, 107
Degsastan 65
Deira 61, 65
Demetia 49, 58
Denmark 125, 129, 169, 180, 182
Deorham 60
Derby 152, 161, 174
Dere Street 43, 62
Derry 81

Deva 16
Devil's Dyke 37, 38
Devon 111, 169, 171
Diddlebury 174
Dinas Emrys 33
Diocletian 10
Domnall Brecc 196
Don valley 159
Donald of Strathclyde 168
Doncaster 86
Dorchester 91
Dore, castle 29, 109
Dover 153
Drumceat 203
Drust 190, 193
Dubglas 40, 43
Dublin 131, 153, 155, 166
Dumbarton 203
Dumfries 193
Dumnonia 45, 75
Dumyat 197
Dunadd 199
Duncan 206
Dundurn 196
Dunkeld 190
Dunmail 161
Dunnotter 157
Dunstable 35
Dunstan 168, 169
Dunwich 93
Durham 96, 161
Dyfed 62
Dyfnwal 202

Eadburgh 114
Eadric 172, 174, 176
Ealdred of Bamburgh 153
Ealstan 115
Earl's Barton 157
East Lexham 185
Ebchester 21
Ebissa 25
Ecgfrith 107
Edburga 126
Edgar 166
Edinburgh 201, 203, 206
Ediovinchus 16
Edmund 'Ironside' 160, 161, 166, 174, 177
Edred 162, 166
Edwin of Deira 194
Edward I 143, 149, 150-153, 154
Edward (Edgar's son) 168, 169
Edward 'The Confessor' 184, 186
Edwy 166
Egbert 109, 133, 135, 137
Egferth 75, 76, 93, 96, 196
Eglwys-Cymmyn 55
Egwina 159
Elchere 112
Elfgifu 166
Elfric 170
Elidyr 62
Eliseg's Pillar 153
Elswitha 148
Ely 133
Emma 177, 182, 184
Eric Bloodaxe 162
Ermine Street 45
Erp 190
Escomb 108
Ethelred 'The Unready' 169, 170-175, 182, 184
Exeter 143, 157
Eyam 84

Fairhair, Harold 159, 161
Farndon-on-Dee 154
Farne Islands 96
Farnham 142
Farr 198
Fercher 'The Tall' 204
Fergus, Oengus mac 197, 202
Fife 190
Flanders 159, 186
Fleam Dyke 39
Fortrenn 190, 198
Franks 15
Frisia 24, 25
Fulham 139

Gabran, Aedan mac 194, 202, 203
Gainsborough 173
Ganhumara 52
Guallauc 62
Gawain 50
Geddington 118
Germanus 24
Gerontius 16
Ghent 168
Gildas 20, 22, 23, 28, 31, 108
Gilsland 9
Glastonbury 50, 52
'Glein' (Arthurian battle) 40
Glen, river 42
Glentworth 180
Gloucester 59, 136, 160
Godwin, Earl of Wessex 182, 184
Godwinsson, Harold 133, 185-7
Goodmanham 86
Gosforth 124
Goths 13
Govan 196
Granwynion 43
Gratian 12, 13
Great Dunham 185
Great Paxton 159
'Great Ridgeway' 120
Great Tey 184
Greensted 163
Greenwich 175
Gregory (Pope) 82, 142
Guestwick 184
Guildford 182
Guinnion, castle (Arthurian Battle) 21
Guoloph 27
Gurness, Broch of 191
Guthfrith 155, 157
Guthrum 134, 136, 139
Gwen Ystrad 43
Gwr y Gogledd 190

Hackness 80
Haddiscoe Thorpe 187
Hadrian's Wall 9, 104
Haesten 142, 143, 145
Halfdan 135
Halley's Comet 187
Halton 130
Halwell 142
Harold Hardrada 187
Harold 'Harefoot' 182, 187
Haroldsson, Magnus 182, 185
Harthacnut 182
Heapham 180
Hereford 157
Hengest 21, 24, 25, 114
Heysham 121
Hexham 92
Hingston Down 109
Hincmar 114
Honorius 15, 90
Horik 129
Horsa 21, 24
Hough-on-the-Hill 154
Huda 113
Huns 13
Huntingdon 133, 153

Iago of Gwynedd 168
Iclingas 91
Icknield Way 35
Iley Oak 138
Ilkley 164
Ine of Wessex 100
Inverness 206
Iona 82, 90, 199
Ipswich 170
Ireland 109, 130, 131, 159
Irthing, river 9, 106
Isca Silurum 16
Islay 199
Isle of Man 206
Isle of Wight 137, 173
Ivar 133

Jaenberht 102
Jarlshof 193
Jarrow 96, 130
Jedburgh 191

Julian 12
Jutes 23

Kay 50
Keillmore 200
Kenneth of Alba 168
Kennet, river 118
Kent 71, 78, 151, 171
Kesteven 133
Kiev 124
Kildonan 200
Kincardine 157
Kingarth 200
Kintyre 202
Kirby Hill 163
Kirkdale 166
Kirk Hammerton 112
Kirkleavington 130
Kirkmadrine 198
Kynan 15

Lanbay Island 130
Lanchester 21
Langford 78
Lea, river 146
Ledsham 112
Leeds 86
Leicester 153, 160, 161, 174, 176
Leogaire 25
Lewannick 58
Lichfield 102
Liddington Castle 45, 46
Limerick 135
Lincoln 33, 161, 174
Lindisfarne 94, 96, 108, 129, 130
'Linnuis' (Arthurian battle) 40, 42
Liskeard 107
Liverpool 121
Llanaelhaern 55
Llanerfyl 58
Llangadwaladr 59
Llangian 53
Llangybi 55
Llanilltud Fawr 57
Llantwit Major 149
Llywelyn ap Griffyd 58
Loarn 202
Loire, river 131
London 114, 145, 146, 151, 153, 166, 170, 173, 175
Lot of Orkney 50
Lothar 130
Louis the Pious 129-130
Louth 131
Lucius 50
Ludwig 130
Luna 131
Lupicinus 12
Lydford 145
Lyminge 84
Lynton 138

Maccus 166, 168
Maelgwn (Mailcunus) 25, 56, 193
Maen Madoc 59
Maes Cogwy 71
Maes Howe 193
Malcolm I 161
Malcolm II 181, 206
Malcolm III 206
Maldon 153, 170

Manau Guotodin (Gododdin) 25
Marden 125
Margate 24
Margram 114
Marianus 48
Marton 177
Masham 80
Maximus (Prince Macsen) 14, 15, 22, 50
Maximian 10
Mayburgh 155
Medraut 50
Medway 176
Melbury 125
Melsonby 121
Men Scryfa Down 58
Mercia 134, 137
Merioneth 48
Meredune 121
Mersea Island 145
Middleton 130, 163
Midgeholm Moss 9
Moncrieffe Hill 196
Monkton 96
Monkwearmouth 95
Moray Firth 190
Morcant 62, 75
Morcar (Earl) 186
Mote of Mark 199
Mount Agned (Arthurian battle) 43
Mount Badon (Arthurian battle) 44

Nechtansmere 196
Nectan Morbet 193
Nennius 20, 25, 37
Nevern 59
Newent 100
Newton by Castleacre 185
Newstead 21
Niall 16
Ninian of Whithorn 193
Normandy 173, 177
Northly Island 192
Northumbria 134, 145, 146
Norway 125, 127, 130, 171
Norwich 183
Nottingham 153, 157, 161, 174
Novgorod 124
Nunburnholme 163

Ochta 25
Offa 97, 100, 102, 104, 106, 107, 151
Oldbury Camp 28
Old Sarum 147
Ordulf 169
Orkneys 111, 190, 194
Orphir 191
Orwell, river 176
Oscytel 136
Osbert 133
Osric 117
Oswald 11, 72, 91
Oswestry 71
Oswulf 97, 166
Oswy 72, 92, 93, 196
Oundle 94
Ouse 153
d'Outremer, Louis 159
Ovingham 161
Owain 62, 157, 159

Owen 181
Oxford 151, 173, 174

Palladius 25
Pannonia 13
Paternus 25
Patrick 25
Peada 72
Pelagius 24
Penally 107
Penda 69, 72, 99, 133
Penmachno 60
Penrith 162
Penselwood 175
Penzance 171
Peredur of York 62
Pewsey, Vale of 60
Picts 12, 196
Piercebridge 21
Pilton 145
Pisa 131
Portchester 133
Portland 169
Portsmouth 11
Powys 24, 65
Praen, Eadberht 107
Prestatyn 106

Raegnall 153, 161
Ragnall 204
Ramsbury 115
Ramsgate 24
Ravenna 16
Reading 118, 120
Reculver 76
Redwald 80, 136
Repton 95
Restenneth 198
Rey Cross 166
Rhufawn 'The Tall' 64
Rhun 57, 194
Rhydderch 62
Richard I of Normandy 170
Richborough 13
Ripon 93, 95, 161
Risingham 21
Rochester 90, 139
Rome 113, 114, 180
Ross-on-Wye 177
Roughton 184
Rowley Burn 71
Ruthwell 195
Rutupiae 24

St Albans 22
St Andrews 200
St Brice 171
St Wilfred's Minster 161
Salisbury Plain 137, 138
Sancreed 171
Sandbach 84
Sandwich 170, 172, 174
Schleswig-Holstein 12
Scotti 12, 202
Seaham 109
Seckington 99
Senlac 49, 206
Severn, river 145, 152
Severus 105
Sexburga 24
Shaftsbury 149
Shannon, river 131
Shelford 178
Shetland 111, 204

Shoebury 144, 145
Sigurd 205
Sihtric 155
Singleton 136
Sittingbourne 142
Skipwith 80
Sockburn 114
Solsbury Hill 45
Somerton 137
Sompting 171
Sourton 60
Southampton 169
South Cadbury 50
Spain 131, 161
Springthorpe 177
Stainmore 166
Stanton 171
Stapleford 176
Stanwick 63
Stilicho 16
Stoughton 183
Stow 79
Strathclyde 78, 97, 153, 159, 161, 181
Strathmore 190
Strethall 184
Suebi 16
Sutherland 111
Sutton Hoo 77, 80
Swansea 79
Sweyn 172, 175
Swithun, Bishop of Winchester 117

Taezali 190
Taillefer 49
Tamar, river 157
Tamworth 99, 155, 160
Taplow 74
Tara 76
Tarsus 93
Tavistock 60
Tay, river 78
Tempsford 152
Thames valley 91, 118
Thanet, Isle of 24, 113, 168
Theodore 93
Theodosius 13
Thetford 133
Thorfinn 206
Thorgils 131
Thorkell 'The Tall' 136
Thornhill 200
Thurferth 153
Thurketil 152
Thurkettel 152
Tintagel 41
Torksey 135
Tostig 185, 186, 187
Towcester 152, 153
Towyn 106
Traprain Law 197
Trent, river 153
Tribunus 49
Trusty's Hill 195
Tryggvason, Olaf 170, 205
Turf-Einar 205

Uffington 120
Ulfketil 133
Uppsala 125
Urien of Rheged 43, 62
Usk, river 59
Uther Pendragon 50

Vacomagi 190

Vandals 16
Valens 12
Valentia 13
Valentinian 12
Venicones 190
Venta Icenorum 30
Verulamium 22
Vikings 124 et seq
Vinovium 43
Visigoths 13
Vitalinus 27
Volga, river 13
Vortigern 22-5, 31, 190
Vortimer 29
Vortipor 56
Votadini 21, 25

Wallingford 147
Wansdyke 59, 71, 104
Warden 161
Wareham 136, 139, 168
Watchet 111
Waterford 131
Watling Street 36, 145, 152, 153
Wat's Dyke 99, 106
Weald, the 142
Wearmouth 96
Wessex 109 et seq
West Stow 23
Wexford 131
Wharram le Street 163
Whitby 95
Whitehorse Hill 120
Whithorn 198
Wickham 170
Wighard 93
Wiglaf 112
William of Malmesbury 50, 115, 162
William of Normandy 133, 184
Wilton 135
Wimborne 150
Winchester 77, 115, 116, 140, 142, 157, 166, 173, 182, 184
Windsor 124
Wing 107
Winterbourne Steepleton 171
Wodensbeorg 99
Witham, river 42, 153
Wlencing 30
Wootton Wawen 175
Worcester 166
Worth 170
Wroughton 109
Wroxeter 34, 38
Wulfhere 74-5
Wulfryth 168
Wulfnoth 172
Wulfstan 162

Yeavering 65-6
Ygerne 50
Ynglinga 125
York 21, 65, 83, 96, 133, 153, 155, 157, 159-163, 164, 165

Zosimus 17